D1756736

This book is to be returned on
or before the date stamped below

1 2 NOV 2002

CANCELLED

INTER-SITE LOAN
plymouth

University of Plymouth Library
Subject to status this item may be renewed
via your Voyager account
http://voyager.plymouth.ac.uk
Tel: (01752) 232323

90 0517777 7

Communities across Borders

Communities across Borders examines the many ways in which national, ethnic or religious groups, professions, businesses and cultures are becoming increasingly tangled together irrespective of national origins or identities. This is a result of the vast flows of people, meanings, goods and money that now migrate between countries and world regions. Now, the effectiveness and significance of electronic technologies for interpersonal communication (including cyber communities and the interconnectedness of the global world economy) simultaneously empowers even the poorest people to forge effective cultures stretching across national borders, and compels many to do so to escape injustice and deprivation.

The consequences of constructing new, or replenishing older, transnational communities of nationality, interest or symbolic power – either for those directly involved, or for the countries and cultures on which they have an impact – are varied, as the case studies in this book testify. Topical themes analysed include:

- symbolic forms of resistance against earlier eras of cultural imperialism
- the experience of host discrimination or unequal political systems
- the dilemmas for governments faced by multiple transnational communities whose members are engaged in loyalties outside their borders
- the expression of subtle personal or social relationships drawn together from several sites to form new hybrid cultural forms and identities

Students of sociology, politics, development and cultural studies, as well as scholars and the travelling public – interested in the issues raised by globalisation, cultural and economic interdependency, and the opportunities offered by new technologies and the implications of the rise of ever more vibrant communities straddling borders, peoples and lifestyles – will find this book both engrossing and revealing.

Paul Kennedy is Reader in the department of sociology at Manchester Metropolitan University and director of the Institute for Global Studies. He recently co-authored *Global Sociology* and co-edited *Globalisation and National Identities: Crisis or Opportunity*. **Victor Roudometof** is Visiting Assistant Professor with the department of sociology, Miami University, Ohio. He has held appointments at Princeton University and Washington and Lee University. He is author of *Nationalism, Globalisation and Orthodoxy*, and co-editor of *American Culture in Europe* and *The New Balkans*.

Transnationalism
Edited by Steven Vertovec
University of Oxford

'Transnationalism' broadly refers to multiple ties and interactions linking people or institutions across the borders of nation-states. Today myriad systems of relationship, exchange and mobility function intensively and in real time while being spread across the world. New technologies, especially telecommunications, serve to connect such networks. Despite great distances and notwithstanding the presence of international borders (and all the laws, regulations and national narratives they represent), many forms of association have been globally intensified and now take place paradoxically in a planet-spanning yet common arena of activity. In some instances transnational forms and processes serve to speed-up or exacerbate historical patterns of activity, in others they represent arguably new forms of human interaction. Transnational practices and their consequent configurations of power are shaping the world of the twenty-first century.

This book forms part of a series of volumes concerned with describing and analyzing a range of phenomena surrounding this field. Serving to ground theory and research on 'globalization', the Routledge book series on 'Transnationalism' offers the latest empirical studies and ground-breaking theoretical works on contemporary socioeconomic, political and cultural processes which span international boundaries. Contributions to the series are drawn from Sociology, Economics, Anthropology, Politics, Geography, International Relations, Business Studies and Cultural Studies. The series is associated with the Transnational Communities Research Programme of the Economic and Social research Council (see http://www.transcomm.ox.ac.uk).

The series consists of two strands:

Transnationalism aims to address the needs of students and teachers and these titles will be published in hardback and paperback. Titles include:

Culture and Politics in the Information Age
A new politics?
Edited by Frank Webster

Routledge Research in Transnationalism is a forum for innovative new research intended for a high-level specialist readership, and the titles will be available in hardback only. Titles include:

First published 2002
by Routledge 11 New Fetter Lane, London EC4P 4EE

Simultaneously published in the USA and Canada
by Routledge
29 West 35th Street, New York, NY 10001

Routledge is an imprint of the Taylor & Francis Group

Typeset in Baskerville by
Prepress Projects Ltd, Perth, Scotland
Printed and bound in Great Britain by
Antony Rowe Ltd, Chippenham, Wiltshire

British Library Cataloguing in Publication Data
A catalogue record for this book is available from the British
Library

Library of Congress Cataloging in Publication Data
Communities across borders: new immigrants and
transnational cultures / edited by Paul Kennedy and Victor
Roudometof.
    p.cm. – (Transnationalism ; 5)
  Includes bibliographical references and index.
    1. Intercultural communication. 2. Transnationalism. I.
Kennedy, Paul T., 1941–. II. Roudometof, Victor, 1964–.
III. Series.

HM1211 C65 2002
303.48′2–dc21   2001048589

ISBN 0–415–25293–8

Communities across Borders

New immigrants and transnational cultures

**Edited by Paul Kennedy
and Victor Roudometof**

London and New York

Contents

Contributors

Hans van Amersfoort is a professor of cultural geography and population geography at the University of Amsterdam. His main research interests are in international migration, the social position of immigrant groups, the role of ethnicity in the modern state and the relation between research and policy-making. He has written extensively on all these issues, including 'Regulating migration in Europe: the Dutch experience, 1960–1992', *Annals of the American Association Political and Social Science*, 534, 1994 (co-authored with Rinus Penninx); 'Migration: the limits of governmental control', *New Community*, 22, 1996; and *International Migration: Processes and Interventions* (co-edited with Jeroen Doomernik, Het Spinhuis, 1998).

Val Colic-Peisker holds a BA and an MA in politics, an M.Phil. in women's studies and a Ph.D. in sociology. Before migrating to Australia from Croatia she was a journalist and radio producer. She has published extensively in the areas of literary criticism, the sociology of education and the sociology of migration in Croatian and English. She is currently teaching sociology part time at Murdoch University in Western Australia while undertaking a variety of academic tasks.

Oscar Contreras is a Research Professor at El Colegio de Sonora, Mexico, and a Visiting Professor in the Department of Sociology at the University of Warwick. His main research topics concern the local impacts of transnational corporations in Mexico, industrial learning within the North Atlantic Free Trade Agreement (NAFTA) region and the implications of information technologies for employment and labour relations. He has published one single-authored book, four co-edited books and more than fifty articles.

Jeroen Doomernik is a senior researcher at the Institute for Migration and Ethnic Studies at the University of Amsterdam. He has published on Turkish Islam in Europe, on Russian Jewish immigrants in Germany and on Dutch and European migration and integration policies. At various times he has also worked in collaboration with the International Labour Office, the European Commission, the Dutch Home Office and Justice Ministry and the United Nations Research Unit for Social Research.

Anne-Marie Fortier is a lecturer in the sociology department at Lancaster University. Her work stands at the crossroads of cultural studies, queer studies and diaspora studies, and revolves around the formation of émigré identities. Recent publications include: *Migrant Belongings. Memory, Space, Identity* (Berg, 2000), and 'Re-membering places and the performance of belonging(s)', *Theory, Culture and Society,* 16 (2), 1999, both on Italian émigré identity formation in England. She has also written extensively on theories of diaspora. Her current research is on the impact of migration, multilocation and multiculturalism on ideas of community, home and belonging; it includes a study of reimagined communities in 'queer diasporas'.

Elizabeth Grierson is a Fellow of the Royal Society of Arts, principal lecturer in art history and cultural theory and head of research at the School of Art and Design, Auckland University of Technology, New Zealand. Her Ph.D. from the University of Auckland investigated the politics of knowledge and post-structuralism in relation to visual arts education. She is editor of the *ANZAAE Journal,* president of the national association of art educators and is an overseas advisor to the Global Studies Association. Her present research is concerned with visual practices and the reimagining of local identities in a global context.

Anna Karpathakis is an assistant professor of sociology at Kingsborough C.C., of the City University of New York. She researches and writes on Greek immigrants in the United States and has published widely in this area, including such topics as binational identifications and Greek immigrants' political integration into USA and Greek immigrant women's changing family roles and understandings. She has recently co-edited a volume with H. Psomiades and S. Tsemberis entitled *Greek American Families: Traditions and Transitions* (Pella Publishing Press, 1999). Another book, *New York Glory: Religions in the City*, edited by Tony Carnes and Anna Karpathakis was published by NYU Press in 2001.

Marian Kempny is associate professor at the Institute of Philosophy and Sociology, the Polish Academy of Sciences, Warsaw. He has recently completed two research projects in the field of globalisation, tradition and identity. He has published several articles on identity and ethnicity based upon these studies in addition to several earlier books published in Polish on social theory and cultural analyses.

Paul Kennedy is a reader in sociology at the Department of Sociology at Manchester Metropolitan University and is the director of the Institute for Global Studies. His publications include *African Capitalism; the Struggle for Ascendency* (Cambridge University Press, 1988), *Global Sociology* (co-authored with Robin Cohen; Macmillan, 2000) and *Globalization and National Identities: Crisis or Opportunity?* (co-edited with Catherine Danks, Palgrave, 2001). He is currently the secretary of the newly formed Global

Studies Association. His present research interests include work on transnational professional collaboration and the politics of consumerism.

Martin Kenney is a Professor in the Department of Human and Community Development at the University of California, Davis, and a Senior Project Director at the Berkeley Roundtable on the International Economy at the University of California, Berkeley. He has studied the globalization of the electronics industry and is currently working on the evolution of venture capital in the USA and globally. He recently edited the book *Understanding Silicon Valley* (Stanford 2000) and is editing a book *Locating Comparative Advantage* on the globalization of various industries. He is the author or editor of four books and over 100 articles.

Kim C. Matthews recently received her Masters in sociology from Concordia University in Montreal, Quebec, where she is currently a faculty member in the department of sociology and anthropology. Her thesis was entitled 'Shiftings of the self: towards a deterritorialized view of identity and belonging. The case of African–Asians in Canada'. Her research interests include globalisation, identity construction and representation, and religion. Her article 'Deconstructing place and space: towards a deeper understanding of the "social" ' was recently published in *The Colloquium*, Vol.1, 2000.

Alan O'Connor teaches in the Cultural Studies Program at Trent University in Canada. He is the author of *Raymond Williams: Writing, Culture, Politics* (Blackwell, 1989) and a series of articles on community radio in Ecuador and Bolivia. His current work is a long-term project of multisite ethnography of youth subcultures and resistance to globalization.

Victor Roudometof is visiting assistant professor of sociology in the Department of Sociology, Gerontology and Anthropology at Miami University, Oxford, OH. His research interests include the study of globalisation, transnationalism, nationalism and ethnic conflict. He is the author of *Nationalism, Globalization, and Orthodoxy* (Greenwood, 2001) and *Collective Memory, National Identity, and Ethnic Conflict in the Southern Balkans,* (Praeger, forthcoming). He is the editor of *The Macedonian Question: Culture, Historiography, Politics* (East European Monographs, 2000) and co-editor and co-author of *American Culture in Europe* (Praeger, 1998) and *The New Balkans* (East European Monographs, 2002).

Manuchehr Sanadjian is an anthropologist. He has carried out research among the Lurs of south-western Iran and on Iranian diasporas in Europe. His publications include the role of violence in local–national articulation, and class and national identity in diaspora. Currently, he is conducting research into music, food and national identity among Iranians in Britain and Germany. He is a part-time teacher at the Department of Anthropology, Manchester University, UK.

Lloyd L. Wong is an associate professor of sociology at the University of Calgary, Canada. A graduate of York University in Toronto, he conducts research in the areas of migrant labour, Chinese capitalist migration and ethnic entrepreneurship, transnationalism and citizenship. Among his recent publications are 'Globalization and transnational migration', *International Sociology*; 'Chinese immigrant entrepreneurs in Vancouver', *Canadian Ethnic Studies*; and a chapter in *Street Protests and Fantasy Parks: Globalization, Culture and the State* (edited by J. Stein and D. Cameron, 2002).

Acknowledgement

Anne-Marie Fortier's chapter was originally published in the *International Journal of Canadian Studies*, no. 18, Fall, 1998, pp. 31–49, under the title 'Calling on Giovanni: Interrogating the Nation Diasporic Imaginations.'

Abbreviations

EU	European Union
FYROM	Former Yugoslav Republic of Macedonia
MNC	Multinational Corporation
OCL	Orthodox Christian Laity
YMCA	Young Men's Christian Association

Preface

This volume is based on the papers presented at the 1999 international conference on Globalisation and Identities, which was organised by the Department of Sociology and the Institute of Global Studies at Manchester Metropolitan University. During the course of the conference, we realised that many of the papers shared a concern with the broader issues of transnationalism, globalisation and identity. After the conference concluded, we contacted the participants and indicated our interest in publishing the presentations as an edited volume. We would like to thank the contributors for their patience while we were negotiating an agreement for the publication of the volume. Also, we feel we should thank the contributors for the timely submission of their final essays.

Paul Kennedy
Victor Roudometof
November 2001

1 Transnationalism in a global age

Paul Kennedy and Victor Roudometof

> Cultural diasporas ... are no longer confined to the rich. In dress, in religious or political orientation, in music, people in the poorest ghettos link themselves to transnational 'communities of taste' in an active way.
>
> (Giddens 1994: 188)

This collection of readings endeavours to extend the frontiers of our understanding concerning the increasing significance of transnationalism in national and global life. Most of the literature on transnationalism to date has concentrated on the experience of new immigrants. These experiences suggest that their ethnic, religious or national diasporic relations and connections span national borders, thereby establishing the claim that such relations represent a qualitatively new phenomenon. As important and interesting as this rapidly expanding literature is, it cannot encompass – nor does it claim to do so – the actual range of transnational communities increasingly shaping the everyday lives of people across the world. While lip-service is often paid to the need to widen our explorations of transnational communities beyond migrants and diasporas, little research of this kind has so far been conducted (for an important exception, see Sklair 1995, 2001).

Our contribution to this on-going debate on the meaning, definition, nature and basic features of transnational communities rests on our claim that transnational communities and cultures need to be understood as constituting a much wider and more commonplace phenomenon than the existing research might lead us to suppose. We argue that transnational relationships have to be understood as manifestations of broader social trends that are not confined to the experience of immigrants; rather, they are extending into and shaping the lives of people engaged in many other kinds of associations, clubs and informal networks as well as into cultural life at large.

This selection of readings aims to furnish evidence in favour of a common conceptual framework that is capable of accommodating the growing diversity of vibrant transnational communities and cultures flourishing in global social space and to incorporate case studies as valid examples of this framework. Therefore, our discussion in this introductory essay will provide for a general theoretical and conceptual framework. We shall begin by discussing the current state of affairs in the related literature on transnationalism, globalisation and diaspora. Our overview is meant to highlight the achievements as well as the contested points in recent research and to lay out the fundamentals of our approach toward the topic. Next, we turn to the concepts of 'community' and 'culture' and critically examine the manner in which the decoupling of locality from territory has caused important transformations in the meaning and nature of these two central sociological concepts. Then, we proceed to outline our classification of the new transnational and global communities, including the reasons for drawing a distinction between the two, as well as the reasons the two should be considered within the same broad category. Towards the end of the chapter we also indicate briefly the manner in which the individual essays in this volume relate to the central themes of our argument.

Transnationalism, globalisation and diaspora

Despite important contributions focused specifically on enhancing our understanding of transnationalism in a broader and deeper sense (Appadurai 1990, 1991, 1995; Giddens 1990, 1994; Hannerz 1992, 1996; Lash 1994; Beck 2000a), the theorisation of the transnational experience (and its ties to globalisation) remains incomplete. The strong leaning of the literature has been directed towards research mainly concerned with migrants, diasporas and transnational nation-state building (Basch *et al.* 1994; Danforth 1995; Cohen 1997; Smith and Guarnizo 1998). This tends unwittingly to accentuate the special significance of such communities in world culture and politics while downplaying the contribution of other equally important non-ethnic/national communities in the global arena. There are also important terminological issues, which remain unresolved. Namely that some (mainly US based) researchers have used the term 'transnationalism' to designate the experience of post-1945 new immigrants into the USA. In contrast, other (predominately British) researchers have opted for the term 'diaspora', a word that has expanded its reach to include new groups of expatriates, refugees and immigrants (including such cases as the Kurds, Palestinians, Armenians, and so on) (Safran 1991; Anthias 1998; Van Hear 1998).

The arguments about transnationalism have reflected the general tenor of the debate between proponents and opponents of globalisation (Held *et al.* 1999). That is to say, the assertion that transnationalism is a novel phenomenon, intimately connected to the social, economic and cultural transformations of our global age (Albrow 1997), has been criticised by researchers who have pointed out that the transnational experience pre-dates the post-modern world of e-mail, faxes and instant wireless electronic services (Dominguez 1998; Hanagan 1998; Mintz 1998; Van Hear 1998: 241–56; Danforth 2000; Roudometof 2001). Historically, transnational connections, cultures and communities were the 'normal' state of affairs. This ubiquitous quality was temporarily concealed during the relatively recent age of the modernising nation-state. Affiliations and supranational organisations based on religion, ethnic diasporas and transregional trading associations were among the many transnational collectivities that preceded the modern nation. Alongside numerous local and subnational identities, such collectivities were suppressed, submerged and rendered deviant compared with the myth of a single, national people asserted by the ascendant modern nation-state (McNeill 1985; Vertovec and Cohen 1999). In any case, it was the rise of the nation-state that accelerated and massively deepened the processes associated with globalisation (Mayall 1990; Held *et al.* 1999). Moreover, the global formation of an international society of nation-states compelled many ancient diasporas to seek and to assert a new 'national' relationship to their homelands, in many instances marginalising yet other ethnic minorities and other subgroups so that they were driven to seek security by migrating elsewhere (Roudometof 1999).

In this regard, Anderson's (1983, 1993) work on modern national community is of direct relevance to our argument. Anderson (1983: 6) suggests that 'all communities larger than "primordial" villages of face-to-face contact (and perhaps even these) are imagined'. It follows, therefore, that even vast entities such as nations are communities based on imagined bonds. Indeed, this is the only way a nation can experience commonality, shared goals and a boundary; namely, as an imagined community constructed around the idea of a 'deep, horizontal comradeship' (Anderson 1983: 7). Of central significance for nation-state building was the arrival of the printed word in the vernacular, harnessed to market capitalism. Through the development of a mass market for books and newspapers – boosted eventually by state-sponsored mass education programmes – it became increasingly possible for the members of a national community to experience the 'simultaneity' (Anderson 1983: 39) of their shared experiences with numerous others far beyond the immediacy of the small face-to-face community.

As Hannerz (1996: 20–1) reminds us, Anderson's insights convincingly demonstrate how 'the leap out of the local' was made possible by the ability of people to engage in a 'common intelligibility' through developments in media technology. However, he goes on to point out that while writing binds together those of the same language it also creates discontinuities between nations and peoples who employ different languages. On the other hand, the new symbolic codes associated with the advances achieved in, and the dissemination of, the visual media technologies of the last hundred years have proved to be far less bounded and restrictive (Castells 1998a). In Anderson's (1993) view, mass migration and mobility – stimulated by the technological advances of the last decades – lead to pervasive feelings of nostalgia for the homeland. Such feelings permeate immigrant communities, thereby giving birth to the 'long distance nationalism' of ethnic diasporas, refugees, *Gastarbeiter* or illegal immigrants. This interpretation flows from Anderson's (1983) earlier work – with the important difference that now place of residence and locality have become disjoined.

Obviously, none of the above is meant to refute the fact that many transnational communities have been born out of the experience of social injustices, global inequalities and chronic insecurities. Global economic restructuring, the post-1989 capitalist boom and the ascendancy of neoliberal economic policies have further accentuated such experiences. Migrant encounters with radicalised social exclusion in host countries have further intensified the exposure of people everywhere, but especially in poor countries, to conditions of great economic and social uncertainty (Goldring 1998; Smith and Guarnizo 1998). Thus, as Schiller *et al.* (1992: x) remark, 'transnational migration is shaped by ... the encompassing global capitalist system' and 'is becoming increasingly a global phenomenon as populations in capital-dependent countries are everywhere forced to migrate to centres of capital in order to live'.

Indeed, membership and participation in such migrant or diasporic communities have long provided strategies of escape from poverty, discrimination and oppression for both individuals and their families – even if many kin remain behind in the home village (see, for example, Chan 1997; Smith 1998). Migrant communities have often offered a way of vitiating the worst aspects of poverty and oppression experienced by entire regions, countries or peoples (for example, Cohen 1997). In Portes's (1997, 2000) formulation, the transnational communities of the new immigrants represent a process of empowerment for the underprivileged groups – or what he calls 'globalisation from below' to be sharply contrasted with 'globalisation from above', i.e. global financial integration and the spread of capitalism worldwide.

As we will suggest later on, however, transnationalism is not only an escape mechanism or a mode of coping with global capitalist transformations for migrants. It may be equally valuable to other disadvantaged groups of non-migrant origins living permanently within the heartlands of many nations. Consider, for example, the cases of discriminated and disadvantaged groups (such as women or stateless and tribal peoples) whose demands for land rights, regional and cultural autonomy or independent statehood have been persistently ignored or marginalised. Such groups have often striven to seek the attention and support of global human rights or environmental or development groups in an attempt to strengthen their national or local demands (Boli *et al.* 1999: 75–6). At the same time many such underprivileged communities (such as the Kurds or Palestinians) are involved in a variety of activities that display a global frame of reference. Such groups simultaneously might demand independent statehood (in their appeals in global forums) while orchestrating transnational political solidarity as well as cementing cultural ties built around family networks spread across a number of nations.

Nor are some Third World governments averse to taking a leading role in cultivating transnational connections (Basch *et al.* 1994; Smith 1998; Smith and Guarnizo 1998). The motive for adopting a strong state presence lies in the desire to exploit the economic benefits, i.e. foreign exchange earnings from remittances, investment flows into impoverished villages and regions and the export of home products to satisfy the needs of nationals living abroad. 'In the face of the neo-liberal storm' (Smith and Guarnizo 1998: 7), these goals have assumed a new significance during the last two decades. Alongside this state-fostered economic transnationalism, certain Third World governments (such as Mexico) also seem intent on promoting the status and presence of their national culture in the world as a whole. Referred to by Smith (1998: 228) as the 'global nation', this image consists of a worldwide community of nationals with their shared cultural meanings and identities. In Mexico's case, this is accompanied by all the signifiers which denote 'Mexicaness' – and which are always and immediately recognisable as instances of 'the Mexican global nation' (Smith 1998: 229).

In this regard, the constitution of transnational national communities provides an excellent example of what Robertson (1992) has referred to as the global construction of locality, i.e. the construction of local identity drawing upon, and with specific reference to, globality. While the construction of national identity provides a solid example of this process, we should point out that the conceptual opposition between globalisation and the nation-state obscures the foundational role played by the nation-state in the institutionalisation of key political, economic and cultural features of contemporary globalisation. Furthermore, confining one's attention to the nation-state and the transnational flows of peoples detracts attention from the equally important flows of cultural practices ranging from popular music or ethnic food to types of social movements.

Thus, our approach toward the entire genre of transnational studies aims to rectify the strong emphasis of the US-based literature on 'new immigration'. We aim to accomplish this goal in a twofold manner. First, our volume includes studies of groups traditionally not included under the definition of transnationalism, either because they were conceived of as 'older', more established ethnic communities or because they are residing outside the USA (in Canada, Australia or the UK). Second, our goal is to open up the theoretical space in order to allow for the examination of additional transnational groups that do not fall within the category of 'new immigrants'. Such groups have not been traditionally included in the study of transnationalism.

Our purpose in presenting both immigrant and non-immigrant studies in a single volume is to emphasise the strong similarities that exist between all kinds of transnational and global communities irrespective of their migrant or non-migrant origins and experiences. Until now, we believe, much of the existing literature has ignored or played down these important shared characteristics and experiences. In this volume, we hope to move towards remedying this deficiency. In order to stress these shared features, our enterprise is organised equally around the themes of both transnationality and community. Indeed, we begin by discussing the nature of community and how it is that communities remain valid and viable in late modern societies.

Community in an age of globalisation

Communities are units of belonging whose members perceive that they share moral, aesthetic/expressive or cognitive meanings, thereby gaining a sense of personal as well as group identity. In turn, this identity demarcates the boundary between members and non-members. Communities therefore are constructed symbolically through an engagement with rituals, signs and meanings; they provide a container within which individual members negotiate meanings and construct and reconstruct different kinds of social relationships over time (Cohen 1979: 15–20).[1]

The classical sociological tradition stressed the 'withering away' of community under the forces of modernisation. Following Ferdinand Tönnies's *Community and Society* (1887), the division between *Gemeinschaft* 'communal' relations and *Gesellshaft* 'modern' social relations provided the backdrop for the theorisation of community (for a discussion, see Featherstone 1997). The conceptual opposition between the two types of relations was particularly popular in the first half of the twentieth century. In the second half of the twentieth century, a more nuanced perspective gradually evolved, stressing the interpenetration of 'tradition' and 'modernity' and suggesting that the use of these concepts as ideal types should not degenerate into them turning into caricatures or stereotypes (Bendix 1967). Sociologists such as Talcott Parsons or Edward Tiryakian (1991) argued that communal relations remain important for contemporary social actors. Indeed, modern units like the nation provide for 'societal communities' that serve the same function as the older, more 'traditional' premodern communities.

The new transnational connections enshrined by globalisation bring about further important changes in the nature, orientation and character of communal relations. Indeed, there are important differences between premodern and early modern communities and the communities of late modern (or post-modern) societies, and it is only by clarifying these differences that we can hope to understand how and why communities are able to flourish in global social space.

First, the communities of premodern and early modern societies were mostly based on what Beck (2000a) – with intended irony – calls 'natural' relations of narrowly defined allegiances. These relations might be compulsory (Beck 2000a: 164), but they might also involve a strong sense of inclusiveness based on 'natural' criteria. Such criteria included blood lines or descent (kinship), locality and residence (neighbourhood) and – once modernity was firmly under way – the nation and its association with what Beck calls 'state-organised citizens' solidarity' (Beck 2000a: 155, 163).

Second, in premodern and early modern societies, communal relations were basically relations of locality, thereby allowing for the construction and maintenance of all-embracing, multipurpose and intertwining relationships based on direct, face-to-face contacts. Thus, territory and social propinquity in everyday life coincided. Third, as Hannerz (1996: 26) suggests, such locally circumscribed communities were likely to endure. They could offer their members 'broadly inclusive long-term relationships', highly charged emotional relations and mutual understandings. In addition, they might typically involve 'close surveillance' of members and highly effective mechanisms of social control. In other words, there was a broad symmetry in terms of the scale and directionality of interaction flows taking place among members (Hannerz 1996: 96–7). Last, because locality could more or less guarantee that any community was endowed with a 'clearly demarcated system of communication' it also generated understanding, security and common experiences (Beck 2000a: 155–6).

It is therefore clear that physical proximity, defined by locality and residence, was central to the conventional understanding of community. Of course, it was far from the only structural constraint. Other constraints were also important. These included the restrictions on people's rights to move (including kinship, religious, customary and positional loyalties and obligations); the limited range of economic opportunities elsewhere against the immediate availability or prospect of land, employment, mutual assistance, protection or charity; and the impediments of cost, danger, risk and inconvenience associated with physical mobility and communications. To a considerable extent most, if not all, of these constraints have declined in significance for the majority of people across the world.

Unlike the era of the first state-led drive to modernity, with its scientific certainties, neat territorial containment of society, economy and nation, continuing compromise with the traditional structures of class, gender and family and the unquestioned assumption that nature could be bent in the service of human need in perpetuity, we are now in transition to a new, more 'open, risk-filled modernity characterised by general insecurity' (Beck 2000a: 19). This second or reflexive modernity must confront an entire array of new phenomena, including the information revolution with all its repercussions, a revolution in gender relations, the rise of widespread environmental threats, the reconfiguration of state sovereignty and a growing trend towards post-national citizenship (Beck 1992, 2000b; Soysal 1994; Castells 1996; Sassen 1996, 1998).

These multiple challenges and the risks associated with them both compel and allow us to pursue a path of individualisation, constructing our life paths and identities more and more free from traditional structural constraints. However, although risks must be partly tackled individually, there is also considerable scope for, and perhaps many potential advantages to be gained from, engaging in new types of 'community-bonding through the sharing of risks' (Beck 2000a: 163–4). Constructed as bulwarks against the collapse of family support, the end of secure employment, the loss of national identity or the growing threat of environmental catastrophes, Beck (2000a) argues that the new communities are founded on shared cultural outlooks and values. They are fundamentally political in intent and are likely to be increasingly transnational in scope and power. In the light of these changes, in what ways are communities different in the era of reflexive modernity and globalisation?

First, community today is actively generated by its members in much the same way that trust in social relations has to be 'energetically treated and sustained' (Giddens 1994: 186). Neither the emergence nor the continuity of community can be taken for granted by its members. Second, the reflexivity of communal connections is revealed in the voluntary involvement of individuals who choose to set up a community or to seek membership in it (Lash 1994: 161). This reflexivity stands in sharp contrast to the more 'traditional' communities where membership was allocated according to fixed criteria ascribed by birth and social position. Following on from this voluntarism, participation in communal relations neither is a once-and-for-all decision nor is continuity assured or inevitable. Instead, participation is likely to engender a conscious reconsideration of the nature and purpose of a community, perhaps leading to a process of 'constant reinvention'.

Third, there is a relative shift from material resources and ends toward symbolic, informational and cultural resources and goals (Lash 1994: 161). Fourth, reflexive communities are no longer all-embracing. They do not provide a totalising life programme or schema designed to cover all events and purposes and they may overlap with other communities (Beck 2000a: 164). Nor are they necessarily permanent or even long lasting and intensely emotional. Finally, underlying the above-mentioned features lie deeper and more important shifts in the connections among space and community. In order to gain a better and deeper understanding of these shifts, we need to take into account the transformation of the other main corollary of 'community', i.e. the notion of 'culture'.

Rethinking culture, locality and community

Over the last twenty years or so, the increasingly obvious exposure of societies, economies, cultures and peoples to each others' practices, needs and meanings has led to extensive revisions of the social scientific discourse on the connections among locality, culture and community. Within anthropological discourse in particular, this revision has led to the open questioning of the connection between culture and locality.[2] In the new revisions, anthropologists have raised a twofold argument. First, they have argued that the traditional anthropological notion of 'culture' – as essentially localised and moored to a particular place while existing as a self-contained, internally coherent, all-inclusive package with clearly defined borders – is misguided. Second, the idea of 'culture' as fixed through childhood socialisation – to be later reinforced by unchanging and uncontested external social pressures – fails to take into account the social actor's reflexivity.

On the first issue, Rapport and Dawson (1998: 4) claim that the 'localising image of separate and self-sufficient worlds' found in much anthropological analysis was 'never more than a useful ideology that served the interests of (some) anthropologists'. According to Clifford (1988, 1992), earlier ethnographers tended to construct and represent the cultures they were studying in spatial terms so that villages were seen as 'bounded sites' (Clifford 1992: 98). This tendency to localise cultures – to tie them to concrete places – yielded a view in which the natives appeared to be imprisoned or confined 'through a process of representational essentialising' (Clifford 1992: 100). Ethnographers overlooked the fact that it was actually their own methodological needs and strategies which generated this result, e.g. the use of the village as a manageable unit for purposes of eliciting information and for providing a convenient focal point from which to construct a picture of an entire culture. At the same time, anthropologists forgot that they were only able to function at all because numerous external influences and changes had previously prepared the ground, thus making their travel and sojourn possible while many of their key informants were only able to play their roles because they had already acquired a sufficiently cosmopolitan outlook. In all this the true existential character of cultures as simultaneous sites of both travel and dwelling and subject to multiple anchorages – always exposed to numerous external influences and the movement of people in and out and often sites of negotiation whose members were engaged in continuous encounters with other cultures – became largely hidden from view or side-lined.

On the second issue – namely the supposedly fixed, internally coherent and externally imposed, non-negotiable nature of culture – various writers have challenged such conceptualisations. Thus, for example, Swidler (1986: 273) argues that culture needs to be seen as providing a ' "toolkit" of symbols, stories, rituals and world views, which people may use in varying configurations in order to solve different kinds of problems'. Similarly, Hoben and Hefner (1991: 18) argue that 'tradition' is too often understood as a set of meanings, which provide fixed standards against which all changes have to be measured and justified. But, what tradition actually requires is to be renewed, modified and remade in each generation.

This rethinking of the traditional notion of 'culture' suggests that cultures may never have possessed the degree of solidity and firm attachment to localities attributed to them by many social scientists. Moreover, there seems little doubt that they have become even less coherent than formerly, and much of this is because cultures are being 'delocalised' – lifted from particular and familiar places and thrown into the 'global post-modern' maelstrom (Hall 1992: 302). As Featherstone and Lash (1999: 1) declare in their introduction to an excellent collection of essays on contemporary cultural experience, the declining viability of the notion that cultures possess a degree of coherence sufficient to guarantee stable identities is the result of globalisation.

In this context, it is important to draw a distinction between older periods of globalisation and the increased contact among peoples, cultures, economies and regions of our information age. First of all, in the pre-1500 period, globalisation was a gradual, uneven and highly contested process that did not, for the most part, penetrate deep into societies and cultures. Then, following 1492, the pace of globalisation gathered considerable force, culminating in the modern period of globalisation (1840–1945) (Held *et al.*

1999; see also Robertson 1992). In the post-1945 period, this process culminated in the construction of a truly global economy. During this period, Castells (1998a) argues, the world produced the technological infrastructure required for a truly global economy to function as 'a unit on a planetary scale', i.e. information systems, telecommunications, microelectronic-based manufacturing and processing, information-based air transportation, container cargo transport, high-speed trains and international business services located around the world. This global economy is an economy whose core activities work as a unit in real time on a planetary scale – as the case of capital markets aptly illustrates.

Fuelled by the information revolution (Castells 1996) of the last thirty years, the rapidly accelerated pace of contemporary globalisation has generated 'new spaces' where cultures clash and mix both across and within nations.[3] Communication technologies are a crucial causal agent involved in this radical delocalisation of culture. The power of the mass media in the global arena – especially the extraordinary intensity and reach of the visual media of television, film and video – has massively enhanced the influence that imagination can exert over the everyday lives of ordinary people everywhere (Appadurai 1991). Because of the mass media's global penetration into all cultures and societies, we can no longer easily continue to inhabit entirely localised worlds even if we wish to do so. Simultaneously, the media facilitate the social production of fantasy, whereby the line between simulated reality and the 'real world' is erased (Baudrillard 1983). Thus, even those trapped in the most demeaning and impoverished circumstances can no longer experience reality as a 'given'. For example, the image of the 'global city', broadcast around the world (including the most impoverished nations), acts as an incentive facilitating actual migration in search of one or other imagined alternative.[4]

According to Welsh (1999), so profound have been the changes inflicted on cultural experience, at both the macro/societal level and the microlevel where individuals grapple with problems of personal identity, that we need an entirely new way of understanding it. Clearly, the traditional notion of single, entirely separate and homogeneous cultures embedded in an ethnic or folk core is now completely unacceptable. But, Welsh (1999: 197) also rejects the idea of interculturality and multiculturality since both continue to presume that we live in a world made up of separate, distinctive and internally coherent cultural 'islands or spheres' where social actors are nevertheless engaged in exercises designed to achieve mutual understanding, peaceful coexistence and a degree of interlearning. Instead, he suggests that the reality of living today with cultural conditions 'largely characterised by mixes and permeations' (Welsh 1999: 197) demands an alternative conceptualisation, namely the idea of transculturality. Thus, ours is a world of complexity and difference produced by endless amounts of cultural 'interpenetration' – while, at the same time, cultures increasingly overlap and interconnect with one another through 'external networking'. Accordingly, '[l]ifestyles no longer end at the border of national cultures ... [and] ... are found in the same way in other cultures' (Welsh 1999: 197–8).

We have already alluded to the changing nature of communities in our global age. Thus, communities today are consciously constructed and continuously reinvented; their membership is voluntary and may be impermanent so that continuity is not guaranteed. Material goals and resources remain important but the balance is likely to tilt more towards the informational and cultural concerns of members. That is to say, the advancing technologies of transport and communication transform the nature of social interactions among community members. Membership no longer needs to be only or even mainly based on direct, face-to-face interactions.[5]

In addition, we want to suggest that communities today are further influenced by the shifting nature of 'culture' or, to put it more precisely, by the delinking between locality and culture. The production of locality, of 'neighbourhood' and the *Gemeinschaft* social relations it engenders, has never been easy – even in premodern societies (Elias and Scotson 1965; Appadurai 1995). Ceremonies and rituals concerned with multiple boundary demarcations, with protecting resources, with trying to ensure loyalty and continuity and prevent fission and with much else besides were frequent and important.

Under globalised conditions, locality, no longer necessarily rooted in particular places, has become highly problematic. The traditional unifier of the modern era, the nation-state, is now under siege by two other forces: first, by the despatialisation of social relations (i.e. the fact that subjectivity, territory and social relations no longer necessarily need to coincide directly), and, second, by what Appadurai (1995: 213) calls the separation of 'spatial and visual neighbourhoods'. Despatialisation is the inevitable outcome of numerous migrations and increased global mobility at large (Bauman 1998: 6–26, 77–102). Both factors have dispersed, displaced, mixed and brought into conjunction, whether in harmony or conflict, disparate cultures and peoples across cities, regions, countries and continents.

Beyond mere physical mobility, it is the electronic mass media that have completed this process by enabling small, dispersed communities to communicate as groups through film, theatre and other forums. In this process of producing 'spatial and visual neighbourhoods' lie immense opportunities for effective interpersonal, microlevel communication and collaboration – operating independently of states and corporations. Such opportunities extend through access to home-made video, cassette and camera or through facsimile and electronic mail to more and more individuals and families. As the incidence of virtual neighbourhoods across the world grows, it will be increasingly possible for their members to 'create more effective national and global strategies of self-representation and cultural survival' (Appadurai 1995: 218). Such processes of delocalisation create numerous uncertainties as well as possible permutations in terms of different kinds of social relationships. Thus, as Beck (2000a: 29) vividly suggests, people may live in local isolation with respect to some groups – 'as if they existed on different planets' – but they may enjoy social nearness and closeness to others living thousands of miles away, thus merging 'into a single social space'.

The range of possible situations and ways of coping with delocalisation, social fragmentation and the pluralisation of meanings brought by globalisation has been explored by the contributors to the research project carried out on London as a global city in the mid-1990s (Eade 1997a). Some white residents found themselves increasingly isolated, alone and unable to adapt when faced with the settlement of large-scale migrant communities from other countries and the death or exodus of older natives like themselves. They tended to resent life in a multicultural society. Others who had been born in the locality made some approaches to the newcomers, kept in touch with other elderly white residents through local amenities while participating in national and global friendship networks through letter, phone and holiday visits abroad. Some, mostly younger, white locals embraced migrant social life as a result of shared experiences based on school, youth or other common connections. Some individuals, on the other hand, knew hardly any one at all, whether white natives or migrants, but felt no resentment because to them the locality was simply a site of temporary accommodation while their important relationships were scattered across many other locations elsewhere (Durrschmidt 1997). A similarly wide range of variations with respect to local and global affiliations was equally apparent among the migrants (Eade 1997b).

As a final point to the argument advanced in the preceding paragraphs and in order to avoid misunderstandings and misinterpretations of our thesis, we need to add three important qualifications. First, our argument obviously does not imply a negation of the significance of the physical locale. Everyone continues to inhabit one or more locale at any one point in time in the obvious sense that we all need a place to eat, sleep, store our possessions, find shelter and pursue our interests and needs for leisure and recreation. Moreover, most of us also participate in a place of work. Although for many types of employment this may not necessitate confinement to any one particular location but may instead involve fairly continuous travel, work normally requires places of residence and rest within easy reach, however temporary such places might be.[6]

Second, the declining dependence of more and more people on their immediate locale as their only or main source of direct, interpersonal relationships does not mean that we do not continue to romanticise the local. Indeed, its traditions seem to exist in 'limitless supply', and while the global often appears to be rather 'shallow' the local retains depth and substance – at least in our imagination (Hannerz 1996: 28). Third, it is necessary to highlight the sociological significance of the distinction between locality (in the sense of 'place' or physical proximity) and territory (or what might be referred to as 'soil' or 'homeland' or ancestral birthplace). For the delocalisation of many communities does not imply a loss of significance for territory. For example, diaspora communities continue to be primarily defined and organised around ethnic or national affiliations and maintain a strong sense of attachment to their homelands. Indeed, the histories of these groups are deeply grounded in particular territories (see Danforth 2000).

Communities across borders: people and cultures

In our global age, communities have become liberated from dependence upon direct interpersonal relations and, like cultures, from the need to operate primarily within the limits set by particular physical locations. Locality is no longer the only or even the primary vehicle for sustaining community. The subversion of physical locality and its reconstitution in a deterritorialised fashion is a task carried out by the migration of people and cultures across borders.

The 'new immigrants' of the global age, variously defined as 'transmigrants' or 'transnational' peoples, have provided the traditional research site for the study of transnational connections (Schiller *et al.* 1992; Basch *et al.* 1994; Guarnizo and Smith 1998; Portes 2000). Many observers (for example, Smith and Guarnizo 1998; Portes *et al.* 1999; Vertovec 1999; Vertovec and Cohen 1999) have argued that the new forms of communications technology and mass transport are giving rise to unparalleled opportunities for the members of migrant national communities to opt for the perpetuation of active transnational linkages between homeland and host country in preference to assimilation because such technologies have placed the power to create a simultaneity of experience and feeling right into the hands of migrants themselves (Smith 1998: 213). Moreover, second-, third- or fourth-generation migrants might be empowered to reinvent and revitalise their former national cultural identities long after it seemed that they had moved firmly in the direction of host society assimilation (for example, Schein 1998).

However, just like people, cultures can and do migrate, increasingly assisted by electronic communications and the mass media in addition to being carried through interpersonal social exchanges. Transnational cultures lead to the formation of communities of 'taste', shared beliefs or economic interests – to list a few of the factors that work on a global scale. This mobility of cultures, people, economic resources and much else besides necessarily both requires and creates deterritorialisation – an increasing number of situations in which social interactions take place across, beyond, outside and frequently without any reference to particular nations, borders and identities (Appadurai 1990). In effect, transnationalism is necessary, unavoidable and advantageous. It has become a built in feature of the cultural, social, political and economic lives of many people everywhere.

Appadurai's (1991) concept of 'ethnoscapes' has meant to provide a vehicle for conceptualising the deterritorised 'spaces' occupied by multitudes of transnational or diasporic migrants as well as by tourists, professionals and experts, entertainers and cosmopolitans along with the members of corporations, associations, interest groups and political movements.

Accompanying and following these ethnoscapes – and often independently of them – are numerous mobile flows (Urry 2000) consisting of meanings, ideas, images and information but also goods, finance, informal and organisational arrangements and all the other baggage which human beings both need and generate as a result of their local and worldwide interactions.

Reflected in the division of this volume, our thematisation of the transnational experience consists of classifying the delocalised, deterritorialised communities of our global age into two groups: the new immigrant groups of the post-1945 migrants, and the groups organised around transnational cultures. We should stress that traditional or 'old' diasporas or ethnic communities should, at least in our view, be considered as examples of transnational cultures. Hence, the second- or third-generation ethnics of many immigrant nations provide examples of transnational culture. Our recommendation aims to provide a general framework capable of allowing the examination of delocalised culture in addition to the experience of recent immigrants. Moreover, the persistence and intergenerational reproduction of ethnic difference should not be viewed as a phenomenon of the last twenty years since a rich literature does exist pointing out the long history of this phenomenon (see, for example, Jacobson 1995; Morawska and Spohn 1997; Hanagan 1998; Roudometof 2001).

It is tempting to suggest that the first group consists of the new 'local' or transnational national communities; while the second group consists of truly 'global' communities – at least in the sense of them not being tied to a 'national' community, but rather being organised around a different set of orientations that explicitly transcend the national divide.[7] Such an interpretation would be dangerously close to a false opposition between the local and the global, for the two are mutually dependent upon each other and, therefore, to view them in isolation is misleading at best. In our view, such a distinction is unhelpful and misleading. There are several reasons for this.

First, it may be possible to distinguish between transnational links across and between two or more countries that are constructed primarily around specific ethnic or national loyalties, affiliations and concerns – defined by ties of blood, territorial origins and citizenship – and yet others that are not defined in strictly ethnic or national terms at all but are rather shaped according to ties and affiliations determined by sport, leisure, lifestyle, business and so on. Very little research has been conducted on the last, but that does not mean that such transnational associations do not flourish. Indeed, it is our contention that such ties do exist but that they are rarely taken into account in the literature – with the rather obvious exception of the Americanisation debate (see Epitropoulos and Roudometof 1998).

Second, as our own case studies demonstrate, migrant and diasporic communities are extremely heterogeneous both with respect to each other and in terms of internal differences among their members. Class, education, occupation, generational cohort or even the particular leanings towards varying religious preferences are factors likely to generate considerable heterogeneity within any particular ethnic or national group over time. Such differences may ultimately create a situation where subgroups within an ethnic community share a lifestyle and personal aspirations which bear a stronger resemblance to those evinced by members of the 'dominant' host society than to the members of their own migrant group. At the very least, such individuals are likely to 'accept that identity is subject to the play of history, politics, representation and difference ' (Hall 1992: 309) and learn to live within the fragmented, ever-changing and plural realities of a multicultural – or transcultural (Welsh 1999) – existence shaped by multiple identities and affiliations.

Third, given that participation in community has become much more open, flexible and subject to negotiation, it is perfectly possible for an individual to participate in more than one kind of community at the same time. By the same token, the focus of a person's allegiance between such communities may also shift over time, depending upon the specifics of individual biography (for examples and further discussion, see Hedetoft 1999). In other words, community allegiances contain diachronic and synchronic aspects, thereby demanding situational analysis. Thus, even the most loyal and passionate member of a deterritorialised ethnic or national community may nevertheless also offer strong support to a human rights, green, religious or other cause committed to solving global problems and to engaging in global co-operation and campaigning strategies. Similarly, individuals with strong attachments to ethnic or national diasporas might also demonstrate powerful loyalties to a professional, scientific, political or business identity and ethos which has obvious cosmopolitan and universalistic leanings and implications.[8]

The reverse may also be possible. Thus, individuals whose primary loyalties and identities are defined by membership of a cosmopolitan professional ethos and whose families enjoy ancient non-diasporic roots to a single nation may develop a sudden and unexpected feeling of national pride – perhaps prompted by loneliness or by a sense of being overwhelmed by engulfment in a foreign society and culture during a period or during employment abroad. Such feelings may give rise to the impulse to seek out local members of the expatriate national community, to openly declaim and reaffirm national origins and identities and to keep alive, revive or even intensify long-standing links to friends, family and others who have remained in the homeland. However, these strong tendencies towards transnationalism on the part of such individuals may prove to be short-lived – they disappear or fade once other friendships with non-nationals have had sufficient time to develop or with the prospect of a return to the home country. Moreover, they may prove to be perfectly compatible with an equal and parallel participation in a worldwide community of friendships constructed around earlier and continuing shared professional experiences. The range of possible situations and permutations here, and the scope for individuals and groups to engage in multiple affiliations and to negotiate between several non-exclusive identities, is vast.

Last, as stated above, many disadvantaged tribal or ethnic peoples and groups – lacking a homeland and/or independent statehood, some of whose members are dispersed across many counties – have been simultaneously engaged in using global forums as one key vehicle for seeking worldwide support while maintaining concrete cultural and kinship ties across several countries built around primordial identities. Moreover, their involvement in global strategies has often bought such groups into close alliance with and dependence upon other non-ethnic/national groups with an entirely global agenda such as human rights or the environment such that the different causes become partly merged at times. Something like this synergy took place at the Earth Summit in Rio in 1992, but there are numerous other examples.

In summary, it appears that proposing or maintaining a clear and watertight distinction between 'truly' global as opposed to 'purely' transnational national communities is difficult, sometimes impossible and not very helpful. Moreover, both types of communities share specific experiences that, in our view, justify their inclusion into a single category. These include the following:

1   *More or less equal exposure to global flows and processes.* All the individuals and groups participating in transnational communities and cultures are exposed to globalising forces from multiple and similar sources, including a global economy; the mass media in all their forms; the particularistic cultural flows originating from many parts of the world; the vast movement of people as tourists, entertainers, commercial agents and so on; and the influence exercised by goods, information, values/ideas, commercial temptations and much else besides. Migrants, of course, constitute part of these forces and expose host communities to their values and lifestyles. But the reverse is obviously also even true if migrants are prevented from assimilating or do not desire to do so fully or at all. Thus, global influences reach 'locals' who have never moved from their place of birth and those caught up in recent or earlier migrant flows in equal part, while both constitute part of those same global flows with respect to each other's experiences. 'Local-ness' has become relative.

2   *Bringing the local and the global into conjunction.* Everyone is compelled to live with and negotiate the paradoxes and complexities arising from the simultaneous exposure to local/national and global influences. Similarly, however cosmopolitan and mobile we may be – used to moving between and living and working within a series of temporary, short-lived social situations and locales – at any one moment in time we all nevertheless reside in a particular place insinuated with numerous meanings and interact with a given set of 'others'. Retaining a foothold at the local level while juggling with global forces and connections is a condition no one escapes.

3   *A universal frame of reference.* Whoever may be the subject of investigation – either migrants or permanent, long-established locals or globe-trotting

middle-class cosmopolitans – everyone shares common points of reference which lend some structure and meaning to their lives: a place and nation of birth, parentage and family ties; citizenship (whether single, dual, uncertain, contested, unwanted or whatever); perhaps a preferred, ultimate or ideal homeland or place of destination; and a current locale where a livelihood, a habitat and some degree of sociality, however temporary, superficial or undesirable, may be sought (for further discussion, see Robertson 1992).

4   *Technological advances offer new resources to everyone.* In recent times, the interpersonal and symbolic/imagined exchanges involved in community life have been transformed by the possibilities inherent in communications and transportation technology. It is important to remember, however, that everyone can benefit from recent advances in technology in terms of cementing ties and orientations over huge distances, forging or enlarging new attachments or enhancing the sense of shared meanings between those deemed to be members of the same community. Thus, technological empowerment enables lower-class youths in Mexico City who have never experienced overseas migration to participate in and borrow from global popular culture while forging their own brands of punk – as Chapter 10 demonstrates. As the discussion in Chapter 6 reveals, educated UK-based Iranians join in a global sports event, like billions of others, thereby temporarily neutralising their enforced loss of social status as non-citizens while becoming symbolically reunited with their countrymen. At the same time, videos, photos, e-mails and all the rest enable far-flung middle-class cosmopolitans to keep in daily touch with their families back 'home', with their friendship clusters in several countries and with their co-professional community sharing the same ethos across the world (Bauman 1998). It is not just the lives and interactions of migrants engaged in maintaining transnational national communities that are being transformed by advancing technology.

5   *Disadvantage stemming from common exposure to macroforces.* Both migrant and non-migrant populations experience different degrees of oppression, deprivation, insecurity, marginalisation and inequality, whether this emanates chiefly from the national location where people are currently situated, from the global economy and polity or from both of these at the same time. Moreover, these experiences may have historical links and continuities. We outlined some of these earlier: racial/ethnic prejudice from the host society and/or state and the existence of obstacles to assimilation or citizenship participation; class discrimination and deprivation; a long history of communal exile, exploitation and imperialist oppression and denigration; increased exposure to global, hegemonic–political and/or economic controls and ideologies such as neoliberalism which prevent or inhibit attempts to develop home economies or which inflict deprivation on migrants and non-migrants alike – especially,

women, the unskilled, the rural landless peasants, those employed in traditional industries – across many countries.[9]

6   *The opportunities and resources generated by globalisation.* The formation of new communities and the growing participation in established ones may provide key resources which enable disadvantaged groups to partly neutralise, resist or even reverse some of the forms of oppression to which they have been subjected. Thus, participation in such cultures and communities can be and frequently is empowering for both individuals and groups. Sometimes, what may begin as a desire to harness global community support for purely local goals and needs may culminate in a decision to pursue global goals and causes, seen as valid in their own right but also useful for the attainment of local aims. Such transnational mobilisation is going to be an important feature of organisational life in the twenty-first century. It may involve alliances of trade unions across the world with churches, environmental or women's non-governmental organisations or via human rights groups working with migrant communities, stateless peoples and the representatives of marginalised Third and First World groups. Again, the local and the global reveal a capacity to become merged and inseparable.

In different ways, the scenarios outlined in 5 and 6 are demonstrated by most of our case studies. Here, we briefly outline some of these examples. In Grierson's study in Chapter 11, artists from several Pacific islands were trying to recover and assert their unique local identities while celebrating hybridity as well as their strength and dignity through expressing their transnational unity. The Polish Silesian Lutherans in Kempny's study (Chapter 8) were engaged in symbolically retrieving their 'lost' place identity as a reaction to their engulfment in the turmoil created by vast changes taking place in the societies surrounding them and which have continuously disrupted and disadvantaged them over many years. O'Connor's work (Chapter 10) on young people in Mexico City shows how, as non-migrants experiencing political and class oppression, they were participating on their own terms in a global punk subculture which, wherever it has appeared, has tended to be associated with the symbolic criticism and even rejection through music of conventional politics and social life. In this sense its potential to subvert the established order or to press for alternative, radical values unites members everywhere on a similar basis, even though – as O'Connor shows – the actual content of this criticism and the political form it takes may vary considerably across countries. In the Mexican case, punk was a means of symbolically subverting the dominant class and political hierarchies in Mexico and the latter's agenda for pursuing conventional development strategies that do little to help the poor. Roudometof and Karpathakis (Chapter 3) show how recent lower-class Greek emigrants to the USA are more likely to adopt a direct political stance with respect to their affirmation of continuing identity with their Greek homeland than the more religious and cultural expressions of diasporic belonging revealed by second- and third-generation migrants. This is related to the fact that members of the former group are finding assimilation difficult and they experience a sense of ethnic/national as well as relative class deprivation in relation both to the non-Greek population and to the longer established members of the Greek diasporic population in America. Finally, the middle-class Iranians living in the UK discussed in Chapter 6 had been 'de-classed' as a result of the discrimination to which they were exposed in Britain since they were compelled to pursue occupations below their educational levels. They were also exiled from an oppressive homeland regime – an experience which had halted their pursuit of upward class mobility towards bourgeois status since this is difficult to attain outside one's own nation. To them, enjoyment of the global game of football, based on equality of participation in an open competition and their pride in seeing their national team beat the superpower's team in a fair and just match marked by a spirit of generosity and good relations, offered a medium for reasserting their belonging to and pride in a 'lost' national identity and some temporary compensation from the humiliations involved in living abroad.

7   *The local/national and global impact of transnational communities.* Irrespective of their orientation and character at any one time, most transnational and global communities have a potential to shape nation-states and local economies as well as global political, social and economic life. Such communities have long been a formidable component of the global flows which increasingly connect peoples, cultures, economies and nations to one another and, again, the literature on migration, diasporas and the numerous examples of active transnational nationalism has led the way in exploring this issue. The interactions of people and meanings to which they contribute may have wider implications either for conflict or cohesion. Thus, long before the surge of cross-issue and multinational political collaboration which crystallised strongly and unambiguously around the theme of global economic injustice at Seattle in December 1999 – and which has continued to have an impact on key world forums ever since – there had been numerous earlier campaigns over such issues as nuclear power and weapons, environmental issues, apartheid in South Africa and corporate irresponsibility. Although these were mainly aimed at national governments they also succeeded in attracting global support or had worldwide repercussions (see, for example, Hegedus 1989; Scarce 1990; Clapp 1997; Roseneil 1997; Rodman 1998). For example, the Jubilee 2000 campaign against Third World debt, formed in 1990, has clearly been very successful not only in orchestrating and synchronising numerous global organisations but also in welding together an influential worldwide political community. By the end of the year 2000, it was able to muster a petition signed by 23 million people from affiliated groups spread across more than 100 countries. Moreover, by harnessing the media

influence exercised by several key celebrity figures – who are immensely influential in the world of popular and youth culture – to the campaign, the organisers have demonstrated the huge potential for exploiting the vast reservoirs of untapped 'political' support among ordinary people everywhere.

Many of the papers in our collection discuss concrete examples of the immediate or potential impact of transnational communities on local and national life. But, again, the examples are not confined to transnational national communities. Here, briefly, we mention just three instances. Grierson shows in Chapter 11 how artistic endeavour provided the basis for empowering and bringing together the representatives of many disadvantaged and dispersed local Pacific peoples. But this experience has enabled the participants to rediscover and reinvent both their separate and collective meanings and social identities while celebrating their long history of cross-Pacific hybridisation. The Mexican managers in Contreras's study (Chapter 9) were members of a global professional community created by and linked to corporate capital. Participation in this business ethos had enabled them not only to improve their personal career structures but also to become members of an increasingly confident cosmopolitan local élite. Their ability to embed into and adapt their acquired professional business skills, connections and experiences to the needs of Mexican economic life helped to deepen the national industrial base, thereby helping to counter some aspects of regional underdevelopment. Wong's study (Chapter 12) of immigrants in Canada explores the potentially adverse consequences for immigrant groups, for their descendants and also for the national and global economy that may arise given the recent attempt by the Canadian state to reverse its diminishing authority over citizenship by imposing narrower and more territorially linked criteria for future citizenship claims. In a country built upon flourishing transnational and intergenerational networks of people who live within its boundaries, but who retain multiple national affiliations, such a policy seems contradictory and likely to threaten long-term national prosperity.

Toward a tentative typology of globalised communities

All contemporary globalised communities are inevitably different from their predecessors. Nevertheless, ignoring key differences would be just as counterproductive as ignoring similarities and much of our discussion has loosely referred to – or has assumed the existence of – five major types of communities. These are defined in terms of the primary concerns and orientations of their members and are:

- Transnational national communities of the kind discussed by Basch *et al.* (1994) and the contributors to the readings edited by Smith and Guarnizo

(1998). Here, members are primarily concerned with the articulation and reproduction of common, ethnic and national interests, economic linkages and cultural similarities. The ties among community members connect those based in the homeland with those members dispersed across specific national host territories. Membership is mainly or perhaps entirely defined in terms of common ethnic or national origins.

- More widely dispersed and probably older national and ethnic migrant groups constituting a diaspora whose attachment to a homeland is more symbolic in nature and whose members have become assimilated to various degrees into one or more host societies. The Italian Canadians discussed by Fortier in Chapter 7 as well as the older, established communities of Greek Americans briefly discussed by Roudometof and Karpathakis in Chapter 3 provide examples of such groups.
- Communities (mostly but not entirely) of meaning cohering around shared lifestyle orientations and practices involving aesthetic, affective bonds and understandings such as sport, celebrity, musical and artistic followings and fanzines. O'Connor's discussion of the punk subculture in Chapter 10 provides a solid example of such communities. We should add that punk is only one subculture, and there are other musical subcultures that are popular worldwide – ranging from heavy metal to hip hop, techno and rap.
- Communities based on a political, moral or ethical perception of local or global injustices and problems, where the search for solutions necessarily engenders and requires transnational collaborative action leading to the construction of a 'global' culture based on voluntary action and oriented toward problem-solving (Boli and Thomas 1999).
- Groups bonded by a shared professional or occupational ethos based on the notion of service to others and duty to clients, a set of mutually respected skills and exposure to a common set of organisational experiences and obligations which empower them to cope well with mobility and to negotiate global cosmopolitan spaces with relative ease.

The first two types of community are constructed around the so-called 'natural' ties of blood, race, ethnicity and nationality. In this, they are obviously different from the rest of the communities in the above list. Here, indeed, migrant and diasporic communities do seem to exhibit a formidable cluster of features that mark them out from other kinds of transnational and global community and which go a long way towards explaining the attention they have received from researchers. Even so, there are several reasons for suggesting that we should not allow this to distract us from the need to place all types of globalised communities within a single theoretical frame.

First, it is essential to bear in mind all those experiences, opportunities, potential impacts, a common frame of reference, the structural constraints, technological changes and so on which expose every type of community to essentially similar realities under globalised conditions and which we examined in detail earlier. Second, the situation with respect to cultural/ aesthetic, professional/business and political/ethical communities may change dramatically in the future as the interconnectivities brought by globalisation, including technological advance, rapidly intensify, thereby increasing the need and the potential to build much more durable links and structures approximating more closely to those displayed by migrant and diasporic communities. Third, a considerable and growing amount of heterogeneity is apparent both within and between different transnational migrant communities. This is readily apparent in several of our case studies, e.g. in the chapter by Roudometof and Karpathakis on the complex religious and cultural differences displayed by members of the Greek diaspora in the USA. Another instance is discussed by Dommernik and van Amersfoort in Chapter 4, where they consider the varying degrees of success and determination with which Turkish migrants and their descendants have sought assimilation into Dutch life and intermarriage with native Dutch people alongside the manifestation of very different forms of Islamic religious practice and militancy. In addition, some members of national/ethnic communities seem to display cosmopolitan and professional leanings and attitudes which differentiate them sharply from their less well-educated and more nationalistic fellow members, as Colic-Peisker's discussion (Chapter 2) of middle-class Croatian migrants in Australia clearly shows.

Fourth, there has long been an argument in the literature on transnational ethnic/national communities to the effect that migrants have always been confronted with two sets of alternatives. On the one hand, they could resist full assimilation into the host culture and retain a high degree of ethnic separatism or seek such assimilation in the long term. Alternatively, they could pursue a degree of absorption into the host society but alongside this maintain an attachment to their diaspora's history, its traditions, nostalgic longing for the homeland and some degree of continuing transnational connections to ethnic or national members dispersed across the world. However, this supposed bipolarity between diasporic experiences versus the assimilation–ethnic separatist option has increasingly been challenged. Faist (1999), for example, attacks what he calls the 'container concept of culture' (Faist 1999: 31). Here, immigrant lifestyles and meanings tend to be seen as something forever being 'figuratively packed and unpacked, uprooted (assimilationists) and transplanted (cultural pluralists)', always existing either as a whole or in a state of dismemberment but never, apparently, surviving in multiple transnationalised forms in conjunction with other equally translocal and hybridised cultures across many borders (Faist 1999: 32). Several of the chapters in our collection also take issue with this viewpoint. Fortier, for example, shows that the Italian presence in Canada is often understood in terms of both migration and a claim to be indigenous, i.e. to have created a second Italian homeland in Canada. Drawing on work by Brah (1996) and Gilroy (1993), Fortier suggests that what is really important to many individuals is not so much the need for a concrete homeland as the homing desire as such, and that the diasporic imagination often involves the search for routes as well as roots and the need to negotiate continuously and understand the state of being in-between place of origin and place of destination.

Finally, and following on from the last point, a central theme explored by a number of our contributors concerns the importance that diasporic members attach to the construction of their own ethnic or national community. Yet, more often than not this occurs without the need to imagine community as tied to a particular location. For example, this delocalisation may revolve around what are essentially 'floating' cultural sites, often linked to shared religious rites, icons or temples, as Matthews shows in Chapter 5 for the case of Asians living in Canada, many of whom had previously migrated several times between different countries and may never have lived in their original 'homeland' at all. Shared religious interactions, beliefs and ceremonies also helped to symbolise community for many of the Turks living in Europe (discussed by Doomernik and van Amersfoort) as well as for the second- and third-generation Greeks in the USA (discussed by Roudometof and Karpathakis). The latter are engaged in intense internal debates over how best to represent Greek identity through different versions of Orthodox church culture. Alternatively, Fortier shows how community was created for many Italian Canadians by relying on historical memories and the dissection of different claims concerning the nature of migratory experience. Colic-Peisker's chapter reveals yet another strategy for symbolically constructing community adopted by the mainly older Croats in her study who had migrated to Australia from small villages; namely, their nostalgic yearnings for, and their idealisations of, an idyllic but now lost rural background in post-war Croatia. Kempny's Lutheran Silesians (Chapter 8) now live officially in catholic Poland, but in reality they occupy a borderland region subject to centuries of upheaval, regime changes, in and out migrations, religious threats and shifting frontiers. Indeed, since 1918 – after Polish independence – they have become virtually a host minority besieged in their 'own' land both by 'foreign' newcomers and an increasingly pluralistic culture – a sort of 'transnational' national community in reverse whose members never left their original region of settlement. This long experience of chronic insecurity has heightened the potential significance of locality and historically occupied territory as the sole remaining, potent source of community identity. Yet, even here, we find that though 'place' has indeed retained that role it has become delinked from territory – its defining power rests on the fact that it has now become a symbolic construct self-consciously used in order to represent a space of cultural distinctiveness rather than a geographical entity.

Conclusion

The ways in which its members experience community today is different from the forms of community that flourished in premodern and early modern societies. Nevertheless, none of this undermines the capacity of 'community' to meet the needs of its members. In an age of globalisation, 'culture' and 'community' have become separated from locality. Indeed, the deterritorialisation of culture is in large part responsible for transforming people's notions of what constitutes a community. Community now assumes a more fluid nature. This opens up opportunities for groups to reconstitute themselves around various kinds of shared identities despite their dispersal over considerable distances. In a global age, distance is no longer an impediment to community.

Indeed, far from globalisation jeopardising the possibility of viable communal life, it has probably given the latter a new lease of life. *Thus, transnational communities are almost destined to provide the most significant form of 'community' in the future.* It may be that most future communities will not only derive numerous advantages from operating with a transnational or global orientation but this will be increasingly necessary, perhaps even inevitable, if they are to fulfil the needs of their members adequately.

The fact that more and more communities are now transnational in intention and practice does not mean that 'locality' has ceased to be significant. For one thing, at any one moment in time everyone occupies a locale with its attendant life-world no matter how much they travel or participate in multiple worldwide networks. However, it is also the case that globalisation compels the local to rethink itself; globalisation relativises and changes the local even as localisation not only presupposes but also, in turn, revitalises and informs the global (Robertson 1992).

Following on from the last point, the continuing salience of territory is especially evident in the case of migrant, ethnic/diasporic, transnational communities. However, in these instances, locality is normally experienced symbolically; it consists of an imagined homeland or place understood through nostalgia, memory, history or constructed cultural sites and it is precisely this quality which enables such transnational communities to survive and remain viable for its members.

It seems to us that this delinking of communal identity from specific places or territories by so many (migrant and non-migrant) groups provides powerful evidence in support of our claims concerning the increasing similarities between all types of globalised communities under globalising conditions. Thus, 'place' is replaced by an imagined or symbolic unity built around shared meanings. Locality does not evaporate. Rather, it is a purely symbolic notion of locality that becomes the focus of community formation. Although it is essential to identify and explore the crucial differences that exist between certain types of transnational communities, it is equally important to discuss the overarching similarities between them. It is these similarities that, in our view, justify placing all kinds of transnational communities within the same theoretical frame.

Notes

1 This central significance of shared meaning is stressed in the literature. Hall (1998: 182), for example, observes that the main ingredient for a national or any other kind of viable community is 'the idea we have of it, … the meanings we associate with it, the sense of community with others we carry inside us'. Similarly, for Lash (1994: 157), and in contradistinction to Giddens and Beck when – in the same book – they talk about the essentially cognitive knowledge of the world possessed by separate individuals under the condition of reflexive modernity, reflexivity in relation to community necessarily involves 'hermeneutic knowledge'. But 'the latter is only possible when the knower is in the same world as and "dwells among" the things and other human beings whose truth she seeks'. Thus, community is based in everyday habits, routine practices, shared understandings, tools, goals and emotions and is guided by some mutual acceptance of 'what is regarded as substantively good'.

2 For example, Abu-Lughod (1991: 139) is one of the authors who have argued strongly against earlier anthropological notions of culture, claiming that these have outlived whatever explanatory usefulness they may have had. She suggests that, as a discipline, anthropology was 'built on the historically constructed divide between the West and the non-West'. While the West was unproblematic, the non-West consisted of largely powerless 'others' whose 'discovery' by the West required an investigation in order to chart and understand the nature of their different identities.

3 As more 'voices demand to be heard', the assumption that national cultures are uniform 'begins to be seen as a myth'. Mass migration leads to a break up of the traditional notion of culture, leading to the simultaneous coexistence of multiple cultures within a given territory. By the same token, the intruding cultures then become multilocal, i.e. based in several countries. Alternatively, other transnational cultures – especially those defined by a strongly professional, business, scientific, artistic or political ethos – are increasingly extending worldwide primarily through the avenues generated by global capitalism (Friese and Wagner 1999: 106).

4 Furthermore, communication technologies permit people to send messages to each other without the need for physical contact. But, more importantly, they make possible the self-conscious construction of the world as 'one single field of persistent interaction and exchange' (Hannerz 1996: 19).

5 Indeed, social closure has ceased to require or to depend upon geographical proximity. As Beck (2000a: 156) suggests, 'the persons we experience as significant others are no longer restricted to those we know from direct encounters within a local community'. Putting this another way, social life has been despatialised (Beck 2000a: 24).

6 Also, most individuals will tend to imbue even the most temporary and lonely locales with some degree of meaning and are likely to try to establish at least a minimum of relationships, however shallow and fleeting, while, for most of us, the locale we currently occupy will actually contain rather more than this in the way of meaning and social bonds.

7 Before we proceed any further, we should point out that our classification is not meant to incorporate the entire range of possible transnational groups, but rather those groups that we deem most closely connected to the globalised notion of community. One rather obvious group of people associated with the transnational mode yet clearly not forming a 'community', as such, would be tourists.

8 Other instances of such overlapping, alternating or shifting alliances and priorities as between the different levels pertaining to the local/national–

transnational–global communities are not difficult to find and have been widely discussed in the literature (for example, Friberg and Hettne 1988; Robertson 1992; Oommen 1997a).

9 When such systemic deprivation engulfs entire regions or countries, mass emigration in search of the economic opportunities in the advanced industrialised countries is likely to become endemic, giving rise to effective transnational national networks – such as those described by Basch *et al.* (1994) and Schiller *et al.* (1992). Nevertheless, such inequalities of wealth and opportunities as well as social exclusion, persistent discrimination against religious or other minorities, unemployment and political repression shape the lives of millions of people living in an increasingly integrated global economy – irrespective of whether these people are migrants or non-migrants.

Part I
New immigrants

2 Migrant communities and class

Croatians in Western Australia

Val Colic-Peisker

This chapter seeks to explore the links among migration, class and community using a case study of Croatians in Western Australia (WA). Mass movement of people across the globe has been an important feature of the contemporary world. Migration has special significance in Australia, which is second only to Israel in having the highest proportion of immigrants in the total population (Bessant and Watts 1998: 200). WA is the Australian state with the highest proportion of immigrants: one-third of the total population according to the 1996 census (*Perth Social Atlas* 1997).

Migration into a different social and cultural environment disrupts people's community life as well as their sense of identity and belonging – the things that are tightly connected in everyone's life. Following migration, new communities need to be formed and a sense of identity re-established to provide a sense of continuity with the previous self. Two waves of Croatians in WA, who migrated only two decades apart, have gone through these processes in distinctly different ways.

Croatians form one of the largest migrant communities in Australia (Collins 1991; Kipp *et al.* 1995), but are under-represented in Australian migration studies. Until recently, they have usually been included in either the category of 'Yugoslavs' – since Croatia was a part of federal Yugoslavia until 1991 – or the even larger category of 'Southern Europeans'. The other reason for the lack of research on Croatians is that the Croatian community in Australia has only recently developed a critical mass of 'organic intellectuals', either from the second generation or from the recent wave of migrants. My research deals with the two post-Second World War cohorts of Croatian voluntary migrants (non-refugees). The first represents the largest influx of Croatians that ever reached Australia, in the 1960s and early 1970s, and the second is a 1980s/early 1990s migrant cohort.

Migrant communities and identities of the two cohorts

The overwhelming majority of Croatians who migrated to Australia during the 1960s and early 1970s were people from rural areas (Evans 1984: 1064; Nejašmic 1995: 216–17). Prior to migration to Australia, most of them lived off the land as small farmers and rural workers, or combined a blue-collar job with agriculture. They started emigrating on a larger scale in the late 1960s after an unsuccessful market reform in Yugoslavia in 1965 had slowed down the extensive industrialisation and movement of the rural population to the cities (*Demografski i prostorni* ... 1968; Mežnaric 1991: 40; Castles and Miller 1993: 108). In these circumstances, emigration represented an alternative escape route from the bleak prospects of rural life. A large majority of the 1960s wave of Croatians came to Western Australia from Dalmatia, the Croatian coastal province and traditional emigration area which includes the Adriatic islands and immediate hinterland (Holjevac 1967; Nejašmic 1995). After the Second World War, internal economic and political problems combined with opening of the borders in the 1960s resulted in the largest exodus of emigrants among European communist countries (Slany 1990).

A factor that facilitated emigration was so-called 'chain migration'; in the Croatian case, this was a firmly established pattern that had continued for at least a century (Holjevac 1967; Denich 1970: 133; Živkovic *et al.* 1995). Many people had relatives or friends, earlier emigrants, who could assist and sponsor their move. Although in the 1960s the majority of emigrants headed to West Germany and other Western European countries in search of 'temporary work migration' (*Gastarbeiters*), the late 1960s were also the peak of Croatian migration to Australia (Collins 1988: 25; Madden and Young 1992: 4).

The rural–urban movement had been the predominant pattern of international migration until the 1970s, when not only immigration demand in developed countries changed but also the emigration supply in developing countries (Phizacklea 1983: 1, 108; Slany 1990). Developed countries did not need so much manual labour any longer and Croatia had more skilled labour to offer. Tradespeople, white-collar workers, professionals and intellectuals created during the 1960s and 1970s Croatian education boom, and who could not find employment in the undeveloped service sector of the state-controlled economy, often opted for emigration. This was the migration context of the recent cohort of Croatians.

This cohort consisted of predominantly urban dwellers, with a higher level of education and better knowledge of English than the previous cohort. The emigration of the 1980s/90s was triggered by an abrupt deterioration of the economic, social and political situation in ex-Yugoslavia during the 1980s. Young urban professionals with high expectations suddenly faced shortages of consumer goods, huge inflation, unemployment, low salaries and an increasingly unstable political situation. Education, the main channel of social mobility in post-war Croatia, became a cul-de-sac. By this time, Western European countries were much less welcoming to Southern Europeans, so overseas countries, and primarily Australia, became a more realistic immigration target. According to the Australia migration statistics, this cohort of Croatian migrants, which reached its peak in 1988/9, consisted to a considerable degree of professional people (see Meznaric and Grdešic 1990; *Settler Arrivals* 1994–95).

My initial observation of the two migrant cohorts was based on professional interpreting work and private contacts. It brought me to the realisation that the two groups of migrants were significantly different in terms of socioeconomic background, motives for migration, lifestyle and their relationship with Australia as well as with their homeland.[1] An early result of my participant observation was that Croatians in Perth, WA, did not form a single ethnic community in any sociologically meaningful sense. The migrants from the recent urban cohort remained apart from the organised forms of community life that took place in Croatian clubs and churches. In addition, the ethnic community life of the 1960s migrants comprised separate political factions with different ethnic identifications (e.g. Yugoslav–Dalmatian vs. Croatian). The tension between them tended to ease as the war in the homeland halted in the mid-1990s and the political situation normalised.

What an outsider's gaze usually identifies as a single 'Croatian community' is in fact a conglomerate of diverse groups: some of them tightly knit and some only loosely connected; some formalised in associations and clubs and some entirely informal and private. The divisions within these groups run along political as well as class lines. The two cohorts of Croatians whom I am dealing with in this chapter form not only separate but also thoroughly different migrant communities. The two migrant groups also experience different processes of identity change following migration. In the case of the earlier cohort, during the 1990s, these processes were strongly influenced by the tumultuous political developments in their homeland.

The 1960s wave: communities of place and local–ethnic identity focus

According to Croatian migration literature as well as to Australian migration statistics, the majority of the 1960s wave of Australo-Croatians lived in traditional, parochial 'communities of place' prior to migration (Meznaric 1991; Nejašmic 1995). Catholicism was the main factor in the preservation of the traditional way of life in rural communities. The central features of this traditional way of life were the patriarchal family, tight social control, strong kinship and neighbourhood ties and an understanding of the village as an extended kinship network. Individual status came from belonging to a certain family and individual identity was largely ascribed, determined by birth, and for women also by marriage (Erlich 1966). The great majority of the 1960s migrants whom I met through my research came from such rural communities.

Social mobility was limited in such an environment: the way to improve one's social position, as well as one's ranking in the community's marital market, was to leave the community and migrate to the city. In post-Second World War Croatia, this was considered a smart move: until the late 1960s blue-collar jobs were plentiful and the city was a place of opportunity. One could also keep in touch with the community of origin by travelling back and forth, visiting for the weekends or spending holidays there (Simic 1973).

Emigration abroad, however, was considered to be a mixed blessing: it was economically more rewarding but migrants had to sever their local ties and set off into an alien world. In the case of migration to Australia, the enormous distance reinforced the tragedy of separation. Young men, who were usually leaving by themselves, were seen off as if they went to war. Their return from the faraway land was uncertain and sometimes even news about their life overseas was sparse. One interviewee said: 'When I went around the village to bid farewell to people, everyone wept, especially elderly folk' (Mr V. J., migrated in 1967).

Nevertheless, most of the interviewees told me that they were convinced they were leaving temporarily and would be back in several years after they had earned sufficient money to improve their circumstances at home. However, most people from this migrant cohort remained in Australia permanently. Some of them never even made a return visit, and most visited their place of origin very few times, usually after they had spent decades in Australia. For these traditional people, letters and the telephone were an inadequate means of keeping in touch with their native communities; other people's return visits and their stories upon return to Australia seemed to have provided a more substantial connection. In any case, the outcome of migration to Australia was a feeling of separation and loss of the native community.

Croatian written poetry and folk songs reflect the feeling of tragedy and irreplaceable loss of 'one's own people' as a consequence of international migration. This feeling is preserved and nurtured among migrants as a 'culture of nostalgia' in which the old country appears to be a 'lost paradise' (Skrbiš 1994: 134–6). In the case of young women, who as a rule migrated only to join their husbands or fiancés, the 'tragedy of emigration' was, at least in its initial stages, mitigated by the 'naturalness' and joy involved with reuniting with their men. Most of the interviewees from the 1960s cohort reported that they never stopped feeling the longing for the old 'place':

> No, I never felt at home here ... my first thought every morning is my old courtyard back home in Blato, it's an incurable illness, and it's actually getting worse over time.
>
> (Mr A. M., migrated in 1970)

However, nostalgia did not seem to be all that bad: it was an important element of the maintenance of a sense of community and belonging in people who never really felt integrated into the mainstream Australian community. The feeling was shared with others and represented the 'emotional cement' of the ethnic community. Most people from this wave came from the region of Dalmatia, spoke a similar dialect, ate similar food and played the same card and sport games, and this helped to 'materialise' the nostalgia more easily. In this way, the migrant community was embedded in the common place of origin and the shared knowledge and memories that reinforced the local–ethnic identity focus.

The relative importance of their place of origin compared with the host environment in the cognitive and emotional map of the interviewees was detectable in the way they talked about the two environments. Their home village was viewed 'through a magnifying glass' and every little detail was important. For example, the fact that two people did not come from the same village but from two neighbouring villages on the same little Adriatic island was usually emphasised. On the other hand, the host environment was usually seen through 'reversed binoculars' and referred to as 'Australia' – closer qualifiers, such as 'Western Australia', 'Perth', or the suburb they lived in were rarely used. Also, the interviewees rarely made a distinction between different English-speaking nationalities and referred to all native English speakers, including those born in Australia, as 'English', which was part of the same 'reverse binoculars' syndrome.

Migrant community activities and occasions in Croatian clubs in Perth were usually past-orientated, celebrating the old country's customs and holidays, traditional sports, folk music and food. Community life was imbued with myths about the homeland. This seemed to be one of the numerous ways in which organised ethnic community life[2] substituted for the traditional village community as well as for the mythical homeland itself. Besides the identity-preservation purpose, the migrant communities served various additional practical purposes in the life of this migrant cohort, such as finding housing and employment, especially at the early stages of settlement. This community dynamic resulted in residential concentration and the preservation of traditional cultural narratives and practices within the migrant communities. This finding is in tune with the image of migrant communities as more traditional, patriarchal and socially conservative than the wider environment, confirmed by other Australian studies (see Bottomley 1992: 161).

The 1980s wave: deterritorialised communities and professional identity focus

Communities of the urban cohort of Croatian migrants were formed following different patterns and to meet different needs. First of all, migrant communities – the communities based on the ethnic principle (common origin) – were not predominant in this group of migrants. The communities they belonged to reflected their feeling of identity, which had a translocal and transterritorial focus. For this generation of city dwellers – all except one of the interviewees from this wave came from the four largest Croatian cities, and the majority came from the capital – spatial mobility has been a fact of life. These migrants grew up in a modern urban environment and were not born into a 'community of fate'. Rather, they felt the communities they belonged to were something they, as individuals, could create and recreate. In their modern outlook, the individual was an ideological starting point, and the collective was a derivation. The individual was a 'unit of identity', not the family, the kin or the local community.

Owing to the strong penetration of communist ideology, Croatian cities were largely secular in the post-Second World War era (Dyker 1977: 91–2). The traditional Catholic focus of social life was thus seriously undermined. Also, because of the relative openness of Croatian (Yugoslav) society, this generation was socialised under the influence of Western capitalist culture through film, music, literature and fashion, with individualism being one of its central tenets.

Individualism is noticeable in this cohort's pattern of migration. The chain migration pattern dominant in the previous migrant wave gave way to independent migration; recent urban migrants were mostly self-reliant upon arrival. Most of the interviewees knew someone before they came here, but the practical assistance they received was minor, usually limited to the first couple of days in the new country. Unlike the previous rural wave, they had an appropriate cultural 'tool kit' containing English language proficiency, professional education and 'urban skills' that enabled them to function in the Australian environment immediately upon arrival. Hence, the 'ethnic community' did not assume a prominent role in their Australian life.

By emigrating, this group of people joined the ranks of the 'global professional middle class' (Stubbs 1996). Their professional skills – which I argue were the axis of their identity – were transferable, conditional of course on their English proficiency. In other words, their professional as well as everyday 'urban skills' were of a global variety and enabled them to live as 'itinerants' (Gouldner 1989: 401) if they chose to. They were members of the globally dominant culture that was defined by English as a global language and by professional and urban skills, and their process of acculturation in the Australian environment was far less difficult than in the case of the 1960s rural migrants. Ethnic communities were not necessary to meet either the practical or the identity needs of the urban migrants.

When the interviewees from this cohort spoke about themselves or mentioned their acquaintances, they tended to emphasise the professional element of their identity – 'a friend of mine, who is an engineer ...' – whereas interviewees from the previous wave would usually say 'another man, who came from the same village'. Finding an appropriate job and therefore recreating their previous – or new, but still acceptable – professional identity was the main criterion in the appraisal of the 'success' of their migration to Australia.

The paramount importance of professional identity, which, unlike ethnic identity, defines a person in individual terms, is arguably the central reason why the 'ethnic community' assumed little importance in the Australian life of urban Croatians. The interviewees reported that they found the ethnic community based on a common place of origin and 'common blood', which was already firmly established in Perth when they arrived, incongruous with their feeling of identity. With only two exceptions, they reported having no connections with the life of Croatian churches and clubs. Most of them had visited a Croatian club once or twice but could not find much in common with the 1960s generation of migrants that dominated there.

> I've never been to Croatian clubs, am not even sure where they are. I went to a Croatian Catholic church once out of curiosity, St. Lawrence's church in Balcatta, but people I saw there were the kind of people my parents might fit into, and my grandparents definitely would, nice people, but I felt we had very little in common.
>
> (Ms V. B., migrated in 1995)

> We went to Croatian clubs three times in ten years. At one occasion it was the celebrations of the 900th anniversary of Zagreb, someone invited us to come ... we do not attend Croatian or any other church because we are atheists.
>
> (Mrs A. V., migrated in 1988)

In this migrant wave, the profession as an eminently modern phenomenon took the place of traditional, locally defined ethnicity as a primary source of affiliation and identification. Živkovic *et al.* (1995: 89–92), who studied Croatian migrants in the USA, also reported the 'weakening of ethnicity' in better educated and higher status migrant groups, who identified more with the 'dominant group'. These migrants might find more in common with other people of similar education and social status than with their 'ethnic community' (Harvey 1997: 124).

The Croatian networks that these professional people developed following migration did not fit into the idea of the 'ethnic community'. They could rather be described as loosely knit, 'native-language networks' that existed outside ethnic venues and operated with little reference to their common 'ethnic belonging'. Illustrative of this is the fact that a network of people who came to Perth from the same Croatian city began to develop when two of them 'met' on an Internet 'chat line'. E-mail was a way of exchanging news and useful information and keeping in touch rather than attending Croatian clubs and churches. Most of them reported that ethnicity or common place of origin did not feature in their choice of friends and that they regularly socialised with people from different cultural backgrounds. The communities they formed, 'virtual' as well as face to face, were essentially translocal and transethnic. Professionally based networks were apparently important in their social life.

The issue of diaspora

An important point of difference between the communities of the two migrant cohorts pertains to the issue of diaspora. The diaspora, or diasporic community, is usually defined by its emotional–nostalgic and sometimes practical–political connections to the homeland (Safran 1991). Following such a definition, I argue that the communities of the 1960s cohort of Croatian migrants conformed in many ways to the concept of diaspora, whereas the 1980s professional cohort did not follow such patterns.

The myth of return and the fact that their community and identity had been firmly bound to the homeland/native village as 'constitutive elsewhere' or 'heterotopia' (Karskens 1999) were conspicuous features of the communities of the 1960s migrant cohort. Most of the interviewees from this subsample told me that they planned to return to the homeland 'one day'; they were adamant that at least their remains would 'rest in the native soil'. Tölölyan (1996: 14) has maintained that this desire to return is a necessary part of the definition of diaspora. The 'myth of return' also seems to provide a sense of control over one's destiny.

For these people, the homeland was a close, almost physical presence – 'elsewhere' – imbued with smells, colours and sounds. Homeland was the place to which their feelings of identity were anchored. In emigration, the essence of life, symbolically, remains forever elsewhere, separated from everyday existence like the body separated from the soul, and emigration becomes a form of death. This almost spiritual experience of separateness from the place where they feel they belong feeds the diasporic consciousness. As already argued, nostalgia is the emotion that binds the diaspora: there is a faraway place, a lost paradise, where they all belong.

The leadership of the diasporic communities of the 1960s migrant wave invested considerable ideological work in the preservation of the concept of an ideally continuous and ethnically based 'natural' community (see Tölölyan 1996: 17). The Catholic Church and clergy played a primary role in this ideological work (see Kolar-Panov 1997: 85). During the Croatian political and military struggle for independence the leadership of the migrant community was able to 'tug at the heartstrings and purse strings' (Tölölyan 1996: 19) of its flock.

For several years Croatian clubs in Perth were much livelier than before and the community became more cohesive, bound by the awoken patriotism. For many people, this was the final stage in the development of their ethnic identity from local to national. Turbulent developments in the homeland confirmed and reinforced the Croatian ethnic community as diaspora (see Kolar-Panov 1997).[3]

It may be suggested that this process of diasporic consciousness-raising largely mirrors the 'imagining' involved in the processes of building modern nations in the last two centuries, as analysed by Gellner (1983), Anderson (1983) and Hobsbawm (1990). As Hobsbawm (1990: 46) argued, the 'imagined community' is created to 'fill the void left by the retreat or disintegration or unavailability of real human communities or networks'. In the case of the 1960s migrant cohort this applies to the loss of their native communities. Also, as all the three authors argued, the creation of the imagined community involved considerable 'social engineering', part of which is the ideological work that invokes myths of common ancestry, history and interests.[4] In this process, the role of leadership is crucial; in the case of the Croatian ethnic community in Perth, the role of the priest and religion as connecting agents was paramount.

The cohort that arrived in Australia in the late 1980s seemed to have a less emotional relationship to Croatia, as well as to the notion of homeland. They were emigrating at the time when old communist myths were being deconstructed while new nationalist myths were replacing them. Having left the troublesome, myth-saturated land in search of a more 'rational' environment,[5] they were not ready to join with the political myth building going on in the diaspora, prompted from the homeland. Some of the interviewees from the 1980s cohort helped with fundraising or attended protest rallies because they 'felt their interests were involved there', but without necessarily looking for an ideological or emotional justification for such involvement. In this migrant group the very idea of homeland was less bound to the mythical place of childhood and youth and more to a pragmatic attitude: *'ubi lucrum, ibi patria'* or 'where the money is, there is your home country'. Rather than looking back to their native land, they directed their gaze towards the host society and establishing themselves in it, practically and emotionally. They did not see themselves as part of a diaspora.

The connection to the old place and its cultural peculiarities seemed to be an eminently individual experience for professional migrants. They drew a part of their creative energy from the connection to their culture of origin and from their experience of the encounter of two cultures, but the essential *collective* aspect of a diaspora was absent. Their shared feeling of belonging was embedded in the shared sphere of cultural knowledge and a shared discursive approach to reality through that knowledge, rather than in a sense of belonging to the same place.

Tölölyan (1996) and Bhabha (1994) described a 'new' type of professional and intellectual diaspora that consisted of urban, educated people who migrated to ensure the best use of their knowledge and expertise or to find freedom for artistic expression. I am not inclined, however, to see the professional Croatian migrants within the notional framework of diaspora. For these people, the homeland seems to be a diffuse idea that becomes a part of their creativity through their bicultural and hybrid identities. It should be kept in mind that this process of cultural hybridisation starts before migration and does not pertain only to migrants: the post-modern, urban world is multicultural, and cultural hybridity can be developed without moving to another country. Only isolated traditional communities can be monocultural in the strict sense.

In the development of a hybrid identity the homeland loses its immediate presence and mixes new and 'foreign' ideas to result in complex intellectual/ artistic forms and emotional attachments. In this process of 'creative translation' the idea of homeland loses its emotional impact (loss, pain, nostalgia) and becomes a cultural legacy that upholds cultural, intellectual and artistic creativity. This process of translation of faraway homeland/ otherness into creativity/biculturalism rather than into pain/nostalgia, and the non-participation in collective diasporic types of political and cultural interaction in favour of an individual and thus 'uncontrollable' relationship to the homeland, makes the usual notion of diaspora inadequate in the case of professional migrants. If culturally hybridised (which may well mean 'Westernised') migrants declare themselves to be a part of a diaspora (as in the case of Bhabha, Tölölyan or Rushdie), this seems to be an act of embracing the symbolic space of the homeland rather than embracing its political space or its interests and problems. Their interaction with the homeland (which would then allow them to call themselves a diaspora) happens in a symbolic cultural (as well as virtual) space – where cultural elements can be transformed through creative processes beyond 'ethnic' recognition – rather than in ethnic clubs and churches where collective loyalties, a *sine qua non* of the diaspora, are demonstrated.

These creative processes of scientific, intellectual and artistic production, being eminently individual, cannot be the connective tissue of the community. The diaspora of this type of postmodern migrant, unlike the case of traditional people coming to an urban environment, exists in discursive rather than in real space. It is an 'imagined' rather than a real diaspora.

The relationship to the hostland of the two migrant groups had an important, although not so readily observable, role in determining the relationship to the homeland and the dynamic of diaspora-building. For the 1960s working-class migrant cohort, integration into the wider Australian community remained limited; the emotional preservation and practical recreation of the ethnic community was crucial. Limited English and low occupational and social status in the mainstream English-speaking community seemed to be important factors in the processes of identity maintenance and identity change following migration, as well as in the processes of community-building; the links and intersections between class and ethnicity are significant (see Pinches 2000). This more disadvantaged and isolated group of Croatians had a more pressing 'identity need' to locate its rather fragile 'ethnic bubble' into the wider context of the Croatian homeland. The ethnic identity of these Croatians gained a new authority after Croatia became independent. On the other hand, the more globalised professional group felt more comfortable in the Australian context and did not need the emotional and identity props of the diaspora with its inherent claim to be a part of the homeland as a larger and more powerful entity.

Conclusion

My research indicates that rural–urban (traditional–modern) and class backgrounds are of paramount importance to the way that migrants create communities and recreate their feelings of identity and belonging following migration. The different ways in which these processes unfold for the two cohorts of Croatians are the case in point. Ethnic origin, i.e. that they all came from the same country, seems to be less relevant in this respect: the two groups hardly have any contact with each other, and the ways in which they have formed their respective communities are based on different principles, much as these communities meet different needs.

The identity of the 1960s wave of Croatian migrants, the people of *Gemeinschaft*, seems to be firmly embedded in their native community, which is defined by the place of origin. Their migrant communities are construed to substitute for the native 'community of place' lost in the spatial and temporal distance because for these people the loss endangers their sense of identity. In the alien environment and under the influence of developments in their homeland (Croatia becoming independent in 1991) these concrete face-to-face migrant communities also came to represent the imagined national community of Croatians. This enlargement of community/identity can be viewed as the modernisation and transcendence of the traditional community that is defined by exclusive blood ties and common territory. At the same time, the premodern ethnic principle is maintained in the imagining of the diasporic community of Croatians as an ethnonational community. This was reinforced by the fact that the newly independent Croatia was defined as an 'ethnic state'. Therefore, the modernising effect of the process of the enlargement of the migrant identity from local to national remains ambiguous: the national community is, in principle, as exclusive as the traditional local community used to be.

The ideas of ethnic belonging and diaspora are peripheral in defining either the communities or the identities of the 1980s wave of migrants. Their modern professional identity rather than a territorially defined one is the central point from which they address the exigencies of migration. For this mobile group the integration into the Australian (Western) environment started back in Croatia, through the Western influences to which they were exposed during their formative years. Because of this, they seem to adopt the narratives and practices of post-modern capitalism relatively easily, and in this process develop a complex transcultural identity. The communities they form in the Australian environment are integration-oriented, unlike the nostalgic ethnic communities of the previous wave.

The two cohorts of Croatians have vastly different migration experiences and form separate communities. This challenges the notion of the ethnic community as it is perceived from the outside. A closer 'insider's' look reveals that there is no such thing as a single 'Croatian community' or 'diaspora' in

WA: class, rural–urban and political differences clearly overshadow the 'ethnicity principle'.

My research suggests that the notion of diaspora fits better into the migration experience of rural migrants coming to an urban environment and may be inadequate to describe modern educated itinerants. Authors such as Tölölyan (1996) and Bhabha (1994) claimed that the notion of diaspora has significance in the life of middle-class educated émigrés. However, as analysed, this seems to be a rather different notion compared with the idea that feeds the nostalgia of the people who left their traditional communities to migrate to alien cities.

In the globalised world of the late 1990s the frontiers of national states remain the most obvious but probably not the most important social, political, economic and cultural divides. In the post-industrial and post-modern world the most important social divides seem to be cutting across national boundaries, primarily between social groups that have been 'globalised' and 'Internetised' and those that have been left behind in these processes. The two groups of Croatian migrants seem to inhabit two different sides of this socioeconomic divide.

Notes

1 Data collection was mainly based on semistructured interviews and participant observation. I conducted interviews with twenty people from each migrant cohort and spoke with many more on various occasions during the period 1996–9. The sample of interviewees consisted of an equal number of men and women and was collected by a snowballing technique. All but four interviews were conducted in interviewees' homes, which provided an opportunity for participant observation in the interview setting. Part of my fieldwork involved attending social gatherings in Croatian clubs as well as outside 'ethnic' venues. Two interviews with the functionaries of the central Croatian club in Fremantle were conducted in the club's office, which provided an additional opportunity for observation and insight into the club's activities and rules. It is important to note that only the rural (1960s) cohort of migrants attended these venues and gatherings.

2 By 'organised community life' I mean the activities that take place in Croatian clubs, churches and other public venues, outside private homes, whether they are organised events or just spontaneous socialising.

3 As Tölölyan (1996) argued, every diaspora is an ethnic community, but not every ethnic community is a diaspora.

4 This is also reflected in a concern raised by several members of the 'leadership' of the community from the 1960s wave about my 'political position' and my willingness to act as an advocate for the community in order to rectify its unfavourable public image. They usually referred to a stereotype, reinforced through the Australian media, about Croatians as fierce nationalists and terrorists, as well as uneducated 'wogs' (Australian pejorative term for Southern Europeans) who only speak broken English (see Skrbiš 1994: 3–7; Hughson 1997).

5 What I found particularly interesting in this group of interviewees was that a considerable number of them argued that they fitted better into the Australian environment than their native environment.

3 Greek Americans and transnationalism

Religion, class and community

Victor Roudometof and Anna Karpathakis

Over the last decade, transnationalism has become a topic of extensive discussion in the scholarly community (Glick Schiller *et al*. 1995; Basch *et al*. 1994; Smith 1994; Smith and Guarnizo 1998; *Ethnic and Racial Studies* 1999). In this chapter, we will examine the dynamics of the Greek American community and, in particular, the recent post-1965 Greek immigrants' situation.[1] We argue that the recent post-1965 Greek immigrants can be viewed as a transnational national community, no different in this regard from the other well-publicized instances of transnationalism. However, this is only part of the story. These immigrants' sense of belonging and understanding of who they are bring them into direct conflict with the older, more established generations of their fellow Greek Americans. These older immigrant generations have developed a more romantic or nostalgic attachment to Greece, and for them it is religion rather than ethnicity that forms the foundation of their identity. In this sense, transnationalism constitutes a bone of contention between older and recent immigrant cohorts. Just as with the Australian Croats (see Chapter 2), it is the (more recent) lower-class immigrants that display the stronger attachment to their homeland.

First, we should situate this community in the context of the Hellenic diaspora worldwide. This diaspora consists of approximately 3–4 million people globally. Australia, Canada, and the USA account for half of these communities; while the USA alone is home to around 30 percent of the Greeks abroad. However, there are significant differences in these communities' profiles that are most acutely observed in the attitudes of their communities toward marriage and the homeland. Australian and Canadian Greeks express a deep longing for their original homeland and wish to return. Such feelings are less pervasive among Greek Americans. Of the families who expressed a desire to return to Greece, the overwhelming majority consisted of those where both spouses were of Greek origin. Yet, such families are far more typical in Canada and Australia than in the USA.[2]

These differences reflect the slower pace of acculturation for the Greeks of Canada and Australia and can be attributed to the historical origins of the different communities. The US migration was part of the large wave of southeastern European emigration at the time; indeed, official US statistics show a total of approximately 500,000 Greek immigrants by 1932. In sharp contrast to this early wave of immigration, post-1945 Greek immigration was directed towards western Europe, Australia, and Canada. Consequently, in contrast to the post-1945 Greek immigrants in Australia, Canada, and western Europe, Greek Americans have a history dating back to the early twentieth century. Therefore, the US Greeks have developed their ethnic identity away from modern Greece for a considerable period of time. Additionally, they have a higher socioeconomic status than their Canadian and Australian counterparts, for they have had more time to acculturate into US mainstream and to achieve higher social mobility within their host society.

However, after a sharp decline in Greek immigration to the USA between 1930 and 1950, a new wave of immigration took place between 1951 and 1975 (Karpathakis 1994: 102) and this helped to slow the pace of assimilation. It also contributed to a rupture in the community between second- and third-generation Greek Americans and the more recent immigrants and their children (Karpathakis 1993). This latter group has closer, more complex ties to Greece and a lower socioeconomic status than the older upwardly mobile immigrants (see Rosen 1968; Tavuchis 1972; Dinnerstein and Reimers 1982; Monos 1986; Vegleris 1988; Moskos 1989a: 25–37; Katsas 1992). Our research has investigated the situation of this latter group: a group of immigrants that displays some similarities to the well-publicized Latin American cases (Glick Schiller *et al.* 1992, 1995; Basch *et al.* 1994; Smith 1994).

Post-1965 Greek Americans as a transnational national community

Perhaps the most important feature of the post-1965 Greek Americans is the extent to which their experience is directly linked to their involvement and interest in issues relating to their original homeland. Journalists, mass media personalities, businessmen, and other public relations personnel hired by the Greek government, academics with strong and multiple ties to Greece, embassy and consulate employees, leaders of local chapters or groups related to Greek political parties, and officers of regional secular immigrant organizations make up the community's "identity workers." These identity workers perform three functions. First, they translate Greek affairs to the community. Second, they translate immigrant concerns to Americans; and, finally, they interpret American affairs to the immigrants. While many of these "identity workers" are immigrants themselves, the American born and educated immigrants are now beginning to take over many of these positions. While this new generation brings with it a new sensitivity to American politics and affairs, its frame of reference remains Greek national politics.

The "identity workers" are involved daily in constructing a variety of identities for the immigrants and their descendants. It is an inherently political process, and all identities constructed are ultimately political, regardless of the "efficacy" of each of these identities. Many of these "identity workers" emerged during the 1980s and 1990s as they worked to mobilize immigrants around home society national and territorial concerns. There are over 180 secular Greek immigrant organizations in New York City alone (excluding those in nearby New Jersey and Connecticut), 60 percent of which are based in Astoria and Brooklyn. While these organizations are philanthropic in their goals, they are nevertheless important public institutions in which home society concerns are played out. Furthermore, by 2001, all but one of the larger political parties in Greece has a "Friends of ..." organization in New York City. As the political landscape of Greece changes, so does the city's immigrant community. In addition, there are five radio programs produced in New York City. These include a satellite radio program produced in Greece, a Greek-owned and -operated television cable channel, a daily television program sponsored by the Greek government on a public access channel, a satellite television program received from Greece, two Greek language dailies, two weekly English newspapers (with national distributions), and a bilingual monthly magazine. While one weekly newspaper is based in Philadelphia, the rest of the ethnic press is based in Astoria, New York.

Immigrant organizations tend to mobilize around political and national crises in Greece, thus stressing their own Greek identity (Hicks and Couloumbis 1980). Perhaps the most spectacular recent manifestation of Greek transnational national pride has been around the post-1991 Greek dispute with the Former Yugoslav Republic of Macedonia (FYROM) over the use of the name "Macedonia" (Roudometof 1996). In this regard their mobilization and attitude appears quite similar to the Australian and Canadian Greek Orthodox communities. During the 1990s, these communities took the lead in opposing the FYROM's official recognition, owing to the fact that their communities were situated in cities which also hosted Macedonian immigrant communities (Danforth 1995). The Macedonian conflict illustrates the transnational nationalism of these immigrant communities as well as the instrumental role of Orthodox religion in defining membership of a deterritorialized nation.

Immigrant associations throughout the world took part in this dispute, acting as "cultural warriors" (Karakasidou 1994) ready to defend the sacred Greek national narrative. During such national crises, US immigrant organizations hold meetings, and journalists and other mass media personnel talk of how "we are Greek. Our interests, our identity as Greeks, with a glorious history, is once again threatened by those who want to partake of this history and take chunks of our country" (guest speaker on "Cosmos" – a Greek radio program – 27 March 1994). Orthodox clergy make it clear that the Church is once again prepared (as a cleric said) to "lead this National struggle." While the Church uses fear of war to mobilize diaspora Greek nationalism, the Left is powerless to construct an alternative identity. In the words of one Left activist:

> There is no way ... we can get on TV and tell the Greeks not to listen to the priests, that these are dangerous ideas. ... All we can do is present ... one way of looking at the issue, the Church another. Theirs is inflammatory – ours is rational. Under the circumstances, which voice is louder? Not the rational.

When Turkey invaded Cyprus in the summer of 1974, it took over 37 percent of the island and soon afterwards began making claims to the Greek islands. These actions resulted in Greek immigrant activists mobilizing immigrants to influence the American national government on behalf of Cyprus's and Greece's territorial sovereignties. This became an "Americanization" campaign, and it was waged on two levels. First, political activists sought to create formal relations with local- and national-level American politicians and parties, and, second, they mobilized immigrants to enter American political structures (by becoming naturalized American citizens, voting, and contributing funds and other resources to political campaigns). Throughout this process, the "identity workers" constructed for the immigrants a binational identity which emphasized their "Americanness" alongside their "Greekness" (Karpathakis 1999).

The most difficult immigrant cohort to mobilize was the post-1965 working-class immigrants who, for a number of reasons, were the most alienated from the American political system.[3] On the one hand, American policy toward Greece, Cyprus, and Turkey was (according to the immigrants) immoral and unethical, and clearly favored the aggressor, i.e. Turkey. On the other hand, as working-class immigrants, this post-1965 cohort lacked the language skills and other resources to even begin imagining itself as a possible element of American society or polity. The organizers worked also to incorporate their American-born children, who were similarly outside the American polity. This binational identity is acutely reflected in the attitudes of the immigrants' children. Students enrolled in the Church-sponsored parochial schools in the USA and Canada were asked to write essays on the topic of "When I realized I am Greek" in the early to mid-1990s. These essays were edited by a Greek-born journalist and published under the title *When I Realised I am a Greek Child* (1997) by a well-known philhellene of Nigerian descent. Like the adults' constructions of their transnational identities, the children similarly use religion and secular histories interchangeably, and they also often fail to distinguish the historical periods of Ancient Greece, the Byzantine Empire, the Ottoman Occupation, and the War of Independence in 1821. As one child wrote of his summer trip to Greece and his Sunday outing with his grandmother to the Acropolis:

> When we got there, my grandmother began to talk to me about the people who lived in those ages [i.e. the colloquial expression similar to "back then"] and who made this incredible "theama" [sight]. She explained to me that the Greeks in those days had the Acropolis as a place where they

hid from their enemies. Then we went to the Parthenon. The Parthenon, she told me, in the older years, was a large Temple, built before the birth of Christ. As my grandmother talked to me about those people who built the Acropolis and the Parthenon, for the History they have, something strange inside me began to be born. She explained to me about all those years and the great difficulties that Greeks had. But they also had a deep love for their "patrida" [homeland] and their religion so that they overcame all of these [problems], no matter what they were.

(*When I Realised I am a Greek Child* 1997: 5; translated into English from the original)

The Ottoman occupation and the current Turkish threats to Greek islands are pronounced themes throughout many of the essays. A number of the children made direct connections between Turkey's threats to Greece's territorial sovereignty, and the implied threats of war and dangers that could be faced by loved family members and friends living in Greece. Anger, fear, resistance, and immense pride characterize the children's responses to previous and current Turkish claims on Greek territory. One eleven-year-old girl from Brooklyn, New York, whose parents were from the island of Kalymnos (reached by a one-hour ferry crossing from the coast of Turkey, but by an eighteen-hour crossing from mainland Greece), wrote:

A few days ago I was watching Greek television. I was surprised to see my grandmother in Kalymnos on the screen … my parents explained that the Turks wanted to take an island near Kalymnos … I screamed out, "you barbarians, you took it all from us and made it yours. And now you want more. I will fight you too if I have to …" my father smiled, kissed me and said, "a true Greek." I said with determination, "yes father. A Greek and proud of it."

(*When I Realised I am a Greek Child* 1997: 100–1; translated into English from the original)

Constructing boundaries of identity: religious and secular markers

Greek immigrants to the USA created their religious institutions with three goals in mind: (1) to transmit the Greek Orthodox religion to the American-born generations; (2) to transmit Greek secular culture, history, and language to the American-born generations; and (3) to help new Greek immigrants adjust to American society and institutions (Karpathakis 2001). By the dawn of the new millennium, these three initially contradictory goals led to a number of identity conflicts in the Church and the Greek immigrant community over the relations between religious and secular markers in defining national and ethnic identities.

With its dual religious and secular role, the Church inevitably comes into conflict with the more secular interpretations of modern Greek identity. For example, a major Greek national holiday – 28 October "No (Ohi) Day" (a secular holiday commemorating resistance to the 1940 Italian invasion of Greece) – has been appropriated by and celebrated in the Church as a religious national holiday. As the Church tries to bridge the gap between the secular hometown organizations and its own structures, clergy make a point of visiting and consequently leading some of the secular organizations' celebrations. One priest, invited by an organization to lead the 28 October celebrations, spoke eloquently about the relationship between Greeks and God:

> It is God who has guided us through each and every one of our Nation's troubles. And alongside God has been our Church. Our bishops, our priests, our Fathers who have been our guiding light. God has been our guiding spirit, our Church has been the light we followed through difficult national times. ... From Byzantium to the present, our Church has been the leader of our Nation.

Another organization, commemorating the same event, offered a very different interpretation. The organization's president (a well-known Left activist) described Ohi Day as commemorating the "country's resistance to Nazism and Fascism." Daily events included lectures, presentations of biographies of guerrilla fighters, and detailed accounts of people who joined the resistance and were later persecuted by the Greek government because they were seen as "communist sympathizers" and thereby "traitors to the Greek nation."

These two reconstructions of Greek history employ radically different markers. For the Left, "ordinary men and women" create Greek history, and it is they who have freed Greece and Greeks from the oppressor. For the Church, God and the Church have been the "guiding spirit" and "light" leading Greece out of difficult times; orthodoxy lies at the center of Greek history and thereby Greek identity is defined by a fierce loyalty to God and Church. In the more secular version of the Left, "Greeks" are part of a "country" and "Greece" is delimited in time and space (at least within the twentieth century). In the Church's version, "Greeks" are part of a nation, and "Greece" is transhistorical and exists independently of particular men and women.

While secular organizations not faced with issues of diverse religious or political affiliations among their membership may accept religion as a criterion in demarcating Greek American identity, those groups with members or potential members of diverse religious or political orientations resist this function of religion. The following example illustrates how religious–secular rivalry emerges and is dealt with among the community's members. In the fall of 1993 a group of immigrants from a city in Greece with a large Jewish population held a meeting to form a new organization. It was decided that anyone born in the city or whose parent or spouse was born in the city would be eligible for membership. Mike, the man responsible for spearheading the organization, informed the group that a "Jewish organization" had offered help. As the discussion turned to specific methods of cooperation with this and other organizations, one man (George) interrupted the discussion, which was then joined by Mimis (a writer and Left activist):

George: I want no Jews in this organization.

Mike: Mr ... it's not up to you. We will not exclude anyone because you want it that way.

George: This is a Greek organization. Jews are not Greek.

Mike: These people are Greeks. They were born and lived in ... . They have fond feelings for the city ... as many bonds to the city as you do Mr ... .

George: They're Jews. They're not Greek. Greeks are Christians. Jews are not Christians.

Mike: This is not a Christian organization. It's a Greek organization.

Mimis: I know ... [George]. He's a member of ... organization. The fascists. I am not Orthodox, I am not religious, I am an atheist, a communist, and I am Greek. You have no right to tell us who is Greek and who isn't.

Immigrant activists on the Left as well as the American born who grew up influenced by American liberal ideologies but who remain interested in Greek politics are more inclusive in their definitions of who is a Greek. One woman, who gave up her position as secretary to one organization but who nevertheless maintained a modicum of community activism, articulated the Leftists' and liberal Greek Americans' position on the role of religion in demarcating their group's identity:

> I myself don't go to church. My husband is very religious. Our kids go to Sunday school. But that is irrelevant in this whole argument here. Personal beliefs I mean. Of course there are Greeks who are not Orthodox Christians. There are people who are born in Greece who are Jewish. Others who are Muslims. Others who are Catholic. Even Protestants. Who cares? The important point is that they are Greek. The church can make as many claims as it wants. The fascists can do the same. The truth is that these people do exist. I mean Jews and Catholics and whatever other religion have you. And they have as much right as the rest of those born in Greece to call themselves Greek. For crying out loud, the mayor of Athens is Jewish. Nobody in Greece questions his Greekness.

One man active in the organization discussed above said during the meeting: "When I walk the streets of ... and I see all those shops owned by Jews, down by the market, a lot of those shops are owned by Jews. I don't think that these people are not Greek. Nobody does. It's absurd. This religion thing is here." To the extent that the Orthodox Church has been supportive of Right-wing governments throughout Greece's modern history (Stavrou 1988; Simos 1991), only those on the Right equate Church and nation. Nevertheless, this secular–religious rivalry remains confined within the community's boundaries. When the audience of the particular identity is made up of outsiders ("Americans"), the immigrants offer little resistance to the employment of religion as the main criterion for cultural representation.

The Annual Independence Day Parade (25 March) offers the main opportunity to present a Greek American identity to the wider American public. During planning meetings for the parade, long debates take place over the roles to be played by the central religious authority of Greek Americans, i.e. the Archdiocese of North and South America and the Archbishop himself. Traditionally, it is the Archbishop who leads the parade, thereby representing the Greek American community to the broader US society. During a 1991 planning meeting for the parade, immigrants once again debated Archbishop Iakovos's role. The first argument, from a fifty-four-year-old Left activist, focused on the politics and class structures of the home and host societies:

> We are Greeks. We are also workers. Iakovos supported Bush and badmouthed Dukakis [i.e. in the 1988 US presidential elections]. What kind of a Greek is he? He placed his class interests over our interests. ... Today we're here as Greeks. Iakovos snubbed Dukakis. He snubbed all of us. Do we want him to represent us?

The second argument was made by the president of a secular men's organization. He bluntly stated the issue: "The problem is, is there anyone else in this country besides the Archbishop who is recognized as a Greek? No other leader is known the way Iakovos is." The third argument was made by an eighty-year-old man active in the community organizations since the 1930s: "Yes, we are Greek," he said, "and the Archbishop often does not represent us very well." But, he added, "we are also Greek American and the Archbishop has respect in American society." He then concluded by suggesting that "on this day ... we forget our own internal conflicts and unite as one people. We have to stop our squabbles."

While some used the immigrants' class background or Greece's international and geopolitical history to define Greek identity, others were more concerned with the identity to be presented to the "Americans" within the US social context. Since Archbishop Iakovos was the only leader easily recognized as Greek by the wider community, the Left offered little resistance to his serving as the immigrants' representative during the parade. When the community enters into relations with the larger and vague "American society," the Left finds itself at a loss, and its attempt to decouple religion from Greek identity is defined as petty internal politics which should not be made known to outsiders.

Identities in conflict: post-1965 compared with pre-1965 immigrants

While maintaining some form of allegiance to Greek culture and heritage, the Greek Orthodox Church has long been involved in articulating an identity for the earlier immigrants and their descendants. Encouraged by social ambition, fueled by media coverage of criminal arrests of Greek immigrants and political scandals or problems in Greece, many upwardly mobile second- and third-generation ethnics differentiate themselves from "other Greeks"[4] – Greeks in Greece, recent arrivals, and working-class Greeks. The status interests of these earlier immigrants, still insecure in their newly found status of respectability, predispose them to opt for an identity that mirrors their needs and concerns.

The Church, the earlier immigrants, and the American born active in Church-related groups employ perceived cultural differences (in addition to the mere fact of place of birth) to differentiate themselves symbolically from working-class Greeks (and, inevitably, recent Greek-born immigrants). Simultaneously, the need to distinguish Greek Americans from other ethnic Americans to avoid further intermarriage and consequent shrinking membership leads to the romanticizing and extolling of the alleged Greek cultural heritage, defined as "Love of God, country, and family" (a viewpoint that implicitly coincides with extreme Right-wing activism).

To facilitate a bridgehead between Greek and American identities the Church has appropriated American national heroes (such as Jefferson) into its pantheon, through a form of ecumenical particularism. Immigrants and clergy alike emphasize "American" cultural elements, creating a dual heritage in which they are now of America because of their acquisition of American virtues, but still possess Greek virtues distinguishing them from other Americans. While it is simply taken for granted that other Americans lack this glory or the particular Greek virtues, the interesting argument is that Greeks in Greece now lack these virtues. The somewhat paradoxical claim is that the Greek Americans, through the Church, are maintaining the "true" Greek or "Hellenic" identity, heritage, and traditions, and are thereby "more Greek" than the Greeks in Greece. As one clergy member said, "In Greece they have lost all sense of tradition, of heritage." In contrast, in the USA, "our students are taught and they learn their history … Our children here, we here, the Greek Americans are more Greek, truly Greek, not the Greeks in Greece."

While older immigrants and the American-born upwardly mobile opt for such a narrative of identity, the final outcome of the process is the complete shedding of the ethnonational bond in favor of a clearly demarcated Orthodox universalism. The Orthodox Christian Laity (OCL), a group of second- and third-generation middle-class professionals, has been lobbying for changes in the Church, including the replacement of Greek with English during services (Sfekas and Matsoukas 1993). The OCL's ultimate aim is the creation of a pan-American Orthodox Christian patriarchate to replace and unite the various immigrant and ethnic Orthodox Christian churches (Karpathakis 1994). For this group the nostalgic paradigm carefully nourished by the Church is no longer adequate. Not only is their "space" that of US society, but their own "time" is the present. For them, the context of the US separation of religious and secular domains prohibits the fusion of ethnic and religious boundaries.

The stage is thus set for a conflict between the Greek transnational identity and the pan-Orthodox identity, each of which employs a different sociotemporal framework. Transnational national identity remains committed to Greece, both in temporal and spatial terms. Pan-Orthodox identity endorses the mainstream US present. This rupture pervades the critical issues of cultural reproduction and identity maintenance, evident in the contentious and most fundamental question of how many Greek Orthodox Americans can be described as Greek Americans. While no consensus exists, the answer is probably more than a million.[5] The dispute concerns the criteria employed: should second- and third-generations Greek Americans be considered Greeks or simply Orthodox Americans?

The conflict between the American differentiation of religious and secular domains and the mixed ethnoconfessional nature of the Greek Orthodox Church deeply influences both the Church and its laity. While the OCL views ethnic and religious identities as completely separate, Archbishop Spiridon (in an interview in *Odyssey*, September/October 1996: 25) considers the "Hellenic" identity of Greek Americans to be identical to orthodoxy. Moreover, even where the Church hierarchy might endorse the OCL agenda, it faces important constraints. First, the Archdiocese headquarters is located in New York City, which has the largest, most recent, and most active fundraising Greek immigrant community in the USA. Second, the Church still has many strong and important economic and political ties with the Greek government and the Church of Greece. As one clergy member said:

> [W]e are Greek. We are not Russian. They adopted our religion and alphabet, we did not adopt theirs. I'm not saying this in a nasty way, I'm saying this just to show that there is a history there we cannot deny. But they are Orthodox. We are Orthodox. Their children do not understand Russian in their churches, our children outside of New York do not understand Greek in our churches. Do you lose the children, the next generation that will carry forth the Church or do you change some of the ways things are done? Am I Greek or am I Orthodox? [moment of silence] This is how one of my parishioners posed it to me.

To accept the proposed changes in the Church is to give up the Greek American identity embroiled in the community's secular nature and demands, and to create a new identity based solely on religious criteria. As another clergy member said:

> [W]hen you look at the rest of the country, the third and fourth generation

are Greek because of religion. They know nothing about Greece, they care nothing about Greece. Do you lose these children? The same is going to happen to Greeks here [New York]. ... What is the Church's responsibility? It's people's souls; it's people's spiritual lives. We are a Church; Greek Americans are Greek Americans because of the Church, because of the religion, our beliefs. So let us simply accept this and perhaps also the inevitable [i.e. pan-Orthodox American Patriarchate].

The OCL posits a new potential identity in which religious markers will overshadow the secular. In their attempts to preserve their ethnonational identity, even those closely involved with the Church argue that the social aspects and history of the Church are of equal significance to its religious teachings. According to them, Greek language and history are intertwined with the Church's own rituals. A middle-class woman active in the parochial school's parent–teacher association protested: "how can you read and chant the Byzantine hymns and prayers in a different language?. ... By losing the Greek language you are losing the culture that is in the rituals and the history of the Church."

Another woman, a journalist, employs secular criteria to reflect upon and interpret the theological teachings: "our hymns, our prayers, the way we talk with God in our services, in everything, is through the Greek language. You change the language and you change the religion." Immigrants thus interweave the religious with the secular markers (language, social, and intellectual history of Greece) to demarcate the uniqueness of the Greek, and thus Greek American, Orthodox identity from other ethnic Orthodox Christian identities. This shifting of the markers is carried out by immigrants confronted and threatened by the loss of their Church, their "institution." One forty-eight-year-old man articulated vividly what other immigrants have similarly expressed:

> [I]t's our Church. We built it. We, the immigrants. Giving our hard-earned money so we could have a place to take our children and teach them our ways. Who are they now coming in to take this from us? What did they contribute to the Church we built? ... We are Greek. Our children are Greek. Our children are Greek American. They are not Russian American or other American.

One woman Left activist argued that while other ethnic Orthodox churches would benefit from a pan-Orthodox patriarchate into which the Greek Church would contribute millions of dollars each year, the New York City area parishes would lose, because they raise these funds at the grassroots level. Similarly, many argued that with a new patriarchate, and the ways in which funding is raised and distributed in the Church, the Greek working-class immigrants of New York City and Chicago would be funding smaller parishes of the wealthier non-Greek Eastern Orthodox. As one fifty-six-year-old construction worker argued passionately: "why should my money go to fund the building for those who make over a hundred thousand dollars? Let them build their own church." The OCL, whose leaders are middle- and upper middle-class professionals and successful business owners, focuses on Eastern orthodoxy to define a new higher status identity. In contrast, many New York City immigrants (who are primarily working and lower middle class and small business owners) focus on other ethnoconfessional markers with which to lay their claims to the Church.

Conclusion

Post-1965 Greek Americans form a *transnational national community* in which preservation of Greek ethnic identity is safeguarded via the Church. In this recasting of religion in identity politics, Greek orthodoxy serves as a cultural marker delineating membership of an ethnonational as opposed to a purely religious community and uses Greece as the main point of reference. In order to safeguard its reproduction among the second and third generations of immigrants, diaspora identity assumes an increasingly nostalgic character, in which – while the symbolic space of the homeland remains the same – the temporal dimension shifts from the Greece of the present to the Greece of a distant past. Greek Americans are viewed as the inheritors of Greek tradition. The transnational identity of the post-1965 Greek immigrants comes increasingly into conflict with the emerging pan-Orthodox orientation of the older, established, pre-1965 Greek Americans.

In this sense, the relationship between the meaning of religious markers and the class position of the different immigrant cohorts is not accidental. For the middle-class older immigrant cohorts, religion becomes increasingly decoupled from ethnicity. However, this association remains at the heart of the cultural identity of the recent post-1965 immigrants. Hence, the debate over the status of the Greek Orthodox Church in the USA is in reality a debate over the different notions of community advocated by two groups with distinct socioeconomic profiles.

An important non-US agent influencing the community's affairs is, of course, the Greek nation-state, which has a long tradition of maintaining ties with the Hellenic diaspora. This is carried out through Greek state-sponsored Grecophone schools or classes, radio and television programs, academic programs in modern Greek or Hellenic studies, and other forms of cultural organization. In 1983 the Greek state founded the Secretariat General of Hellenic Diaspora (a special branch of the Greek Foreign Ministry) in order to coordinate action among the Hellenic diaspora communities. In 1995, the World Council of Hellenes Abroad was founded, a non-governmental transnational organization intended to promote the collective and autonomous cooperation of various diasporic associations. The Greek state's interests lie in promoting the transnational national identity of the Hellenic diaspora – in effect, hoping to maximize support for Greek foreign policy in countries with large diasporic constituencies (Australia, Canada, USA).

We cannot venture a long-term prediction of the ultimate resolution of the identity conflict among the Greek American community. In the most recent twist of the dispute, the newly appointed Archbishop of the Greek American Church, Demetrios, approved in February 2001 the constitutional amendments that would result in an Archdiocese largely independent of the patriarchate and also of the Church of Greece. The patriarchate and Church of Greece of course rejected this proposal and made a counterproposal, which was rejected by the American-based clergy.

Finally, the evidence presented in this chapter would suggest that transnationalism is a feature closely associated with the experience of recent immigrants. Indeed, the presence of transnationalism even among an old and established diasporic community (such as that of the Greek Americans) suggests that transnationalism cannot be considered as a phenomenon that refers exclusively to the more recent (and "less white") US immigrants. For example, Dominguez (1998) argues that transnationalism represents a new way for reconfiguring the politics of race and ethnicity in US society, whereby multiculturalism and transnationalism provide for a symbolic acknowledgment of racial difference, while simultaneously reifying such difference. Yet, even a cursory comparison between Australian, Canadian, and US-based Greek Orthodox diasporas suggests that class is an important component for the maintenance and reproduction of transnational connections. Such connections are stronger among the lower-class Australian and Canadian Greeks as well as among the more recent (and therefore of lower socioeconomic status) Greek Americans.

Notes

1 Our analysis is based on qualitative and ethnographic work on the Greek American community of Astoria, New York. Extensive quotations from the respondents have been kept to a minimum to allow the presentation of the authors' arguments. Earlier versions of this essay were presented at the 1998 Easter Sociological Society Annual Meeting, the 1999 American Sociological Association Annual Meeting, and the 1999 Conference on Globalization and Identities (Manchester Metropolitan University, UK).

2 For further discussion and statistics on the global strength of the Hellenic diaspora, see Roudometof (2001). The major wave of Greek immigrants (450,000 people) arrived in the USA between 1900 and 1917. In subsequent years, immigration was greatly reduced, but recovered in the 1966–77 period when 160,000 new immigrants arrived (Moskos 1989b; Hasiotis 1993: 106).

3 As one activist said, "Greeks sit in the coffeehouses of Astoria and philosophize about politics … you know the expression, 'we will solve the Cyprus problem' was made up from these coffee gatherings. For years they would sit and discuss. And discuss and discuss. And nothing would of course come of it. Like true outsiders to the system. Complaining about this and that." Another woman added, "their kids are just the same. They sit at the cafes and talk and talk and talk and do nothing. And when you tell them, go out and do something they say, 'what can we do? We are powerless.'"

4 Working-class immigrants represent a stigmatized category (see Granfield 1991), whose expression can be found in Astoria only in the coffeehouses – traditional

places of meeting for males in Greek culture (Drucker and Gumpert 1990, 1991; for the immigrants, see also Kiriazis 1989; Dickson 1991).

5 Using US census information, Moskos (1982: 19) estimated a maximum 1.25 million Greek American population, later revising this number (Moskos 1993: 17) down to 900,000. Hasiotis (1993: 169) reports two very different figures: around 1 million according to census and embassy reports, and 1.2–2.6 million according to the immigrant associations' estimates. A similar figure is used by the Secretariat General for the Hellenic Diaspora.

4 Emergent diaspora or immigrant communities?

Turkish immigrants in the Netherlands

Hans van Amersfoort and Jeroen Doomernik

During the post-1945 period, the growth of the world's population and the development of modern means of transportation and communication have resulted in unprecedented population mobility. This mobility raises the question of whether it is the numbers alone that have changed or whether the new media of transportation and communication are contributing to the formation of new types of immigrant communities. Instead of the 'classical immigrant community', which in due time shifted its orientation from the home to the host country, the modern immigrants remain oriented to the home culture, giving rise to 'modern diasporas'.[1]

Such a general idea is difficult to prove or disprove. Historical examples of transmigrants as well as people moving around in internationally oriented networks of certain professions (academics, soldiers in previous ages) are easily found. Modern communities with strong personal or cultural links with homelands can undoubtedly be identified. But it is much more difficult to assess the general value of a 'modern diaspora' or 'transnational migration' framework. In their introduction to a compilation of articles around this theme, Vertovec and Cohen (1999) summarise a bewildering amount and variety of uses and meanings of these terms. However fair and impartial they might be, their overview does not help us to formulate concrete research questions. Portes *et al.* (1999) are more selective in their introduction to the special issue of ethnic and racial studies on transnational communities but their approach needs substantial operationalisation before it can be applied to a concrete case (van Amersfoort 2001).

Consequently, the framework suggested by authors such as Sheffer (1995, 1996) and Basch *et al.* (1994) continues to offer an interesting hypothesis that merits further attention and scrutiny. Therefore, in this chapter we want to explore further this framework. Our main aim is to come to a definition and an operationalisation of the terms 'modern diaspora' or 'transnational community'. Subsequently we will apply our definition to the Turkish immigrant population in the Netherlands to determine whether this population can be described as a diaspora in a meaningful way.

Migration and ethnicity

Every individual becomes a member of his or her cultural group by way of socialisation. It is through this process that values are transmitted and sentiments of security and belonging are developed. 'Rites of passage' engage the individual in his/her culture in a way that can never be fully undone. Normally, people are hardly aware of the characteristics acquired in this way. But these same characteristics can become an overwhelming reality when people become confronted with 'strangers', with people who are unaware of what has always been taken for granted, and who do things differently, sometimes even fundamentally differently.

This confrontation is the basis of 'ethnicity' and the genesis of ethnic groups. Immigrants typically find themselves in this situation and this is why migration leads to the institutionalisation of immigrant cultures. Clubs, newspapers, churches or mosques and all kinds of common activities must ensure the continuity of the valued aspects of the home culture.

Initially, immigrant institutions generally have a conservative function. They try to avoid unnecessary contacts with the host society. A defensive ideology develops in which the own culture is made, at least morally, superior to the culture of the host society. But, on the other hand, immigrant institutions want also, in most cases, to help their countrymen to improve their opportunities in the new surroundings. Immigrant institutions see themselves often as forming a bridge between the individual immigrant and the host society.

There is an inherent tension between the conservation of the ethnic identity and the adaptation to the host culture. It is a characteristic task for immigrant leaders to master this tension. If no adaptation at all takes place, the group condemns itself to a marginal position in society, and no group can in the long run remain satisfied with such a position. When too much adaptation takes place the immigrant institutions lose their function and the group will lose its cultural characteristics. Most immigrant groups are, certainly for two or three generations, somewhere between these two poles. The question we want to explore here is how far the modernisation of the media of communication has changed the functioning of immigrant institutions, leading possibly to more permanent immigrant communities that can be described as 'modern diasporas' or 'transnational communities'.

Immigrant communities

When studying immigrant communities in modern societies we often see that they enter at the bottom of the social ladder. The boundaries of the group are clearly defined by citizenship, language and religion. From the side of the immigrants these boundaries are maintained by bringing over institutions from the homeland to ensure continuation of the valued aspects of the home culture. In the course of the generations both the social position and the boundaries generally become more diffuse. In such a case we regard the group as 'emancipating' and becoming 'assimilated'. However, not all groups develop along these lines. Some remain confined to a limited social role and stay on the margins of the society.

From a theoretical point of view the process of incorporation of an immigrant population can be followed as long as we want to. Society never becomes stable and it is difficult to decide when the process of immigrant absorption has come to a conclusion. But, generally, the social processes set in motion by a migration movement lose their force after three generations. This may be prolonged when the migration itself continues for a considerable time, bringing in new members from the homeland who 'refresh' the immigrant institutions (see, for example, Chapter 3). Of course, the final result of immigration incorporation does not depend only on the attitudes and actions of the immigrant group. It is also, and perhaps to an even greater extent, a consequence of the policies followed by the receiving society with regard to the immigrants (Doomernik 1998; see also Wong, Chapter 12, for a discussion of the Canadian case). When we look at historical examples we can distinguish three different outcomes of migration movements with regard to the social position of the immigrant group and the nature of its boundaries.

The first outcome is that the immigrant group has become fully 'assimilated' into the host society. This is not to say that members of this group have lost all memory of an ethnic past. Normally, there is still some faint tie with the 'homeland'. But the ethnic identity has become one among many – as the immigrants' occupation, level of education, place of residence or choice of marriage partners are no longer determined by ethnic belonging. In the Netherlands the descendants of the seventeenth-century Huguenot immigrants from France and the nineteenth-century immigrants from Westphalia are examples of such 'assimilated immigrants'.

The second outcome is that the immigrant group has kept its cultural identity and its members are still guided by specific cultural norms in important areas of behaviour. However, the immigrant group is no longer confined to a specific social position, class location (such as 'high' or 'low') and is not occupying a specific niche. In this case, the group is successful in maintaining its boundaries because of the central role of religious institutions in shaping group identity. Because of the group's adherence to religious institutions, group boundaries remain relatively closed, thereby leading to a high rate of intermarriage. In pre-World War II Netherlands, Orthodox Jewish communities, the descendants of seventeenth-century immigrants from Portugal and of eighteenth-century immigrants from eastern Europe, provided prominent examples of such culturally exclusive ethnic communities.

The third outcome is that the group has remained both culturally and socially exclusive. The social participation has remained restricted. Such a group has become an ethnic minority in Schermerhorn's (1970) terminology (see also van Amersfoort 1978). In the Netherlands the Moluccans who arrived in 1950 after Indonesian independence are an example of an immigrant community that over the generations shows a low social and cultural participation in the wider society.

Diasporas and transnational communities

In the social sciences, terms are often used without a clearly defined meaning. Diaspora is a good example of a term used mostly in an unspecified way with a vague hint that there is some resemblance to the position of the Jews in preindustrial Europe. The classical diaspora as described by Smith (1991) seems to be dependent on a premodern type of political order. All examples come from feudal states in which a mobile, outward-oriented 'minority' could perform functions in trade and finance that were forbidden to the 'real people'; who as an aristocracy were inhibited from meddling with such low-ranking affairs as money making, or as a peasantry were tied to the land. Outsiders perform the functions that do not fit into the ideological structure of these societies. These are societies where eunuchs and diaspora people fill typical niches in the social division of labour (Smith 1991: 34–8). 'Typical diaspora people' are endogamous – residentially and socially segregated and confined to specific occupations and professions. They are oriented to their fellow ethnics in the wider world for trade and marriage relations. Whatever the extent of their success in financial terms as traders, craftsmen, scholars or artisans, their legal position remains always fragile. They are part of a particularistic world in which they have no 'rights'. Diaspora cultures reflect this particularistic world. Indeed, here we see particularistic cultures that do not aim at incorporating others or being incorporated by others.

It is not easy to apply these kinds of characteristics to modern situations. Chaliand and Rageau (1995) make some valuable comments in their *Atlas of Diasporas*, but they do not come to a final definition and, in the end, they include a variety of meanings for the term diaspora. In his editorial to the special issue of *Herodote* on diasporas, Lacoste (1989) makes the interesting suggestion that diasporas make up characteristically the majority of the people concerned, i.e. the number of Jews, Armenians, Lebanese residing outside the homeland has always been higher than the number of those residing in the homeland. This approach would classify both the Irish immigrants and the Palestinians as modern diasporas. However, these groups do not fulfil the same economic functions as the classical diasporas (Lacoste 1989: 4).

When immigrant people specialise in certain occupations, it is sometimes possible to detect a similarity between immigrants and diasporas. But this similarity is weak because the modern immigrants' occupations by no means fulfil the same strategic role as did those of the diaspora traders in feudal societies. Moreover, the great majority of the modern immigrant population does not rely on 'ethnic enterprises' for a living but rather depends on the economy of the host society.[2]

Therefore, when the term diaspora is applied to modern immigrant communities, it is not possible to expect that these groups will display economic and social characteristics similar to those of the classical diasporas. Sheffer (1996: 40; 1995: 19–21) has tried to modernise the concept by adding a number of properties, the most important being the immigrants' political orientation towards their homeland. Unfortunately, Sheffer hastily describes all immigrant groups, however recently settled, as 'incipient' or 'emergent' diasporas. We think it is better to speak of 'potential diasporas' instead and to try to determine those factors leading either to gradual assimilation (or whatever equivalent term is used) or to the formation of a modern-day diaspora.

As is the case with the term 'diaspora', the label 'transnational communities' is readily used but rarely defined. In many instances, the authors who apply the term seem to have in mind much the same as those who prefer diaspora. For example, Basch *et al.* (1995: 7) define transnationalism as:

> ... the processes by which immigrants forge and sustain multi-stranded social relations that link together their societies of origin and settlement. ... We call these processes transnationalism to emphasize that many immigrants today build social fields that cross geographic, cultural, and political borders. Immigrants who develop and maintain multiple relationships – familial, economic, social, organizational, religious, and political – that span borders we call 'transmigrants'.

In this definition the temporal dimension remains relatively unexplored. Instead, the empirical material the authors present in order to illustrate the significance of transnationalism is focused solely on the present. In our minds, transnationalism in itself is not fundamentally new. As already mentioned, previous centuries witnessed close interaction between the European immigrants who settled in the 'New World' and those who stayed behind. For example, Thomas and Znaniecki (1958) have shown that the US Polish immigrants of the early twentieth century managed to keep remarkably close ties to their regions of origin without the benefits of the Internet and fast means of transportation. Of course, this interaction was hampered by the slowness of transport but, still, letters were written, goods and money were sent home, and return and circular migration frequently occurred. Therefore, in the end, the only relevant change between the early and the late twentieth century is in the speed of communication and travel technologies. Whether this factor alone can be held responsible for a completely different outcome in the interaction between immigrant groups and receiving societies is not at all certain. Therefore, we would suggest that, even though transnationalism is a valuable tool for describing and analysing the interaction between post-World War II immigrants and their places of origin, it remains to be seen whether this interaction leads to the formation of an entirely new type of permanent transnational community. Instead, we propose to reserve the term 'modern diaspora' (or transnational community) for ethnic communities that have kept their cultural identity and whose members are still guided by specific cultural norms in important areas of behaviour – such as those groups that were subsumed under the second conceptual outcome in the previous section. Of critical importance for the maintenance of such groups is the degree to which they have successfully transplanted their basic institutions into their new environment, for these institutions fulfil the critical function of preserving cultural continuity and promoting ethnic endogamy.

In the case of the Netherlands' Turks, their identity has been preserved through the local institutionalisation of Turkish Islam. In accordance with our thesis, the long-term effect of this institutionalisation can be measured by their rate of endogamy. The boundary maintenance of an effective Turkish Islam would neglect state frontiers in so far as contacts for the arrangements of marriages would be primarily made with other Turkish communities – either in Turkey or elsewhere in Europe. In this instance, the Turkish ethnic group would resemble the outward orientation of the classical diasporas and could be referred to as a modern diaspora.

The migration from Turkey to the Netherlands

The Turkish immigration in western Europe began as typical labour migration. In its early stages, all parties (i.e. the governments of the sending and the host society as well as the individual immigrants) assumed that migration would be temporary. The almost exclusively male migrants assumed that they would return home after a few years of hard work and frugal living. Their ultimate goal was to invest their savings in the family farm, in a local shop or to open a teahouse.

Reality proved to be different. The immigrants adapted to the higher standards of consumption and the provisions of the welfare state, while the expectations of their families back home rose higher and higher. In the meantime, the galloping inflation and political instability of the 1970s and 1980s made it unattractive to resettle in Turkey. Consequently, 'circular labour migration' changed into 'normal immigration' as wives and children were brought over instead of the fathers returning home. Because of the subsequent changes in the demographic structure of the Turkish population (van Amersfoort 1995), the Turkish migration pattern entered a whole new phase. After 1973, labour migration as such came to an end but the process of family reunification contributed to persistent increases in the number of immigrants. After 1983, the migration of wives and children gradually declined, as the process of family reunification was more or less complete. However, in the meantime, a new population of young unmarried Turks grew up and entered the marriage market. The strong ties of the recent immigrant communities with their home societies gave rise to a substantial immigration of marriage partners. Interestingly enough, the traditional rule of patrilocality did not apply to the marriage partners migrating to the Netherlands. Almost as many Turkish men as women came to the Netherlands to marry a Turkish resident (Muus and Penninx 1991).

This migration process has resulted in 309,000 persons of Turkish origin residing in the Netherlands in 2000 (CBS 2000: 75). Of this population, 131,000 persons were born in the Netherlands, and 12,500 of these had a father who was himself born in the Netherlands. Among Turkish immigrants the naturalisation rate is high, especially in comparison with Germany, the country with by far the largest Turkish population in western Europe (Doomernik 1998). Over half of those persons born in Turkey hold a Dutch passport. Among their descendants fewer than one-third are not Dutch citizens. The present demographic composition of the Turkish population can be seen in Figure 4.1, which clearly shows that the younger age cohorts consist more and more of people born in the Netherlands.

The institutionalisation of Turkish Islam

As all immigrant groups tend to do, the Netherlands Turks created a cultural infrastructure almost overnight. As long as the migration was in its first stage this infrastructure was more or less informal and commercial, providing for typical leisure-time activities or favourite products from the homeland. But when family reunification resulted in the establishment of Turkish communities, the preservation of Turkish culture became a more serious matter. Since most Turks consider Islam to be the centre of their culture, the institutionalisation of this religion deserves attention. It should be mentioned from the outset that we restrict our discussion to Sunni Muslims. This means that we omit Alevis (frequently being ethnic Kurds), who belong to the Shia

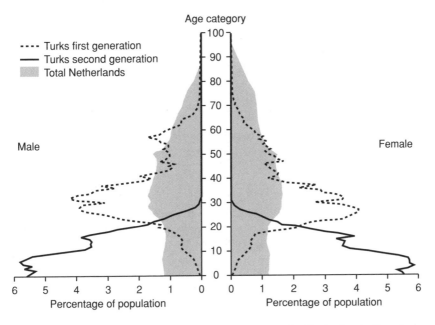

Figure 4.1 Age structure of the Turkish population in the Netherlands (immigrants and their descendants) compared with the entire population, 1998. Note that first generation covers all foreign-born persons with at least one foreign-born parent. Second generation denotes all Netherlands-born persons with two foreign-born parents.

branch of Islam and need few institutional arrangements to perform their religious duties. In effect, few institutional traces of Shia Muslims are found in the Netherlands. It is not known how many Turkish immigrants and their descendants are Alevis, nor, for that matter, how many are Christians or non-believers. We merely know that – in 1989 – approximately half of all Turkish adult males were regular mosque visitors (Doomernik 1991: 116).

When the mosques were first founded they were generally the direct expression of a need felt by the Turkish community at large. However, it was not long before ideological differences became manifest, eventually leading to schisms among sections of the Turkish community. The ideological differences underlying the schisms were related to the ideological orientations of different groups. These groups ranged from those favouring a liberal Islam, to those accepting the secular state and to those favouring extreme fundamentalist orientations.

These ideological orientations have their roots in the political situation in the Turkish republic (Doomernik 1991; Rath *et al.* 1996). After Kemal Atatürk founded the Turkish republic, Islam was banned from the political arena and became controlled by the state directorate of religious affairs: the 'Diyanet Isleri Baskanligi', or Diyanet for short. The secularisation of the state was not acceptable to some of the Turkish Muslims, who organised themselves in various, mostly underground, opposition movements. The 1970s were characterised by intense political conflicts that ultimately resulted in a military coup. This political instability and international developments in the Islamic world stimulated Orthodox Muslims in Turkey to come into the open and once again organise themselves around political parties.

Today, most mosques belong to a wider – national or European – federation of mosques that has a particular ideological colour. The divisions and conflicts we find in the federations of mosques in western Europe can be classified as belonging to three main streams:

1   The liberal line, accepting the secular state, is represented by the Diyanet. In the Netherlands about 140 mosques belong to this denomination. Although the official Turkish Islam was late to respond to the needs of the immigrant population in western Europe, once it started to found mosques it was quite successful and it took over already existing grass roots organisations (Sunier 1996: 61–70). The directorate sends imams to western Europe (generally for a four-year period) to serve the local organisations who subscribe to the Diyanet line.

2   The federation of the Milli Görüs stands for a fundamentalist approach and has, at the time of writing, about 20 mosques. It is to date by far the most active of the 'denominations'. It uses modern organisational techniques and aims especially at incorporating youngsters and women in its ranks. It has close contacts with the Milli Görüs movement in Germany and Belgium, albeit that these contacts have not always been free from conflict. Although at first strongly oriented towards the political

situation in Turkey, the orientation is gradually shifting to take more account of the position of Muslims in the Netherlands. This federation has also experienced a schism whereby a radical branch oriented towards Iran has split from the main body. However, the latter has only a limited influence in the Netherlands (Sunier 1996; Lindo 1999).

3   The Süleymancilar forms the third federation. It is the oldest federation in the Netherlands. This somewhat 'pietistic' denomination originated in grass roots organisations among the guest workers and was very much oriented to the homeland generally and to Turkish politics in particular. It has lost ground first to the Dinayet – when this organisation became active in the 1980s – and, during the last decade, to the Milli Görüs, which because of its more modern forms of organisation is far more successful among the younger generation.

Initially, the committees that run these mosques were preoccupied with the organisation of religious activities and with the ideological confrontations with each other. Furthermore, they generally offered some modest facilities such as a teahouse and some little shops. The mosques were primarily inward looking and oriented towards Turkey. But after about ten years a gradual change became manifest. The membership of the mosques' committees changed from the hands of the 'guest worker generation' into the hands of younger men who were at least partly educated in the Netherlands and had a fair to good knowledge of the Dutch language. These men do not have the idea that they will return to Turkey 'one day' but instead are oriented to a future in the Netherlands.

The change of leadership was reflected in the broadening of the activities of the mosques by, for example, the organisation of Dutch language classes and computer courses to improve the labour market prospects of the unemployed and a growing involvement in (local) politics. One mosque in Amsterdam even organised special bicycling lessons for its female members. Many of these general activities are subsidised by the Dutch state because the local authorities consider them to be of an 'emancipating nature'. The reforming attitude is particularly pronounced among the Diyanet-oriented leaders, who want to perform a 'bridge function' to the Dutch society. The leaders of the Diyanet-oriented federation are openly outspoken. They even think that Dutch-educated imams would be better than the present imams, who come from Turkey. The Turkish imams do not speak Dutch and lack contact with and understanding of Dutch society. In the near future, as the younger members of the community are more Dutch speaking than Turkish speaking, the Turkish imams may have difficulty understanding even their own congregation (reported 2 November 1992 in *Nieuwe Rotterdamse Courant Handelsblad*). It is not unheard of for the Diyanet leaders to argue that their children and grandchildren will be Dutch Muslims, just as there are Dutch Roman Catholics, Dutch Jews and Dutch Protestants.

In sharp contrast, the Milli Görüs do not share this 'assimilationist' approach. They consider such attitudes to be a manifestation of moral laziness and want to preserve a more strict and exclusive kind of Islam. But, as they do not strive to establish a Muslim state in the Netherlands, they have to strike a balance between the prerequisites of modern, urban life and their own strict interpretation of Islam. Indeed, as the debate over a new mosque in Amsterdam (Lindo 1999) illustrates, this group's current leadership argues in favour of a modern Islam, e.g. one devoid of traditionalist gender models. Of this group's followers, only a small minority of extreme fundamentalist organisations totally reject European society. In contrast to them, the third group, the Süleymancilar, are so inward looking that the wider society (at least in western Europe) simply seems irrelevant for them.

In conclusion, judging from the way Islamic institutions have been developing over the last two decades, we are currently witnessing two distinct trends. First, a majority of those Turks who confess themselves to Sunni Islam aim at full incorporation into Dutch mainstream society, giving no reason to believe they will constitute a diaspora. The most interesting group with regard to the possibility of diaspora formation is the Milli Görüs. Originally, they had close political contacts with Turkey and were aiming at transforming Turkey into an Islamic republic. But, gradually, their orientation shifted towards their country of settlement. Over time, contacts with their co-religionists in Germany and Belgium became more important. Their desire to rethink and revive Islam as a religion while living in a liberal Western society sets them somewhat apart from their roots in Turkey.

Migration and marriages

As discussed earlier in this chapter, we consider endogamy to be a constituent property of a diaspora. However, in the case of immigrant groups as recent as the Turks in western Europe, several types of endogamous marriages have to be taken into account. The first type consists of those marriages between partners who were both raised in Turkey. The second type is that between a partner raised in Turkey and a child of a first-generation immigrant. He or she is likely to be socialised in western Europe and may even have been born there. The third type of endogamous marriage is between people who are both members of the Turkish immigrant community, i.e. they are first- or second- generation immigrants.

Our assumption is that, throughout the generations, the persistence of marriages of the second or third type is an indication of the formation of a diaspora. In the case of recent immigrants, these types of marriages can also be seen as an intermediate step towards a greater measure of exogamy. In the case of the Turks in western Europe we cannot be too certain about the interpretation of present-day developments.

The migration waves of the last two decades and the concomitant development of a Turkish social and cultural infrastructure have resulted in a shift in marriage patterns. The first type of endogamous marriage was tied to the first early stage of labour migration. More interesting for the future is the development of the marriage patterns among the first-generation immigrants and their children. In the past, there were a great number of endogamous marriages of the second type, resulting in a migration flow of marriage partners. This pattern was a consequence of the strong ties of the first-generation immigrants with the Turkish homeland. Since most Turkish immigrants have a peasant background they remain tied to a network of extended family relationships. Their emigration was often meant to further the extended family's interests as well as direct personal welfare. These ties between parents and their extended family in Turkey had marked consequences for the children raised in the Netherlands. In Turkish rural areas the custom for arranged marriages (preferably with relatives) still prevails. Because the immigrants are considered to be much better off than their family members in Turkey, their children are seen as very attractive marriage partners. Since it has become more and more difficult to migrate (legally) to western Europe, a marriage to a boy or girl residing in the Netherlands or Germany is the safest way to have an opportunity to emigrate. The desirability of immigrant children as a partner is also reflected in the sharp rise in the amounts of money required as a dowry. Böcker (1992: 68–72) has observed amounts as high as fl.20,000, a tremendous sum of money given the circumstances of those residing in Turkey.

However, over the years, it became more difficult for the immigrants to view their obligations towards their relatives back in Turkey as reasonable. Moreover, a strong resistance is developing among the children raised in the Netherlands against arranged marriages with complete strangers. In particular, teenage girls come increasingly into very bitter and serious conflict with their families over this kind of marriage (Brouwer *et al.* 1992). Hence, the obligations deriving from the traditional Turkish life are becoming gradually less real for the immigrants residing abroad. The only time when they are directly confronted with them is during holiday visits. Böcker (1994) has noticed that several immigrants minimised the frequency of these visits because they found the demands of their relatives to be extremely burdensome.

In the early 1990s, Muus and Penninx (1991: 83–6) came to the conclusion that the number of marriages within the immigrant group was increasing whereas the number of marriages with a partner living in Turkey was decreasing. In addition to the shift towards this type of endogamous marriage, the number of mixed marriages – while still low – is undoubtedly on the increase. In the Netherlands in 1990 there were 1,860 marriages where both partners were Turkish, whereas there were 910 marriages where one of the partners was Turkish. This already amounts to one-third of the total number of marriages – a sharp increase from the 221 mixed marriages in 1987 (Muus 1992: 20). Unfortunately, we cannot follow up this trend using the same statistical source (marriages contracted between nationals and foreigners) because the majority of young people of Turkish descent are Dutch nationals, thereby leading to an insurmountable distortion of the statistics on mixed marriages. Another problem with evaluating these figures fully lies in our lack of information about marriages of Dutch residents that take place in Turkey or at the Turkish embassy or consulates. However, by alternative means (i.e. using a survey of household statistics), Hooghiemstra (2000) found a sharp increase in exogamic marriages during the 1990s: from around 5 per cent to over 15 per cent of all marriages contracted in a given year. Although these figures should be interpreted with some caution (marriages contracted with a Turkish spouse may not immediately lead to settlement of both partners in the Netherlands), they do lend further support to the idea that the Turkish community has slowly started to lose its firm contours.

Conclusion

The Turkish immigrant communities in the Netherlands are a recent phenomena. In the last ten to fifteen years they have shown a shift in their orientation from Turkey to the Netherlands. We expect the Turkish immigrant population to aim increasingly at social participation in and cultural adaptation to Dutch society. In fact, the numerically most important mosque organisation in the Netherlands openly states this as its goal. This does not mean that there will not be a Turkish (transnational) immigrant community any more in the foreseeable future. The members of this community will, however, be largely integrated into Dutch society and, if our prediction is correct, they will become less and less endogamous.

This expectation is very general and has to be modified in two ways. In the first place, we have to point out that the developments within immigrant communities are not purely endemic but are also determined by the reactions of the host society (Doomernik 1998). Until now the response of Dutch society to an emancipating Turkish immigrant population has been positive. Although no society is free from racist groups, racism as a political factor has so far been minimal in the Netherlands (van Amersfoort 1999: 57–60). If and how far this will remain so in the future is impossible to predict.

Furthermore, the development of the Muslim immigrant communities is not only dependent on the situation in the Netherlands or even western Europe, but also on unpredictable events in the world as a whole. For instance, the political tensions in the Middle East can lead to the sudden mobilisation of conflicting emotions with a deep impact on the relation between immigrants and host societies.

In the second place, it is important to note that so far we have treated the Turkish community as a single entity. However, as we made clear above, for reasons of space and availability of data we have excluded the Alevi Muslims and Christian subpopulations from our discussion. For the same reason, we had to disregard the possible effects of ethnic differentiation within the Turkish immigrant population. But even within the Sunni Muslim population Turkish Islam has proved to be far from homogeneous. It may well be that within the general Turkish Muslim community special 'subcultures' will develop that remain culturally closed and that preserve a more traditional form of Islam. It is certainly possible that a range from 'secular' to 'ultra-Orthodox' subgroups will develop within the Turkish immigrant population. It remains to be seen how far traditionalist subgroups can profit from modern means of communication in such a way as to maintain a 'diaspora status'. We predict, however, that the mainstream of Turkish Islamic life in the Netherlands will be of an adaptive nature to which the term diaspora cannot be applied in a meaningful way. The term diaspora (or transnational community for that matter) can be misleading if applied to immigrant populations, suggesting a measure of homogeneity that does not exist. When discussing the Turkish immigrants in the Netherlands it is more realistic, and it will increasingly become so in the future, to describe them as communities in the plural rather than as a diaspora in the singular.

Notes

1   For example, the Israeli political scientist Sheffer (1995, 1996) has presented this view in several publications. In French political geography the same idea is expressed in a special issue of the journal *Herodote* (no. 53, 1989). Using the term 'transnational migration' American anthropologists (Basch *et al*. 1995; Glick Schiller *et al*. 1995) have put forward the same general hypothesis.
2   Bovenkerk *et al*. (1983) have made an interesting study of an Italian entrepreneur migrant community organised around the Italian ice-cream parlours in the Netherlands. But only a small number of the Italians in the Netherlands live by making or selling ice-cream and, if necessary, the Dutch could well do without this service.

5 Boundaries of diaspora identity

The case of Central and East African–Asians in Canada

Kim C. Matthews

In the post-modern era, increased rates of international migration have intensified the problem of identity construction. This intensification requires new ways of conceptualizing space and place. The salience of identity construction and representation is illustrated by members of diaspora communities. This chapter explores the ways in which identity is being and has been negotiated by Central and East African–Asians residing in North America and for whom notions of identity are, for the most part, deterritorialized. The meanings and locations of "home" for Central and East African–Asians of the diaspora are also considered. The complexity of their identity(ies) speaks to the primacy of agency in the development and maintenance of our sense of who we are and where we "belong."

The respondents were Ismaili Muslims, a group which, to date, has rarely been studied. Their responses are textual and illustrative of their experiences as members of a diaspora, and lend themselves well to a broader discussion of identity and belonging. It will become clear that, although their religious background was not the primary focus of the investigation, adherence to the Ismaili faith is an essential component of their lives, sense of belonging, and identity.

Background and methodology

The following is based on a pilot study. Semistructured interviews with five East and Central African–Asians residing in Toronto and Montreal were conducted in Montreal. Criteria for inclusion in the study included: being born in East or Central Africa of Indian descent, adherence to the Ismaili faith, and residence in Canada. From the outset it must be made clear that the goal was not to produce results that could be generalized to the greater population of the diaspora. I sought to glean in-depth knowledge of the individuals included in the study through listening to their stories – producing data that were more in line with case studies. (Case studies are valuable in their own right as they can generate themes and issues that might be explored across a larger population at a later time.) I investigated the interviewees' migration history as well as that of their parents so that I could assess the different countries and cultures they may have been exposed to. The relationship between birthplace and identity was also explored to gain insight into the role the country of birth plays in identity construction and representation, especially under circumstances in which individuals belong to a minority and where political, social, and economic pressures compel people to migrate. Issues revolving around host country and belonging, and the impact upon cultural practices, are also considered. Questions are posed regarding the adaptation to new ways of living one's life in new locales and maintaining one's sense of identity and culture in the process – albeit sometimes in new forms. Finally, various issues are investigated surrounding the notion of home: its symbolic meaning, home as a place of birth, the importance of country of origin, where a family resides, where one has lived the longest, as well as the shifting of home at different points in one's life.

The names of the respondents have been changed for the purposes of this report. Five respondents took part in the study: two men, Imran and Faride, and three women, Arzina, Faori, and Anissa. Arzina (forty-four years old) and Faori (forty-three years old) were born in Bujumbura, Burundi, Central Africa. Arzina moved to Zaire with her parents at the age of two so that her parents could explore economic possibilities. In 1973, at the age of eighteen, she and her family migrated to Canada, where they were sponsored by a relative in British Columbia. They stayed in British Columbia for one month. Arzina and her mother then migrated to Montreal, where she has lived ever since. Arzina speaks Gujarati, Swahili, and the Katchi dialect of Gujarati; she also speaks English and French. Faori was also born in Burundi and moved to Zaire with her parents at the age of seven. Faori studied for seven years in Belgium and then returned to Zaire. In 1973 she migrated to Canada with her family. She lived briefly in France before returning to Canada, where she has lived for the past twenty-six years. Faori speaks eight languages: Swahili, Lingalla, Katchi, Gujarati, Urdu, English, French, and Spanish. There are similar rationales for the migration patterns revealed by the three female respondents: there were political and economic pressures in Zaire in the early 1970s and it became clear to the parents of the respondents that "non-Zairois" were no longer welcome. In addition, nationalization policies were instituted that resulted in family business interests being taken over without adequate remuneration. Canada was selected, in part, because all of the respondents had relatives in Canada and because Canada was accepting applicants from Central and East Africa at the time.

Faride (forty-three years old) was born in Tanzania, where he completed his high school studies before coming to Canada with his parents in 1974 at the age of seventeen. Faride speaks six languages: Gujurati, Katchi, Hindi, Swahili, English, and French. He now lives in Toronto. Imran (fifty-one years old) was born and raised in Uganda. He migrated to Canada as a refugee in 1972 at the age of twenty-three during the Ugandan crisis. Imran speaks four languages: Gujurati, Katchi, English, and French. He currently lives in Montreal.

Situatedness and the role of the other

The ways in which people discuss where they have lived, and are living, are influenced by where they are, and – more importantly – by how they perceive their interlocutor. Yet, although I do have concerns regarding the appropriateness of a white Anglo-Saxon studying the lives and meanings of East and Central African–Asians, much of what the respondents have said to me has allayed my initial concerns. Faride, a respondent born in Tanzania, currently living in Toronto, stated poignantly: "I would much rather talk with you, you do not have the same biases of someone with a similar background." So the potential for Eurocentrism is perceived as less of a threat than the potential bias of someone from within. Faride observed: "I think you are going about this in the right way, you are listening, listening to our stories, that is how we can get towards understanding each other better." I am reminded here of Mikhail Bakhtin's concept of the excess of seeing: "[t]his ever-present excess of my seeing, knowing, and possessing in relation to any other human beings is founded in the uniqueness and irreplacibility of my place in the world" (Bakhtin 1990: 23). Here, Bakhtin is referring to the limited scope of vision, both figuratively and literally, to which each and every human being is subjected. There is always a part of oneself that one may never see in the fullest sense. Only someone outside of ourselves is capable of completing the picture. Likewise, each human being has their own specific way of seeing the world and those around them. The excess of seeing is our ability to see in excess of the one we are looking at. Hall (1991: 48) elaborates on the role of the other:

> This is the other that belongs inside one. This is the other that one can only know from the place from which one stands. This is the self as it is inscribed in the gaze of the other. And this notion which breaks down the boundaries, between outside and inside, between those who belong and those who do not, between those whose histories they have depended on but whose histories cannot be spoken.

So when I ask "How did you identify yourself in Africa, Canada, India," I inevitably must inquire "How did they (the other) identify you?" This is important not so much for how members of the diaspora were identified, but rather their own perception of the opinions of others. Their perceptions will have an impact on their own sense of identity, how they describe it, and the strategies they employ to forge a sense of belonging. The multiple localities that my respondents have lived in, the numerous cultures to which they have been exposed, lend salience to their ability to construct and reconstruct their identity. Consideration of space and place in new forms encourages meaningful analysis of location and identity.

Deconstructing space and place

Concepts for analyzing the relationships between places as well as the social actions and perceptions of spaces have been articulated by theorists concerned with the geography of identity and the politics of place. Yaeger, for example, refers to the notion of deterritorialization as a way of grasping how shifts in our understanding of place and space occur. Thus, "… the boundaries of the physical world have shifted drastically – enforcing the need for new ways to talk about space. … Confronted by the quick metamorphosis of localities into translocalities, by the unmooring of nations and people in real time and space …" (Yaeger 1996: 10, 11), we can contrast past perceptions of space and place – which were fixed and finite, echoing the social expectations of the time – with the new situation. Similarly, Hastrup and Olwig (1997: 12) offer a strategy that encourages an understanding of identity construction in the translocal world:

> By viewing place as a cultural construction that is part of the process of human life, and not as a fixed entity, we will be able to examine critically the historical context within which such constructions take place. This also means that it is possible to examine the hierarchies of power within which such constructions occur and become recognised.

Lefebvre suggests the creation of a theoretical unity between "the physical," "mental," and "social" fields which are usually considered separately (Lefebvre 1991: 10, 11). Lefebvre elaborates on and interrogates the existence of spatial codes and their implications: "[i]f indeed spatial codes have existed, each characterising a particular spatial/social practice, and if these codifications have been produced along with the space corresponding to them, then the job of theory is to elucidate their rise, their role, and their demise" (Lefebvre 1991: 17). Space is not an empty vacuum, but rather the place where social interaction occurs, affecting, and being affected by, the interaction itself; space is where the mental constructs, the symbols, and the imaginary are formed, in the same interconnected manner.

The work of Keith and Pile (1993) is also useful in the present context since they re-vision space and place in order to avoid "the myth of spatial immanence," which contends that there is a singular true reading of any specific landscape involved in the mediation of identity (Keith and Pile 1993: 6). This re-visioning suggests that any given landscape may be read differently by different social agents; the relationship between the social agent and specific landscapes is particularly subjective and elemental in the development and maintenance of identity. Re-visioning space and place involves recognizing the varied meanings that both may hold for social agents at different points in time as they map out their identity.

The construction of identity is derived from the actions of social agents as they negotiate the cultures of the past with those of the present and indeed those of an imagined community. Identity formation is fraught with barriers, as any given identity is constantly acting upon culture and vice versa. "In short, the spatiality of the diaspora is the ground on which momentary and ever-shifting lines are drawn between inside and outside, oppressor and oppressed, the same and other" (Keith and Pile 1993: 18). The lines are not only a distinction but are spaces around which arbitrary closure occurs within hierarchies of power.

A diaspora

> Diasporas usually presuppose longer distances and a separation more like exile: a constitutive taboo on return, or its postponement to a remote future. Diasporas also connect multiple communities of a dispersed population. Systematic border crossings may be part of this interconnection, but multi-local diaspora cultures are not necessarily defined by a specific geopolitical boundary.
>
> (Clifford 1994: 304)

The members of the East and Central African–Asian diaspora I have interviewed seem to fit in with Clifford's distinction of "multi-local diaspora cultures." My respondents invoke India as the site of their common culture, as a social category. The inherent sociopolitical and historical elements of India represent the base of their identity, as it were, the label that they embrace; it represents the source of the culture and practices of their upbringing, despite not being raised there. "So instead, the diaspora is an invocation of communal space that is simultaneously inside and outside the West" (Keith and Pile 1993: 18). The respondents have lived in, and adapted to, many different locales and have connections that span the globe. They may also be considered, consequently, as transmigrants, although not in the way generally described in the literature. Basch *et al.* (1994: 7) define transmigrations as:

> ... the processes by which immigrants forge and sustain multi-stranded social relations that link together their societies of origin and settlement ... Transmigrants take actions, make decisions, and develop subjectivities and identities embedded in networks of relationships that connect them simultaneously to two or more nation-states.

The linkages for the respondents go beyond the traditional definition to encompass many connections and dispersed relationships, including places in which they may never have lived or visited. Parminder Bhachu discusses patterns of migration that involve a series of moves similar to those experienced by the respondents. Accordingly, "... they constitute a transnational people with established international, national, and local connections. These features are critical to the reproduction of their cultural bases and ethnicities and to their engagement with the economies and polities of their countries of settlement" (Bhachu 1996: 290). Arzina, a respondent born in Burundi, relocated to Zaire at the age of two, migrated to British Columbia at the age of eighteen, and now lives in Montreal. She is in contact with family members in twelve different countries; these are the connections of diaspora communities. Arzina's cultural practices are based, in part, on origins that she describes as Indian rather than African. Her society of origin is not where she was born nor where she was raised – not territorial, but rather deterritorialized. Indian as a social category is divorced from a physical site.

Cultural sites and identity

Olwig discusses the effects of "… a world where moving and dwelling are in constant interplay … The displaced do not experience temporary absences only to be confirmed in the well-ordered structure of normal life. Theirs is a more or less permanent experience of not being in-situ, as they negotiate a diversity of experiences in a deterritorialized world" (Olwig 1997: 34). She suggests (Olwig 1997: 35) that:

> Important frameworks of life and sources of identification should rather be sought in the cultural sites which have emerged in the interstices between the local and global conditions of life. These sites encompass and embody the multiple and contradictory spheres of life in which people are involved today.

My respondents are Shia Imami Ismaili Muslims. Ismailis live in over twenty-five countries, with seventy to seventy-five thousand living in Canada from various backgrounds and origins. The mosque is a key cultural site for the respondents not only as a place of worship but also as a site where cultural and religious practises are substantiated. The mosques are accessible only to members of their faith. Truly interstitial in nature, the mosques are found worldwide. Imran, born in Uganda, currently a Canadian citizen living in Montreal notes:

> I can retain part of my Indian heritage, my Indian culture because I still speak the language [Katchi] with friends. I participate in some of the social side, but I can't say the same for my children, and this is why for many of us, we would like to impress upon our children, in terms of culture, food, social activity, movies, Indian cultures, they are a part of that heritage. I think the greatest asset for us in terms of retaining part of that culture is the sense of the Ismaili community. I think more than anything else it is religion that binds us, and takes us back to the culture to the heritage, because communities started from India, and that's where

conversion took place. Even for my children now, if it had not been for the religion, for our sense of community, probably, they would have lost whatever cultural heritage I had carried with me. There is a focal point, where you get together and be a part of yourself and see where your roots are. I think for us, for my community probably it is much more in this country a position, that we are strong here. It is a way of life for many of the people; we retain our roots, what the community has to offer.

All of my respondents reported being very involved with events in their community through the mosque. While all had non-Ismaili friends, the closest friends tended to be Ismaili and from the same towns where they were raised. The respondents have, in a sense, recreated in Canada the communities they had in Africa. The friendship patterns play out at the mosque with groups divided along linguistic and territorial lines, despite the fact that all respondents spoke Katchi, an Indian dialect. The respondents tended to speak English if they were from a British colony, and French for those raised in a Belgian colony. The impact of alternate cultures on their own Indian background is noteworthy. Schooling often took place in systems set up by colonizers, or, in some cases, involved teachers who were trained in the UK and Belgium. While on African soil the respondents were instructed in the ways and customs of places far from Africa. Social groupings were formed with classmates that persisted upon immigration to Canada. Here, moreover, the division along linguistic lines had a very practical effect on the province that immigrants chose to settle in – French speakers went to Quebec and English speakers went to Ontario, British Columbia, and Alberta – although not exclusively.

Imagined communities

One of the ways that minority populations respond to exercises of power from majorities is through the creation of imagined communities. Anderson (1991), in his consideration of nationalist movements, first presented the concept of imagined communities. Anderson examined the ways in which nationalist movements imbue categorical fictive relationships with the emotions and intimacy of face-to-face relationships, strengthening bonds, and their cause in the process. Members feel affiliated to all others in the same movement because they believe they share similar values and beliefs. The social agent has the impression that he/she is part of a group sharing similar hopes, dreams, and aspirations despite never having met. The main difference between Anderson's use of the concept and the way I choose to employ it is that nationalist movements are most often in the majority, imposing their will on minorities. In the case of a diaspora, the imagined community is invoked but not in order to subjugate others who are a minority; rather, it is used to forge a sense of belonging. Interestingly, this need becomes salient when members are faced with opposition to their presence, or simply when faced with alternate and competing cultures.

Imagined communities play a role in breaking free from the arbitrary classifications set forth by majorities bent on situating minorities. Guarnizo and Smith (1998: 23) explore identities forged from below:

> The process of sub-altern identity is a process of constant struggle – a struggle in which discursive communities produce narratives of belonging, resistance, or escape. In these grand narratives of personal meaning, the spaces for forming non-essentialist identities, while not entirely absent, are interstitial – i.e., they open up between such dominant discursive venues as "the nation-state," the "local community," and the "ethno-racial" community.

There can be an empowering aspect to imagined communities, one that lends pride to one's culture and history. The values of their religion play an important role in the lives of the respondents. The Ismaili community is both an actual community and an imagined one; actual in terms of members' interactions with fellow Ismailis here in Canada, and imagined through their solidarity with Ismailis from all over the world. The power of this imagined community is evidenced through the words of one of the respondents, Faride, born in Tanzania and currently living in Toronto: "it doesn't matter where one is in the world, we know we are not alone, we can always meet with someone from our community." It is important to note that by this Faride means that regardless of whether he has met the person before he feels they share a fundamental similarity through belonging to the same religion. It is perhaps not surprising that members of the East and Central African–Asian diaspora have turned to their religion as a main source of identity construction. They have lived in many places and faced opposition, to the point of being expelled in some instances. The formation of the imagined community takes place from a young age through family stories and historical accounts. It is reinforced through the teachings of the community's beliefs and values. More importantly, in the context of the Ismailis I interviewed, the imagined community does not respond or pass judgment – it is called upon to comfort and provide a sense of belonging.

The respondents in this study had not one but two imagined communities that they called upon as part of their identity and as a source of belonging – the second being their Indian origins. Imagined communities play an integral part in identity formation and maintenance, especially for diaspora communities. Identity in this framework takes on a mythical status – divorced in many ways from territorial-based descriptors. The mythical status is not impervious to scrutiny however. There are times, at least in the case of the respondents, that the imaginary slams into reality in the form of visits by members of the East and Central African–Asian diaspora to India or Pakistan, or meeting Indians and Pakistanis from their respective countries in other places. At these times, the question of what it means to be Indian is raised. The meaning for members of the diaspora that I am studying involves Indian as a social–cultural category, while for members of the respective countries it requires living there, or at the very least having been born there. The difference of opinion is not always resolved.

Negotiating identity

Where an individual is living has an impact on how he/she defines his/her identity and on which aspects of this identity are emphasized or, in some instances, which are played down. These situational strategies are employed for self-definition and enable individuals to maximize the possibility that diaspora identity can be used as cultural capital. Imran eloquently describes the aspects of his identity and cultural practises that he stressed while living in Uganda:

> I go back to Uganda's situation, because culturally we wanted to identify both to the Indian community as part of the cultural group that we belonged to and to the British as we were brought up in that system. We tried to get the best out of both the worlds. Now when we are speaking culturally or socially, we would go to films, and people would be interested in going to see an Indian film, and they would also go and see a North American or a British film. For us, we wanted to take advantage of both the cultures in that sense, whenever we could, and here too, you become nostalgic about part of your heritage. I think in the sense of that, you do not want to lose that cultural aspect, and you don't want to become too westernised. English was the dominant language in which to express yourself, with your friends or at school. In a way we as an Indian community or an Asian community in Uganda were in a dilemma, we are an Indian community and yet we are acting more like British in some mannerisms or dress.

Imran acted more British at times and felt comfortable doing so because, in part, the Indian community in Uganda was much larger than his community in Montreal. He notes:

> When I see my children, here in Canada, we speak mostly in English at home, except for at a very early age, you have this inkling that you have to teach them your Mother tongue. When you are exposed to a wider society, it becomes imperative that you have the language of the majority. Back home in Uganda there was not so much of a dilemma because the community was much larger, less of the British influence there in that sense, as opposed to here, with the western way of life. Many of us want to retain part of the Indian culture, by, on occasions, dressing up in Indian costumes, going to the mosque, or taking part in social functions that

have Indian backgrounds, or going to see Indian films, or videos. I guess in a sense that you want to retain part of the heritage of yours, without having to adopt a completely new way of life, a North American way of life. For the Indian community or for a minority group, that is always the dilemma, we have our own ethnic television station, which only appears once a week. I like to catch it to see what is current, what is happening in the Indian film industry, or Indian politics, or life. We go to the internet and there is more opportunity now, but I don't think we can totally identify ourselves in that sense. You are just hanging on to the threads, and you realise that you are living in a society where you have to take the advantages from both of the cultures.

The situational nature of identity construction and cultural practises are well illustrated in these passages. The threads that Imran refers to indicate an Indian background that he maintains as well as he can in a Western setting. The key is that he attempts to glean whatever positive aspects of Western culture he can to improve his way of life. The advantage Imran has over those who have always resided in the same place is that he has been exposed to many different cultures and systems, each with its advantages and disadvantages. He has had the opportunity to gather the habits and practises that he has found useful and, at the same time, he has learned to adapt to many different settings. A common thread remains, however, and this consists of maximizing the benefits from one's cultural repertoire and, here, the larger the repertoire the more likely one is to deal well with new challenges. Getting the best of all worlds is an important characteristic of diaspora identity and it promotes adaptation to new places and enhances self-confidence. Hall (quoted in Pile and Thrift 1995: 10) elaborates on diaspora identity in a fashion that illustrates Imran's coping strategies:

> ... [D]iaspora refers to the scattering and dispersal of people who will never literally be able to return to the places from which they came; who have to make some difficult settlement with the new, often oppressive cultures with which they were forced into contact, and who have succeeded in remaking themselves and fashioning new kinds of cultural identity by, consciously or unconsciously, drawing on more than one cultural repertoire.

Anissa, born in Kenya and currently living in British Columbia and Pakistan, holds British, Pakistani, and Canadian citizenship. In Canada and Pakistan she describes herself as "an Asian from East Africa, I cannot take myself away from East Africa and say that I am a Pakistani I cannot do that." Anissa's experiences in Africa are important to her sense of self. She underlines this as the main difference between herself and Pakistanis, yet she still feels she belongs when she is in Pakistan, and the way she has negotiated this is noteworthy:

People accept me for what I am, differences are there, my way of talking is there, my dressing up is a little different. I wear my jeans all the time. You know, I go on the streets wearing my jeans and my shirt and I just go in the bazaar like most of the youngsters these days do that. It is not like women of my age living in Pakistan. One would not do that, they would wear the cultural clothes, the traditional clothes to go in the bazaar. But for me, I do not have to look at people, and it does not bother me if people look at me, people don't care really as such. I just go out and I do my shopping. Whatever we need to do, I just do, and come home and if people are looking at you and passing comment it just does not make a difference. Believe me, they do not do that anymore. So I just live there, I have accepted the culture, it does not bother me, I fit in very well. I am Asian so I fit in very well. Everyone in Pakistan is brown, we have a lot of ethnic communities as well, so Pakistanis have accepted me for what I am.

This passage is brimming with negotiation strategies formulated in order to forge a sense of belonging. Anissa brings forth similarities between herself and Pakistanis from Pakistan: namely that she speaks the language and she is brown. This allows her to go about her daily routine, live her life as it were in Pakistan as she sees fit. She is Asian and she believes she is accepted despite such differences as the way she speaks and the manner in which she dresses. She links part of this acceptance to the fact that, since there are many ethnic communities in Pakistan, she is simply part of the African–Asian community. It is clear, though, that Anissa does not want simply to blend in with Pakistanis. Interestingly, she tends to wear her saris more often in Canada than in Pakistan. These habits are symbolic and they tend to underline difference rather than similarity – a kind of cultural right of those who reside in more than one place. Perhaps as a defense or a response to the inevitable underlining of difference articulated by those who would define her identity as other than their own, she embraces the difference and makes it her own – something to be treasured and displayed.

By articulating difference – either verbally, or symbolically through dress – Anissa is marking out difference between herself and locals. Anissa is negotiating her identity in a manner that expresses the multiple contexts with which she is associated. In so doing, Anissa lessens the possibility of being judged by the social standards reserved for those from Pakistan. She makes it clear that she has more to offer – perspectives from another place of which she is still a part, embracing the flexibility of an interstitial existence in the process. Identity in this context becomes plural, and context specific. It is such experiences as displacement, reterritorialization, leaving, returning, settling, and moving on that introduce alternate or similar cultural practises to members of the diaspora and, once experienced, no one is ever the same again. One can never truly return to the original ways of "doing." Even the expressed act of attempting to maintain practises in a traditional fashion suggests the recognition that alternate forms exist, and consequently the social agent lives these practises through different lenses from before. Perceptions change, and invariably the meanings of cultural practises shift and evolve even if such a shift involves a recognition of the attempt to maintain "the old ways." This is not to say that the resulting practises do not meet the psychosocial needs of the social agent. On the contrary, culturally reflexive practises help to reinscribe identity as part of a larger community even, or perhaps especially, if these communities are dispersed.

Faori, a respondent born in Bujumbura, Burundi, migrated to Zaire at the age of seven. Soon thereafter, her parents sent her to study in Belgium, where she lived with a Belgian family. At the age of seventeen she and her family migrated to Montreal and she is currently living in Toronto. Her narrative illustrates exclusionary practises and coping skills. While living in Zaire, the local black Africans called her *muzungu* or foreigner. "And I was different, I am Indian, I have Indian blood." Likewise, in Belgium, she did not feel that she belonged. A student whose presence was transitory, she constructed her identity as Indian. The reception she received on her first visit to India and her feelings associated with the events are telling:

> I did not feel good in India. We were seen as foreigners, different from those who live there, not inhabitants. This was a source of extreme sadness as we consider ourselves Indian. They were our compatriots, but they did not feel the same way … It was painful to see our compatriots in such poor conditions.

When I inquired as to how she reconciled the actual events during her visit with her sense of self, she explained that India is the source of her culture and she described herself and others she knows from Africa as "imported Indians" because their travels have changed them. Fundamentally, however, and in her opinion, they share the same culture even if some of the actual practises have changed compared with those living in India. Indian is invoked as a social category. For "imported Indians," one does not have to be from there in order to be Indian, and even this is strongly contested by the indigenous population, who consider themselves to be Indian by virtue of the territory they are living in. When "imported Indians" "return" to India, new meanings are constructed around what it means to be Indian, and the relationship between India as a site and Indian as a social category becomes all the more tenuous.

Home reconceptualized

> Perhaps it is part-and-parcel of an appreciation of the way that individuals live in movement, transition and transgression, that its conceptualization, as "home," is to be similarly paradoxical and transgressive. "Home" we

suggest as a working definition, "is where one best knows oneself" – where "best" means "most," even if not always "happiest." Here in sum, is an ambiguous and fluid but yet ubiquitous notion, apposite for charting of the ambiguities and fluidities, the migrancies and paradoxes, of identity in the world today.

(Rapport and Dawson 1998: 9)

I agree with Rapport and Dawson's definition of home. Their definition contrasts with that of Basch *et al.*: "Transmigrants use the word 'home' for their society of origin, even when they clearly have made a home in their country of settlement" (Basch *et al.* 1994: 7). Among the members of the East and Central African–Asian diaspora that I have interviewed, neither Africa nor India appears to be considered home. Many have never lived in India, all have resided in Africa, in some instances holding citizenship. When we consider the nature of the interactions and the reasons for migration, it becomes clearer why they do not consider Africa as home. Faride explains: "We were considered as the 'Asian people' and the 'Asian people' mostly ran the country after the British left." There were significant social, economic, and cultural differences between the two groups. East and Central African–Asians ("the Asian people") were not considered African by black Africans. Born in African countries, at times refused citizenship, exclusion was part of daily life with very serious repercussions for their well-being in certain instances. This is evident especially in the case of Uganda, where "non-Ugandans" were given thirty days to leave the country during Idi Amin's rule. A desire to embrace the country of one's cultural rather than natal origins as a means of gaining a sense of belonging is understandable in such contexts. Being considered as foreigners in their country of birth led them to generate innovative ways for defining their identity and role in society.

Canada, for the respondents, represents the country of their hopes; "le pays d'avenir" that they sought so strongly when escaping uncertain futures in Africa. Africa, the land where they were born, is described often as a place of transience. Some respondents had spent only a few short years in their place of birth before being sent to study abroad, generally in the West. Even those who lived and studied in Africa relate that they rarely felt secure, viscerally or emotionally, while living there. They felt different from black Africans, Arzina explains: "Africa was more or less home, we were, after all, living there; home in the sense that we had no other choice." Home as where "one best knows oneself" seems to be a much better formulation, specifically in reference to the respondents. When Faride was asked where home is, he responded:

> I came to Canada at the age of seventeen. I found a job, no problem at all, started working in a factory, and it was just great. I think at that point in time is when I discovered myself as a person, and started to learn things on my own, and working ... In terms of the mind opening

up, and in terms of seeing other people as they were, knowing the world as it is today.

I believe it is significant that those respondents who were in their teens and early twenties at the time of their arrival in Canada consider Canada to be home, and consider themselves to be Canadian. Imran, in contrast, who arrived in Canada at the age of twenty-five, was the only respondent to consider himself mostly Ugandan. He cited a lack of closure regarding his departure:

> Maybe I am nostalgic about my home country perhaps it is more because if I had left the country voluntarily, I do not think I would still have sentiments about the country, but because we were forced to leave, I feel that something, that there has to be closure. I want to go back again, and see it once, say to my children "this is where I was born and grew up."

All of the respondents have been living in Canada for, on average, the past 25 years, and no doubt this explains why they consider Canada to be home. They have negotiated their identity in Canada longer than any other place. The respondents who lived out important years in the course of their personal development in Canada identify themselves first and foremost as Canadian. "In short, in a world of movement, home becomes an arena where differing interests struggle to define their own spaces within which to localize and cultivate their identity" (Rapport and Dawson 1998: 17).

Conclusion

Conventional notions of transnationals imply a country of origin and one of settlement. For Central and East African–Asians of the diaspora, origin in and of itself is very ambivalent. Origins may be linked to India – a country the transnationals may never have lived in. The connections – social, political, and economic – experienced by the communities of the diaspora span many borders; they are, in a non-traditional manner, transnationals. A rethinking of place and space enables a broader conception of transnationalism, one that transcends territory as a defining factor.

Identity construction and reconstruction of Central and East African–Asians of the diaspora offers insight into the increasing divorce of place as a physical location and social categories of identification. Geography is increasingly disconnected from identity. Where one lives is not an a priori feature of self-description. This is most evident when one "returns" to the site of origins. Theirs is a deterritorialized identity. "Returning" to India increases the tensions between place and social categories since resistance from local populations is harsh and direct. The ability of members of Central and East African–Asians of the diaspora to negotiate and renegotiate their identity(ies) across multiple borders speaks of their strength and resilience. The interstitial nature of their identity, imposed, initially, from above, is now embraced and employed as cultural capital. In the process they attempt to "get the best from both (or many) worlds."

6 Transnational expansion of 'class struggle' and the mediation of sport in diaspora

The World Cup and Iranian exiles[1]

(In memory of my brother Khosroo.)

Manuchehr Sanadjian

> ... among the people, truth is the property of national cause.
> (Frantz Fanon in *The Wretched of the World*)

A bourgeois transnational link

On a Sunday evening in June 1998, a small crowd of Iranians gathered outside a fairly well-known Iranian confectionery/grocery in London to watch the televised World Cup football match between Iran and the USA. The Iranian residents in the area were known for their relative wealth and were among the first to leave Iran for the West in the wake, or even in anticipation, of the popular uprising that toppled the Pahlavi state in 1978–9. The shop supplied a wide range of Iranian food, raw and cooked, some prepared in the UK and some imported from Iran. The food included fresh 'halal' meat, Iranian delicacies and groceries and fruits and vegetables. Like several other neatly decorated Iranian shops and restaurants in the area, the multipurpose shop presented itself as a place for a cosmopolitan demonstration of taste for quality and imported food. Although the shop served the Iranian customers with a wide variety of 'home' items, their visits to the shop were disguised behind its public image as a provider of exotic food, access to which was an established local bourgeoisie habit.[2] The combined emphasis on imported and quality food evoked the image of a delicatessen where tension arising from foreignness was defused in the quest for the exotic involving the 'modern' experience of 'conjoining of the ephemeral and the fleeting with the eternal and the immutable' (Harvey 1989: 10). This was despite the fact that for the bulk of its Iranian customers the shop provided not so much the site of an ostentatiously bourgeois excursion into the exotic as a surreptitious return to 'home'.

The notably formal language in which the shopkeepers conducted transactions with Iranian customers blurred the difference between the latter's appropriation of goods designated as homely as opposed to exotic products. The shopkeepers granted the customers a respectable status in exchange for the latter's public disavowal of the economically calculated gains in their transactions. The shopkeepers' frequent response to the customers' immanent payment for their goods was, 'It is nothing' (*qabeli nadareh*). The expression was purportedly designed to discourage the customers from paying for the goods by questioning the *acceptability* of the goods they purchased. The acceptability, however, was gauged *not against the price* the buyer paid for the commodity but *the status* granted to him as a person. In this way, the shopkeepers conferred status on their customers by acknowledging that their worth was well beyond the price they were paying for their goods. The customers reciprocated by appearing humbled while insisting on paying and referring to the shopkeeper's offer as 'too kind', 'too generous'. They went ahead with the payment with no further resistance from the shopkeepers. The symbolic rejection of money in the formal exchange between the shopkeepers and the customers shifted the focus in their relationship from the *economic* values of goods exchanged to the *social* status of the givers/takers.

By describing the goods transacted as 'nothing' the shopkeepers acknowledged their Iranian customers' status as incomparable, assessed in non-quantitative terms, with the quantified commodity measured in price. The shift, therefore, reflected a change of emphasis towards the *quality* of goods as the means of gauging the receiver's/giver's status. Similarly, the customers' insistence on the acceptability of the goods purchased involved a reciprocal return of status to the shopkeeper as the giver of *acceptable* (quality) goods. In the course of these formal exchanges the two sides assumed the roles of giver and receiver of a gift whose value was not assessed merely in quantitative terms but as the measure of status (Mauss 1969). Hence, the Iranian shoppers' ostentatious avoidance of bargaining and their tendency to spend less hesitantly. The mutual refusal by the shopkeepers and their customers to acknowledge publicly the potential economic gains and losses at stake in their exchange left intact the actual economic gains achieved by the shopkeepers, who also acted as the cultural agent, a distributor of symbolic goods, through emphasising the acceptability (quality) of the goods exchanged. Thus, by conferring on their customers a 'semi-guest' status the shopkeepers assumed the role of a 'host', whose acknowledgement of the guest's status was demonstrated in the *quality* of the food produced for the guest through skilled and dedicated work (Sanadjian 2000). The mediation of quality goods exchanged between Iranian shopkeepers and customers was homologous with the status negotiated in a delicatessen where the host middle-class men and women visited in apparent search of quality food. Although the food in the shop was not seen by Iranians as exotic, it was, nevertheless, appropriated in a 'war of positions' (Gramsci 1971; Chapter 6) in which they struggled for both a bourgeois credibility and a national identity. As a delicatessen shopper, individual Iranians claimed the place as a publicly defined – objectified – bourgeois space. As an Iranian, however, they visited the place as a more privately defined – subjective – national space. The public, objective, class-based representation of the shop overshadowed its more private, subjective, appropriation by Iranians as national.

The representation of the food in the shop as exotic, a way of demonstrating distinctive taste, served as an alibi for the diasporic Iranians, enabling them to claim the goods as national–cultural items. Thus, the institutionalised 'deterritorialisation' found in the delicatessen allowed the émigrés to redefine the space in the shop, i.e. to 'reterritorialise' it, as Iranian (in contrast to Appadurai 1990). The alibi pointed to the avowal by the émigrés of their 'assimilation' into the host bourgeois society, on the one hand, and yet their simultaneous disavowal of such inclusion through emphasis – even if a muted one – on their exclusion from it as national, Iranian subjects on the other. This 'dual movement of assimilation and exclusion' (Balibar and Wallerstein 1992: 42) was mediated and expressed by the Iranian shoppers, who wore the mask of proprietor purchasing food as a commodity, a domain of universal exchanges, within which were subsumed the social and cultural bearings of the agents involved. Thus, the agents disguised their culturally specific appropriation of the objects behind a bourgeois search for the exotic. The institutional mediation of the delicatessen was conducive to fostering a cosmopolitan atmosphere that placed the cultural objects on sale in the shop beyond the normally polarised construction of cultural distance into 'backward' and 'modern'. The removal of this distance through 'assimilation' was presented in the host British society as 'progress' (Balibar and Wallerstein 1992: 25), while a failure to do this would relegate the excluded to a 'backward' position. Such cultural distance was superseded in a liminal time and space in which cultural objects were freed from the structural constraints that shaped the normal experience of time and space (Turner 1969). This enabled the Iranians to represent their symbolic journey home as 'modern'. The shop, modelled after a delicatessen, saved Iranians from an 'irreducible otherness', the incompatibility with being a European. This was a condition for which they might otherwise have been regarded as prime suspects given the widely accepted identification of Iranians with 'Muslims' – those representatives of a civilisation seen as alien in the West. Thus, Iranians used the bourgeois institution of a delicatessen to disguise their 'home-going', a journey that would render as publicly visible their presence as a *different* people and their resulting hierarchical relation to their English hosts (Balibar and Wallerstein 1992: 56; Sanadjian 1995).

The mediation of ethnic food served to define the difference between those who bought it as a difference between a set of 'similar individuals' (Balibar 1994: 200) who were identified as Iranians. The shop served as an institution that, in the absence of the state, created a sense of community. However, the consumption of Iranian, as opposed to exotic, food demarcated (classified) space and time as culturally specific. This identification (classification) engaged the shopper, who was primarily interested in the exchange of equal values, in a 'war of position' in which the spatiality of an alien presence brought him/her into an unequal relationship with the locals (see Massey 1995). This alien presence invoked the Iranians' insecure ('proletarianised') position in diaspora: their precarious position in the labour market; their questionable professional competence; and their disputed entitlement to the benefits distributed by the welfare state. Thus, for Iranians, any participation in the public domain was fraught with danger – the risk of exposing their increasingly insecure position following their migration to the West in their efforts to overcome the obstacles to the continued construction of a bourgeois identity that the change of political regime in post-revolutionary Iran had brought to a halt.

A plebeian transgression

The 'aesthetic' representation, or 'bourgeoisification' (*embourgeoisement*) (Balibar and Wallerstein 1992: 11), of Iranian national culture fostered by the shop seemed to be threatened by the mobilisation of football 'fans' of the Iranian national team on the street pavement and the likely participation by the plebeians. This mobilisation disrupted the locally developed 'class struggle' that had attracted the well-to-do Iranians to this fashionable part of the British metropolis. This explained the initially negligible presence of the Iranian local residents in the crowd. The latter consisted of a dozen men, mostly young, but also some middle aged, who formed the bulk of the spectators and the stable core of the crowd throughout. The core spectators were known to each other as shopkeepers, their friends and associates. Gradually, more individuals joined the core group and these consisted of predominantly male, casual–peripheral people, including some non-Iranians. Neither those in the core group nor the others seemed to have originally come to watch the match. Although Iranians scarcely missed a World Cup match, they usually kept everyone else at arm's length by watching these at home. The casual–peripheral spectators' length of stay and their number increased particularly after the Iranian team scored its first goal during the first half of the game. Nevertheless, the size of the crowd hardly reached seventy, even at its peak at the end of the match when the Iranian team emerged as the winner.

Most of the spectators, who were predominantly male, had to stand on the street pavement and watch the match on a slightly larger than average television screen placed on the top of an empty shelf outside the shop's adjacent annex – a currently disused butchery which advertised the sale of halal meat in its window. There were a number of chairs irregularly placed in front of the television set which were claimed almost exclusively by the core spectators. Before the game started, when the Iranian players exchanged flowers and gifts with their American counterparts, the crowd showed an unguarded appreciation of this friendly gesture, in sharp contrast to the derision shown towards the Islamic official national anthem sung by the Iranian players. Shortly before the kick-off the shopkeepers and their friends, each equipped with a whistle and one carrying a small drum, moved out of the shop, apparently so that they could sit on the chairs and orchestrate the noisy support for their national team. In so doing, they interrupted daily life by generating a festival 'ferment' (see Caillois 1988/1939: 281). Soon afterwards a plastic carrier bag of tinned beer was brought so that the adult members of the core group could help themselves. The beer-drinkers made no effort to disguise their public consumption of the notoriously non-Islamic substance. The familiar, intoxicating means of initiation into the festival ferment was soon followed by the equally notorious aural one when the men started to shout loudly 'Iran, Iran ...'. The word 'Iran' remained the constant and often the sole component of the repertoire of the 'football songs' shouted by the crowd. Later, the shopkeeper – wearing a white T-shirt embroidered with the Iranian flag, the name of Iran and the picture of an Iranian player – appeared at the entrance to the shop with two enormous pan-lids in his hands and clashed them forcefully as if they were cymbals while generating a deafening noise. The lack of variation in the 'songs' as well as their remarkably meagre content reflecting the poor repertoire for action was compounded by the search for a common denominator sufficiently abstract to appeal to a notoriously divided people. The disproportionately loud noise produced by the core group simultaneously reduced and simplified the positions available to any potential spectators.

Conspicuous among the peripheral spectators, in contrast with the highly active core group, was a meagre kinaesthetic demonstration of sympathy with the activities of the Iranian players (Geertz 1973). For the most part, these casual spectators kept their composure and temperance against the dislodging pressure from the core group to join them. This relatively restrained bodily disposition was, however, interrupted by the outburst of emotion after the Iranian team scored the first goal of the match. Once the goal had been scored, the relatively quiet spectators expressed their hopes and anxieties in words as well as 'wordless' bodily motions. The repetitive, co-ordinated shouts were immediately followed by a deafening eruption of whistling and drumming noise. The blaring noise generated by the 'core' group served to interrupt the spatial and temporal structures which sustained a lived sense of normality in everyday life. The interruption, unlike the one caused by the consumption of exotic food, created a space for transgression. In consuming an exotic object the consumer sought to elevate the ephemerality of the moment of enjoyment (*jouissance*) to the transcendentalism of moments of pleasure (*plasir*) (Barthes 1977). Thus, the 'fleeting' quality of consumption of a good was transformed and expanded through the lasting reflection of the meaning attached to it. It represented a move away from the vulgar expression of ordinary, commercial taste to the distinctive expression of a special, non-commercial one. The transcendental move predicated on the consumption of the exotic served as means for Iranians to avoid an insecure (proletarianised) diasporic presence. The ill-defined, ambiguity-ridden, pleasure-dominated space of the football spectacle, on the other hand, erased the 'dividing line between self and the world' (Debord 1995: 153). The presence of a carnivalesque space, capable of permitting the transgression of the normal socially acceptable rules (Bakhtin 1968; Bennett

1986), was detectable in the signs – the Iranian flags, the football shirts and other paraphernalia of support. These signs served as the direction to which the 'separated' individuals within the spectacle were reaggregated into the Iranian 'communitas' (see Turner 1969). When a non-white, non-Iranian 'casual' spectator quickly moved to claim a vacant seat in front of the television set, one of the shopkeepers promptly turned towards him in front of the crowd to warn the man that he was only allowed to have the seat if he supported Iran. The young man – who found himself facing the whole crowd, witnessing the interrogation – nodded affirmatively. The transgression of social rules in the leisurely, oriented, football space ridden with ambiguities was seized upon by the shopkeepers to reassert their customers' identity as Iranian.

Game and new local–global agency

The interruption of the structured sense of normality through excessive noise enabled the group to draw individuals who were provisionally set free from structural constraints into a game in which each as a supporter was offered an equal chance of success. Participation in this 'artificial space' – the game – and the suspension of mediating structures of normality that 'generally accepted common standards of property and decorum' transformed the match into *an event* (Wilden 1977). Thus, in a place where temperance was cherished, where public visibility was normally sought by status-conscious concert and restaurant goers as well as by delicatessen shoppers, footballers were summoned in order to displace a globally organised, egalitarian game onto a locally circumscribed play (Bourdieu 1990). The organisation of the football spectacle, therefore, replaced the restraints imposed on the normal consumption of time and space in the street by a 'vulgar indulgence' of watching the televised match on the street pavement. Encouraged to abandon their individuated, normal and acceptable 'routine of consumption' of shops and public space (see Thompson 1983: 129), these dislodged consumers were recruited into the collective popular consumption of pleasure (Mercer 1983: 87). Generally speaking, the response of the Iranian passers-by to the noisy 'agitation' was remarkably restrained. It was only at the critical moments of the match, and most spectacularly when Iran scored the first goal, that the crowd erupted in singing and dancing, thus making redundant the distinction between the core group and the peripheral passers-by. Even more Iranians, including women, joined the crowd after the first goal was scored.

The organisation of the football spectacle offered Iranians the opportunity to elude, through equal chance to compete in the 'artificial space' of a game, the differences which usually separated them both *individually*, from each other, and *collectively*, as a displaced people, from others. The reluctance shown by Iranians to assume the role of football 'fans' against the disruptive effect of the excessive noise also revealed a resistance to employing a common notion of culture – one that entailed the relaxation of the prevailing social protocols and a diminution of the normal constraints on fraternisation among Iranians.

Such a relaxation of social protocols called for the use of a popular language that undermined the social distance, the basis on which the exiles negotiated for 'elegance' and 'distinction'. It lifted the 'censorship of the expressive content' and created a sense of 'revelry' which overturned the 'conventions and priorities' (Bourdieu 1984: 34). The game eliminated the distance between the participants by granting them all an equal chance to compete in lending support to their team/players. Indeed, the game's 'artificially created fairness and equality of the chance/competition combination' (Thompson 1983: 131) required the relaxation of the socially inscribed distance that Iranians normally sought to maintain by recourse to a more elitist notion of culture.

After the match had ended and Iran emerged as the winner, one of the shopkeepers brought from the shop a full tray of sweet puff pastry, as he had promised, and distributed it among the crowd and passers-by. Thus, from a commodity that was sold inside the shop as an exotic delicacy the sweet puff pastry became, outside the shop, an object of pleasure for everyone. The shopkeeper's efforts to distribute the sweets widely among the crowd and passers-by were intended to increase everyone's access to an object that had hitherto been associated with the expression of distinct taste and so had been confined to a limited constituency. The shopkeeper who took around the tray of puff pastry offered the sweets to Iranian men by saying, 'Beat it up Mr!' (*bezan Aqa*). The palpable mastery over pleasure conveyed by the 'vulgar' expression of 'beating' was a self-acknowledgement that the public consumption of pleasure – including the drinking of alcohol and sexual gratification – was the exclusive privilege of men. By inviting fellow male Iranians 'to beat' the sweets the shopkeeper actually called upon them to assert their predominant male agency in the public domain. The representation of sweet puff pastry as the object of male 'beating' also allowed the shopkeeper to confer on the good a more plebeian character which had been *deferred* when used solely as the object of a distinct taste. Inside the shop, a highly formalised language used by the shopkeepers and their customers was instrumental in investing such a delicate sweet as puff pastry with an aura of distinctiveness when exchanged between producer and consumers (Sanadjian 2000). The 'vulgar' expression of 'beat' helped the shopkeeper to remove the formality surrounding the exchange of the sweets inside the shop, thus turning the puff pastry into an object of appropriation by the commoners.

Moving the sweet puff pastry out of the shop and introducing it into non-market exchanges changed the shopkeeper's agency from a producer and distributor of Iranian culture, as a domain of aesthetic expression of taste, to a sponsor of the popular construction of that culture. This changing cultural agency was vividly demonstrated by the shopkeeper's spectacular use of the huge pan-lids as cymbals. In clashing the lids against each other, this middle-aged Iranian actually changed the instrument of production of a delicacy into a generator of noise that brought to a halt the structural dissimilarities underlying the differentiated experience of taste on which rested the exotic status of his products. What the shopkeeper's clashing pan-lids connoted was the fact that, in its subsumed position within British bourgeois culture, Iranian culture was not sufficiently *universal* to represent a *national* constituency. Through his noisy announcement the shopkeeper called for the mobilisation of a wider constituency than the one in which he was already acting as a cultural agent. In other words, the disruptive noise was an admission by the shopkeeper that the Iranian culture reproduced through his agency in diaspora was not sufficiently *national*. The spatiality of presence negotiated by Iranians in exile often mediated in the creation of an Iranian constituency that remained ethnic, subordinated to the host national culture. Within this limited, ethnic framework Iranians were effectively unable to aspire to a bourgeois class position owing to the insufficient representation of other classes; and it was only through struggle with these other classes that they could assert themselves as truly bourgeois.

The market mediated in the disruptive effect of the shopkeeper's changed agency as a reproducer of Iranian culture in a diasporic, local situation. In assuming the role of football 'fans' the core group occupied the space outside the shop as an appendage to the 'work place'. This occupation was an additional utilisation of space licensed by the market; the 'realm' of utility (Marx 1967) where the shopkeepers defined themselves as 'local'. The use of this space left undisturbed the continued sale of goods at the shop, which remained open until the match was over. The shopkeepers occasionally interrupted their noisy orchestration of support for the Iranian national team in order to return to the shop to serve their customers. The on-going interaction between the work place and the space for leisure outside bolstered the core group's claim to the public space of the street pavement as a domain in which the shopkeepers were able to take care of their Iranian customers' needs. Thus, the continued organisation of normal business time and space inside the shop by the shopkeepers allowed their associates to embark on a transgression outside the shop – one that disrupted the normal spatial and temporal relations. A respectable bourgeois presence was the basis on which the shopkeepers realised their capital. This normal respectability, however, only allowed a limited Iranian presence geared to exoticism which offered a shared cultural experience of cosmopolitanism. The cosmopolitan sharing of culture defused the tension arising from a global competition between different national cultures which were normally hierarchically ordered into 'modern' and 'backward'.

Proprietor versus citizen

Participation in the game as 'fans' required the Iranians to rework the spatiality of their local presence in transnational terms (see Massey 1995). The recourse to the transnational link evoked the émigrés' narrative of departure from 'home' and their entry into the 'host' country. This entrance and their continued presence resulted in their – Iranians – being identified not so much as people who had *come from* a foreign land as people who had *intruded* into a foreign one. This reference to the Iranians' presence more in terms of their *present* foreign destination than their *past* foreign origins conferred on this presence an invader character. The shift of emphasis from departure to intrusion displaced the perspective of the 'hosts' on voluntary migration into a forced homelessness. Consequently, from the enunciating subject of a global wandering the Iranians became the objects of a narrated invasion and aversion by their 'hosts'. The evoked temporal dimension reinvested the Iranians' diasporic presence with the tensions arising from the continuity/discontinuity of time (Ricoeur 1991). Whereas the universal role of proprietor had enabled Iranians to negotiate a provisional local presence, the resort to the story of abdication from home called for a sustainable presence in the 'public spheres' where the notions of equality and liberty were pervasive (Balibar 1994). The widely reported violence committed by the Islamic state, epitomised by the ordeal endured by Salman Rushdie, had already created the space for a universal political practice manifested in transnational migration. Therefore, an enunciated distance from an Islamic official identity was essential to the émigrés' definition of their migration as 'involuntary' and to claim the global space as a domain of political asylum. The universalisation of politics mediated by the 'public spheres', the battleground for 'the politics of the rights of man' (Balibar 1994), offered Iranians the opportunity to claim, as political refugees, the right to cross international borders and to reside among their British hosts. But the right of asylum, as an integral part of 'the rights of man', could only be exercised by a citizen, an inevitably politically involved figure (Balibar 1994: 211), and this was a position that Iranians normally avoided.

Prior to the revolution of 1978–9 the Iranian middle classes' access to political power was under the state's partially developed juridical rule. The Pahlavi state failed to represent a sufficiently universal interest to enable it to define norms in accordance with which the state could *effectively* enforce contracts covering exchanges in a fast but unevenly developing market economy and society. Moreover, the equality before the law was scarcely tenable under the state's rule in a country where the demands for rights were met with brutal suppression. The areas, therefore, in which the middle classes sought to exercise power were the non-political domains of economy and culture. The Iranian bourgeoisie was ill-equipped to use juridical objectives that were 'tangential' to its class struggle (Engels in Balibar 1988). The combined processes of the accumulation of capital and cosmopolitan consumption were the prime sites at which the Pahlavi state played its role in constituting the bourgeoisie as a social class. Space played a significant role in positioning the aspirant Iranian middle classes, and their on-going negotiation for class identity, who were well aware of the strategic use of distance. To be in the 'right place' strongly influenced the presence/absence of these Iranians, who often felt exposed in a temporal construction of class mobility from a situation of obscurity to prosperity.

After the revolution, the Islamic state inverted the relationship between the bourgeoisie and the state. Not only did the juridical rule, over which the Islamic state presided, exclude the middle classes from politics *but* in addition the state obstructed the exercise of power by the bourgeoisie in cultural and economic fields. It was mainly the result of the limits it imposed on the Iranian bourgeoisie's cultural and economic reproduction by the Islamic state that drove large sections of the middle classes into exile. Thus, in coming to the West these Iranians were primarily concerned to restore their economic and cultural reproduction that had been disrupted by the post-revolutionary restoration of Islamic order at home. Coming to the West was a continuation of the spatial mobility that had characterised the movement of the Iranian middle classes in pre-exodus time from towns to cities and from an urban quarter to a more 'respectable' one. Transnational migration, however, intensified the tension arising from class struggle in a context that lacked a national dimension. At home, the Iranian middle classes pursued their class interests in a 'war of positions' with other social classes. Outside this 'war of position' there could exist no class except as an economic abstraction. The nation-state was the terrain in which the 'war of positions' was fought (Balibar and Wallerstein 1992). Once stateless, Iranians found lacking the (national) framework in which they could articulate their class interests in sufficiently universal terms.

The Iranian exodus to the West in the wake of the revolution of 1978–9 was a further transnational expansion of the class struggle generated by the capitalist development in Iran. It weakened the position of the displaced bourgeoisie in two respects. First, it removed the class from its national breeding ground – where, like any other class, it had come into existence as a 'class for itself'. Second, it also marginalised the diasporic bourgeoisie *vis-à-vis* their host counterparts. The increased competition outside the national context in which tangible class advances were gauged escalated the insecurity of the displaced bourgeoisie. So, it was not only in terms of exclusion, long-term unemployment and the shift towards manual work – represented by the notable presence of educated Iranian émigrés among taxi drivers – that the proletarianisation of the Iranian middle classes in diaspora was detectable. The émigrés' increasingly insecure position was also discernible in their noted drive towards assimilation. The Iranians could not become truly bourgeois unless they pitched their class struggle squarely in the host national context, i.e. unless they became assimilated into the host national framework. The drive towards assimilation, however, was fraught with an acute contradiction as the process of assimilation could only be complete when the émigrés ceased to be Iranians. Hence, the intensified competition among Iranians themselves who in asserting their 'middle-class' identity in diaspora found their fellow Iranians to be prime obstacles to their assimilation within the host bourgeoisie. Thus, any undesirable behaviour by fellow countrymen/-women was considered detrimental to the émigrés' assimilation and, therefore, instrumental in their exclusion from the host bourgeois order; a fact that accounted for the pervasive suspicion found among Iranians in diaspora.

Life in exile for many Iranians was marked by a reluctant entry into politics through wearing the mask of the politically persecuted. Thus, they featured themselves as central figures in a narrative of persecution composed by the 'exiles' in their efforts to represent their transnational migration as a flight from political persecution. Once they secured permission to stay, many Iranians were quick to remove the mask of Iranian citizen in order to exit this political space by resuming their role as proprietor through recourse to a bourgeois repertoire for action, i.e. as a 'concert goer', 'restaurant goer' or 'delicatessen shopper'. The paradoxical entrance by Iranians into exile more as a proprietor than as a citizen was echoed in the complaints made by those Iranian political activists who had helped their fellow countrymen/-women to settle in the foreign country. The activists expressed their disappointment that their compatriots had lost contact with them and had abandoned political involvement as soon as their residence in the host country was officially sanctioned. Implicit in this reference to the Iranians' short-lived appearance on the political scene was the recognition of the immigrants' involuntary entry into politics despite the widespread repression at home that created the space for such politics. Hence, the exiles' fear of it being discovered that there was little behind their valorised status of 'political refugee' and champion of human rights. Dependent on the status of political refugee, a conscientious victim of the suppressed rights of man, was a 'superhuman' place above a 'subhuman' one. The universal right of asylum incorporates, as a universalist discourse, its opposite, namely the *abuse* of such a right (see Balibar 1994). Thus, the *universal* constitution of the politically prosecuted subjects as 'genuine' political refugees was the other side of the *specific* construction of the identified 'bogus' refugees. The elevation to the 'public spheres' and the involuntary involvement of Iranians in the universalisation of politics created tensions within the Iranian diasporic population manifested in a widely expressed aversion to the title of refugee.

Class versus nation in diaspora

The transformation of the football match into a national event required a much larger international audience whose mobilisation was geared to the Iranian players' dedicated part in the game. In the absence of a more universal political practice, the game of football, the 'artificial space' from which was excluded the reference to history and the social divisions sustained by it, promised to represent a hitherto absent national unity. Hence, the heroic role assigned to the Iranian football players. Through the mass media, the internationally mobilised audience was instrumental in driving home this *recognition* of the *witnessing* by the players. Once they had proved their ability on the pitch, each of the players was bestowed with the status of *volunteer* – someone who acts, against the odds, on behalf of the community – a culturally endorsed role demonstrated by the celebrated Islamic and pre-Islamic heroes/ martyrs.

In the course of the match, the Iranian players emerged as 'goodies', a characteristic that gained much wider prominence afterwards. The Iranian players, however, were not admired at the expense of their American counterparts but *as a result* of their non-hostile treatment of the opposition. Thus, the crowd showed not only an appreciation of the Iranian players' ability to overcome the challenges posed on the pitch but also the gratification at the players' successful trial created by the 'moral' challenge from outside the pitch.[3] This moral distinction – or, to use the words uttered by a member of the crowd, the 'good character' shown by the Iranian players in the match – earned the Iranians a place *among* others as distinct from the superiority *over* the other side secured by the Iranians as 'good players'. By proving to be more than a match for the Americans, the Iranians established themselves as 'good players' and credited their fellow countrymen with a collective distinction among others, thus creating a universal space for practice different from the one consequent on the exercise of the rights of man. By acting amicably towards their American opposition, the players demonstrated, rather unexpectedly, a quality of 'good character' that enabled their fellow Iranians in exile to claim credit on shared moral values with others. The praise accorded by Iranians to their players reflected a double surprise. First, it provided a global and dramatic representation of Iranian identity at a marked distance from the irreducible, often threatening, otherness normally associated with the assertion of Iranian identity. In addition, the players acted in contrast to the perceived threat by their fellow countrymen/-women to the assimilation of Iranians in general into the host bourgeois society. The praise reflected an appreciation by Iranians of their players' heroic actions in enabling the Iranians to improve, albeit temporarily, their place in the localities in which they lived. The heroism of the players lay in 'tackling' the opponents to whom a great deal of importance was attached as the powerful promoters of globalisation and the universal domain for practice associated with it. The intensity of the opposition conferred on the match a 'depth', or meaningfulness, and a corresponding space for interpretation that made all the more pressing the Iranians' quest for an equal relationship with Americans.

The competition with Americans evoked a historical narrative which variedly featured in Iranians' accounts of their absence from home. The privileged status conferred on the Iran–USA match as the 'most politicised match of the World Cup' was a direct consequence of the deployment of this narrative in the public spheres.[4] But what primarily concerned Iranians was less to relive the narrated time of homelessness than to reoccupy the space in 'exile' under improved terms. The narrativised conflict with America, and, therefore, the politicisation of the Iran–USA match, evoked Iranians' wanderings in exile – a discursive adventure that jeopardised the exiles' on-going negotiation for a place among the 'locals'. The use and abuse of power inscribed in the evoked narrative called for a mediation of the discourses on the rights of man and popular sovereignty. Recourse to these discourses led the Iranians in the direction of a universal political practice as opposed to the preferred role of *proprietor* and the quest for a *proper place* that had originally driven many of them to diaspora. Thus, in channelling the equal opportunity offered by the game towards their negotiation for *a proper place* among the British hosts, Iranians sought to depoliticise the most politicised match of the World Cup.

The heightened, worldwide publicity conferred on the match bestowed the Iranian football players with the power to represent – to speak for – Iranians in the wider world through the articulation of 'good play' with 'good character' by playing these two distinct roles inside and outside the pitch simultaneously. This articulation, however, was fraught with tension as the players' roles were geared to the construction of two forms of identity. While their demonstration of 'good character' acted as a catalyst in reducing the visibility of Iranian otherness and enhancing their assimilation into the host bourgeoisie, the players' competitiveness was instrumental in the construction of Iranian identity as national subjects. Moreover, without an effective competition, the players' 'good character' was of limited significance for their supporters' 'war of position' in diaspora. Thus, the 'moral' virtue attributed to the Iranian players derived from a contradictory situation in which the players and their supporters forged a shared set of values with others from among whom they simultaneously sought to establish themselves distinctly as a *class* and as a *people*. The 'goody' characterisation of the Iranian football players was based on an effective Iranian/American opposition. At the same time, the effectiveness of this opposition was geared to its acceptance by others. The heroism attributed to the Iranian players' performance by their 'fans' reflected an imagined resolution of the players' incompatible roles, namely representing these fans under terms acceptable to those whose dominant position the players were to overcome in an imminent challenge. For these supporters the players had to win over their American rivals under terms which were more 'American' than Iranian. The sudden outpouring of excitement that followed the victory of Iran over the USA was a temporary resolution of the contradictions that resulted from the struggle by the Iranians to constitute themselves as members of a bourgeois class without the help of a national state – the prime agency of class constitution (Balibar 1988) – through representation of class interests in universal – national – terms. Outside this domain of contested representations, a class failed to become hegemonic and class struggle was subordinated to individuated pursuit of interests by members of a displaced class characterised by the drive towards assimilation.

Game and the universalisation of politics

The Iranian football players, whose competitive ability placed their Iranian supporters on equal terms with those who supported the American ones, were instrumental in uniting the Iranians as football supporters. This empowerment to treat each other as 'comrades' in the 'imagined' space of the game brought into focus the viability of Iranians as a unit *vis-à-vis* other 'imagined communities'. In other words, the Iranians could not seize the equalising chance offered to them in the game without reviving their national–ethnic link that each tried to keep least visible in order to facilitate their locally based adaptation to diasporic conditions. It was this growing tension between local ties and transnational links – between the economically defined class interests and the politically propelled national ones – that burst open in the frenetic celebration which immediately followed the victory over the USA.

Later in the evening and soon after the match had ended, the small crowd outside the delicatessen dispersed following a short celebration during which the shopkeepers served them with the sweet puff pastry. As the shop began to close, some members of the core group took to their cars and sounded their horns repeatedly as they cruised around the surrounding area. The cars were full of passengers who were shouting the name of Iran, waving the Iranian flag and signalling the victory sign with their fingers. Soon, more Iranians were summoned by the jubilant riders and began to join them in their cars. Yet more Iranians from further afield, having been alerted by telephone networks, used public transport to converge on the area in the vicinity of the shop. Eventually, several thousand Iranians gathered in the place and occupied it for several hours before they returned home. The pattern discernible in this spontaneous popular response by Iranians to their World Cup match victory was a pronounced use of public space to secure a maximum engagement with the local population. In seeking to secure their hosts' witnessing of their football victory the jubilant Iranians also negotiated a new presence among them. The Iranians who had been hitherto hesitant to appear in public space either as football fans or as claimants to the rights of man suddenly emerged in that space, compensating with frenetic noise and excitement for their conspicuous absence. Once the Iranian players had demonstrated their competitive ability on the pitch their supporters' often fatalistic, private and subjective conception of time gave way to an objectified, public space as an equalising device and as a means for the universalisation of politics. Thus, the conception of time as a plotter – the agent of a destined wandering in exile that denied chance its equalising role – was replaced by a homogenising time that sustained the artificial space of the game (Thompson 1983). As a displaced people who held time as having 'a heart and a memory' of its own (Thompson 1983: 131), Iranians had narrativised their presence in diaspora that was often hidden from the public domain. Their perception of time was interwoven into stories of fortune and misfortune which militated against the exiles' participation in a dehistoricised space of the game where, in stark contrast, participants were continually offered equal opportunities to compete.

Having found that their players were a real match for their American rivals the Iranians could no longer be held back by a fatalistic notion of time and a weakened position in the political space from joining others. They could now re-enter, wearing the mask of football fans, the local space to reclaim, *en masse,* an equal place among other nations undeterred by the rules that governed the socially circumscribed play that was conducive to a marginal diasporic position. The universalisation generated by the 'deterritorialised', global game, unlike the universalised politics mediated by the expansion of the 'public spheres', was not one in which the drive for equality and liberty (Balibar 1994) was prevalent. The game generated an imagined space in which the participants were freed from the social constraints of class, race, gender and age; the constraints that were taken up in the political space through the quest for equality and liberty. Thus, the universal practice mediated by the global game neutralised the contradictions arising from the transnational migration and the subsequent proletarianisation of the Iranian middle classes.

Conclusion

Transnational migration has played a major role in the expansion of a global space for contested representations in which have featured such figures as proprietor, citizen, connoisseur, fan, Muslim, Christian, healthy, fit, acquired immune deficiency syndrome (AIDS) sufferer, drug addict, environmentalist, enjoyment seeker and so on. The form which this universal political practice takes, as Balibar argues (1994), is not necessarily the result of a drive towards liberty and equality, their combined deployment characterises the extension of the 'public spheres' (Habermas 1989). The effective impact of transnational links does not arise from the notion of globality as a 'master signifier' that overrules local circumstances but from the particularity of a conjuncture in which the subject is historically constituted. Far from being submerged within the 'melting pot of global mixing' (see Anderson *et al.* 1995), 'global ethnoscapes' (Appadurai 1991) may actually exacerbate the tension between class and national relations by depriving class of its national breeding ground. The supersession of the national consequent on transnational migration undermines the universal representations through which class conflicts are fought in terms of a hegemonic, as opposed to a dominant, class position. Paradoxically, global 'bourgeoisification' (*embourgeoisement*) (Balibar and Wallerstein 1992: 11) militates against the exercise of power by a bourgeoisie that could only become a 'class for itself', able to represent its interests, through relations of conflict with other classes. The framework for this class assertion is a national one. Thus, the reduced space for national representation consequent on global expansion limits the 'public spheres' in which the drive for equality and liberty is deployed to challenge the structural constraints based on class divisions. Hence, the shift in global space towards recourse to non-political figures such as the football fan – disarticulated from structural constraints.

The individualism on which the notion of rights is based entails a universalisation of interests (Durkheim 1971: 148) through which the particularity of personal circumstances is superseded and private differences are eliminated in the 'notion of man in general' (ibid.). The conjectural 'limits' to such equality, i.e. the possibility of the dissolution of the particular in the universal, constitute the basis of the 'politics of the rights of man' (Balibar 1994) that are concerned with the constraints imposed on becoming the 'subject' of an agent of the political space.[5] The exercise of rights, including the right of asylum, is an act of insurrection, be it non-violent or otherwise, in so far as the constraints are challenged in the sphere of politics (ibid.: 224). The space for politics is created when particularity is represented in terms of universality. The notion of citizenship depends for its global operation on the scope of universal, contested representations in this space. Thus, the emergence of global politics is marked by the tension arising from the inclusion/exclusion of the various represented groups. The mediation between the locals and their representation in global space is varied and uneven. It involves the ideas of equality and liberty as well as images of the body such as the beautiful, the fit and the healthy. What is at stake in this passage from particularity to universality, from locality to globality, is a reworking by displaced groups of the spatiality of their local presence in transnational terms. The politics of transnational links, i.e. the global dimension of a local presence, is defined at the moment of articulation of the local conditions through a global representation, for instance in a game of football. Thus, the means of representation employed globally may actually serve to unite the representative and the represented, leaving little room for contested representations, a political space *par excellence* and the site of insurrection.

The interplay between local and global presence is highlighted here in the context of equalising opportunity offered in the game of football between Iranians and Americans in the World Cup tournament in France. The interplay became a provisional source of power on which Iranians, as members of a displaced bourgeois class, drew in order to modify their local position in diaspora. This class ambition was frustrated by the absence of a national context where class identity is realised through a hegemonic construction in which the bourgeoisie can define the interest of other classes in terms of its own. It was the absence of a national constituency and the universal interests represented within it that rendered as questionable the recourse by the Iranians to the rights of man, of which the right to asylum was a subsidiary. It was, therefore, of some strategic significance to Iranians that they should maintain a contradiction-ridden transnational presence by assuming the role of global football spectators just at the moment when the gap between the local–global presence was bridged by the Iranian football players. This was the time when the players' heroic action – demonstrating at one and the same time 'good character' and skilful play – allowed their supporters to overcome, provisionally, the impossibility of class promotion outside a national context.

Notes

1 This chapter is based on the material represented in my article published in *Social Identities* (2000, Vol. 6, no. 2). I would also like to thank Pam Sanadjian for her detailed comments on this chapter.

2 In reality, the majority of the shop's food seemed to have been imported from either the Indian subcontinent or other parts of the Middle East. The Iranian products formed the minority of the shop's merchandise.

3 An indication of the Iranians' efforts to negotiate a common moral ground with those among whom they lived was their annoyance that the film *Not Without My Daughter* had been shown on French television. This was presented the night before the Iran–Yugoslavia match on 21 June 1998. The film was based on a popularised and sensationalist account by a female writer of her escape from Iran, leaving behind a damned homogeneous society labelled as 'Muslim' or 'Islamic'.

4 President Clinton's speech before the match, referring to it as the beginning of a new era in the relationship between the Iranian and American peoples, marked a high-profile attempt to seize the equalising opportunity in the game and to denarrativise the relationship between Iranians and American supporters which had previously been fraught with tension and conflict.

5 Significantly, Durkheim, who insists on the social character of morality, confines his analysis simply to the individual's failure to translate a particular interest into a universal one as an 'immoral conduct' (Durkheim 1971: 148). This leaves unexplored the power-laden character of the limits imposed on becoming equal subjects.

Part II

Transnational cultures

7   Bringing it all (back) home

Italian–Canadians' remaking of Canadian history[1]

Anne-Marie Fortier

The renewed currency, in recent years, of 'diaspora' as a theoretical tool has surfaced in the context of contemporary migrations of peoples, capital and cultures.[2] An important contribution of this body of work is to mediate the relationship between the constraining local and the inflated global by conceiving new forms of belonging that are tied in with both local conditions of existence and multilocal ties and connections.[3] Another important contribution of this body of work is to mediate the relationship *between* the constraining local and the inflated global by conceiving of 'new geographies of identity' (Lavie and Swedenburg 1996) that Avtar Brah has called the 'diaspora space' (Brah 1996: 209). Composed of genealogies of displacement and genealogies of 'staying put', diaspora space inserts itself between localism and transnationalism and proposes a conception of identity as a positionality that 'is not a process of absolute othering, but rather of entangled tensions' (Clifford 1994: 307).

I propose to discuss the constitutive potency of 'betweenness', and to interrogate the very terms of this betweenness: homeland and hostland, here and there, indigenousness and migration. These dualities, I argue, emerge from understandings of culture that remain deeply connected to territoriality; a nationalist conception that rests on the congruence between geography, culture and identity.[4] By way of developing my argument, I analyse two contrasting Italian–Canadian narratives on Giovanni Caboto and explore how efforts of settlement and rootings manifest themselves in locally and historically specific ways, and how they articulate with multilocal terrains of belonging. The question is how these multiple connections are rearticulated and remembered in the process of identity formation. In short, I explore how a lived or imagined 'diasporic mode of existence' (Marienstras 1975: 184) mediates the formation of localised cultures, identities or 'communities'. This is my version of exploring the 'diasporic imagination' (Jacobson 1995) of this immigrant population, i.e. the terrain of belonging that spans multiple localities, territories and histories.

The example of Italian–Canadians is particularly relevant because they are most commonly defined as an immigrant or ethnic group.[5] Rather than constituting one *or* the other, I suggest that this 'cultural community', to use the Québecois official jargon,[6] is *both* ethnic and diasporic. Hence, against the tendency to polarise 'immigrants' and 'diasporas' (Clifford 1994; Tölölyan 1996), I start from the premise that immigrant populations experience 'diasporic moments', which, as Caren Kaplan pointedly argues, 'could be further plumbed, rather than marginalized, for links between the historical experiences of migration and displacement' (Kaplan 1996: 137). A large number of *immigrant* populations – not only *migrant* ones, as James Clifford states – share 'forms of longing, memory, (dis)identification' (Clifford 1994: 305) with displaced peoples. The massive scattering of Italians from impoverished rural areas of Italy between 1860 and 1960 consists of a form of diasporisation[7] that has fostered particular kinds of diasporic imaginations in particular settings of (re)settlement. These, in turn, support diverse cultural forms, some of which are examined here.

I begin with the historical narrative promoted by Italian officialdom and Italian–Canadian leaders in their project of rehabilitating Giovanni Caboto as the 'first discoverer' (*sic*) of Canada. The late historian Robert Harney produced an incisive critique of what he called *scopritorismo*, the 'hunt for the Italianità of warriors, priests and explorers of Italian descent serving New France' (Harney 1989: 41). Harney examines this particular identity project as a search for symbolic figures that would support claims of a glorious Italian–Canadian past; one which acquires political potency in the context of multicultural Canada. By casting the official Italian discourse of history against Filippo Salvatore's poetic narrative (Salvatore 1978) addressed to Caboto – examined in the second part of this essay – I reveal that particular historical or cultural figures may be the site of competing definitions within the Italian 'community'. Indeed, Salvatore's poem questions the very significance of Giovanni Caboto for the recovery of a positive Italian self-identity. In short, I use Caboto as a vignette to set up a number of issues related to the critical and creative potency of diaspora as constitutive of identity formation. Hence, the concluding section looks back at my analysis of each narrative to develop further my argument about the limits and possibilities of diaspora. What these narratives reveal, I suggest, is that memory, rather than territory, is the principal ground of identity formation.

From John to Giovanni I: claims of indigenousness

Since 1925, Italian officialdom in Canada has sought to restore the 'real' identity of John Cabot, i.e. the Venetian Giovanni Caboto, and to have him recognised as the 'first discoverer' of Canada.[8] The most recent manifestation was in 1997, the year of the 500th anniversary of Caboto's voyage to the shores of what is today Cape Breton Island. To mark the quincentenary, the Montreal–Italian parish Madonna della Difesa, situated in Little Italy, paid tribute to *Giovanni Caboto, scopritore del Canada* (Giovanni Caboto, discoverer of Canada) in the booklet printed for its annual procession. The biographical note read as follows:

Giovanni Caboto
1497–1997

On June 24 1497, The Matthew, under the command of Giovanni Caboto, arrived to Cape Breton from Bristol. From this day, this land was no longer neglected but discovered, explored, inhabited and today is part of Canada.

There is no doubt that Giovanni Caboto was the first true discoverer of Canada. For these reasons, we of Italian origin proudly celebrate the quincentenary of the arrival on Canadian land of the first great navigator Giovanni Caboto and we do not feel strangers in this big and beautiful country: Canada.

As the above text illustrates, the obsession with who travelled here first still frames the ways in which some Italians create a place for themselves as an 'auxiliary founding people' (Harney 1989: 40). Their repeated efforts to have Caboto officially recognised within the Canadian historical landscape – to the point of attempting to have Caboto Day declared a Canadian holiday (Harney 1989: 56) – are entangled with the founding myths of the Canadian nation, which constitute a 'crucial site in which the terms of "membership" in the national "body" are contested, policed, and ultimately re-defined' (Lowe 1996: 3–4). The contested meanings around the 'true' identity of Giovanni and, more importantly, that of the European state in whose name he travelled (he planted both the British and Venetian flags) testifies not only to the inherent malleability of the past but also to the very criteria upon which national membership is defined.[9]

Narratives of the 'right of blood' are woven through a quest for the patriarchal pioneer that will secure claims of ethnic distinction and national belonging at once. The underlying assumption is that the past accomplishments of 'great men' somehow testify to the inherent qualities of the Italian culture, of which all Italians are the natural bearers. The pronouncement of both a positive ethnic specificity and a national belonging is found in a statement by a member of the Montreal–Italian 'leadership':

> I feel privileged when I meet people … who have nothing but a recent contribution to the development of this country. So it is perhaps a pride in being Italian: in knowing that we have been here since the beginning, that we were amongst the first.
>
> (in Tardif *et al.* 1993: 35; my translation)

Claims of a historical pedigree separate this woman from other more recently arrived immigrants. The evocation of 'origins' – 'we have been here since the beginning' – is possible thanks to the very construction of a history that 'belongs' to Italians living in Canada. By the same token, this woman's statement at once marks the 'beginnings' of modern Canada and establishes a hierarchical system of differentiation among ethnic groups such as Italians, more recently arrived immigrants and native peoples.

Definitions of national belonging, in Canada and Quebec alike, are still grounded in the conflation of genealogy and geography, thus rendering displacement and geographical mobility as the antitheses of national membership. This calls forth the issue of indigenousness – that is, a political claim of national membership founded on past political realities that give some historical right actually to be here[10] – and its connections with notions of migration and displacement. It raises the questions of 'Who is indigenous and what are the terms of definitions of indigenousness?' and 'How long does it take to become indigenous?' The separation of 'immigrant' and 'ethnic' precisely ties in with the tendency to oppose displacement and indigenousness in a way that runs parallel with rootedness and uprootedness, and that reinstates the connections between settlement, rootings, territory and national belonging. The example of Caboto brings to the fore the ways in which Italians relocate themselves as indigenous, thus positing themselves as the 'indigenous other' of more recently arrived immigrants, while claiming some form of equal status in relation to English–Canadians and French–Canadians. This illustrates the extent to which immigration is often the site of struggle over definitions of nation, ethnicity and national belonging, and the ways in which these issues are played out differently in different parts of the world. What is at stake here is the neutralisation of foreignness, as stated in the passage from the church booklet cited above: 'we do not feel strangers in this beautiful country'. Similarly, in the preface to his book *Giovanni Caboto, scopritore del Canada*, Camillo Menchini dedicates it to 'all Italians in Canada, so that they no longer feel strangers in this land' (Menchini 1974: n.p.).

The principal site through which groups lay claim to some kind of Canadian 'indigenousness' is colonisation and conquest of the 'land'. Statements that Caboto saved this land from neglect, that he was the 'first discoverer of Canada', consistently invalidate claims of autochthony of Canadian 'first nations' and rework a hierarchy of immigration through allegations of historical achievements measured in terms of the 'glories' of imperialism. Such was the rationale behind an exhibition held at the David Stewart Museum on Saint Helen's Island, Montreal. Entitled *En Route to the New World: Caboto and the Italian Navigators on Their Journey to the Americas*,[11] the exhibition was funded by the museum itself, with help from the Italian Department of Foreign Affairs and the Italian Department of Culture. It was actively promoted by the Italian Cultural Institute (attached to the Italian Consulate). After some pressure from the Italian Embassy, the exhibition was moved to the Canadian Museum of Civilizations in Hull, Canada, where it opened on 23 June 1998 and remained until April 1999.

Stating that Giovanni Caboto was 'the first modern explorer to set foot on North-American soil', the exhibition was clearly aimed at celebrating the glorious past of Venetian explorers, as testified by the introductory text of Montreal's display:

Our exhibition focuses on the role of Venetians and other Italians as they participated in the recovery of classical geographical knowledge and the diffusing of navigational and cartographic skills which contributed to the discovery of the New World and to the expansion of European dominance.

The historical narrative of Giovanni Caboto reinstates the Eurocentric and colonialist terms of membership to the Canadian nation, while it constructs a history that 'belongs' to Italians and that consequently validates their claims for special status within the Canadian national 'family'. At the same time, this history calls into question the mythic pure origins of Canada's two founding peoples – the French and the English. The recovery of these new bloodlines disturbs, indeed 'contaminates', the lines of descent drawn from John-Cabot-the-Englishman and Jacques-Cartier-the-Frenchman downward. Claims for the status of Italians as an auxiliary founding people are steeped in genealogical tracings of Italian blood within both the Québecois and Canadian national 'bodies'.

This historical reconstruction of Giovanni Caboto is an instance of the diasporic imagination of some Italian–Canadians, which is at once deeply nationalist and transnational; at once a process of constructing and reproducing a national culture and heritage, and a process of hybridisation which, to be sure, is embedded within the European imperial past. This example illustrates how immigrants' efforts for local particularity and recognition are caught up with and defined against definitions of indigenousness (Clifford 1994: 307) that result from the conflation of ancestry and territory, and that guarantee some claims for special status.

From John to Giovanni II: distant memories, moving cultures

An interesting paradox nonetheless surfaces from the repeated efforts to recover Caboto's 'Italianness': the insistence on the indigenousness of Italian–Canadians by virtue of their ancestry relies heavily on a voyage. Claims of ancestry posit Caboto as the first Italian pioneer, thus, by extension, the first Italian migrant to set foot in Canada. Although steeped in nationalist, imperialist and gendered orders of knowledge, these narratives continually reinstate remembrances of migration as the ground of Italo-Canadian identity. At once distancing themselves from 'immigrants', what these narratives also do is to replay the migrant 'origins' of Italians in Canada.

I want to explore this point further by looking at Filippo Salvatore's 'Three Poems for Giovanni Caboto' (Salvatore 1978), in which an ambivalent relationship to migration and settlement, as well as to both Canada and Italy, is expressed. The speaker of the poems addresses the bronze statue of Caboto erected in Caboto Square at the corner of Atwater and Sainte-Catherine

Streets in Montreal. The three poems trace three movements in an emigrant's journey. Movements which contrast starkly with the immobility of the statue.

The first poem is about the emergence of an emigrant consciousness. It opens with the speaker remembering that 'it didn't take much', that 'it took so little' for him to leave Italy, stressing the tenuousness of ties to the 'native land' and the instrumentality of national allegiance. Salvatore further amplifies this point by casting the easy choice to leave alongside the comfortable conditions of his journey:

> Giovanni, I didn't need courage,
> like you, I didn't set sail
> towards the unknown on an unsafe boat,
> ... I travelled comfortably
> with a DC 8 Alitalia plane,
> flew over the ocean,
> closed my eyes,
> dozed for a few hours and
> arrived in the land of my dreams.
>
> (Salvatore 1978)

The speaker looks at Caboto and remarks on how their respective experiences have nothing to do with each other, thus establishing a distance between them. More importantly, this passage reads as a distortion of stories of Italian emigration, epitomised by the sacrifices of leaving one's home and settling in a new country (Fortier 2000). Once in the land of his dreams, however, the speaker found 'plenty of bread, and warm water too', but he also 'discovered what it means/to be an emigrant', facing 'scornful glances, a hostile/environment, an overwhelming/emptiness in my soul' (Salvatore 1978).

The tension between longing to belong, on the one hand, and exclusion, on the other, runs through the second poem, in which the speaker finds some solace in relating to Caboto through the image of the emigrant – that person whose dual belonging is stamped down by the national forces of homogenisation:

> Giovanni, they erected you a monument,
> but they changed your name; here
> they call you John. And you
> look at them from your stony
> pedestal with a hardly perceivable
> grin on your lips.
>
> (Salvatore 1978)

A character with two names, John/Giovanni symbolises the struggles between two competing imperialisms: English cultural imperialism (Ianucci

1989: 219) – 'they changed your name' – and Italian expansionism – Giovanni grins and looks down on the English from the heights of his pedestal.

> The speaker queries Giovanni:
> Where are you looking to?
> Towards the new or the old world?
> You don't answer me, of course,
> you remain standing at Atwater and
> keep on gazing afar.
>
> (Salvatore 1978)

William Boelhower suggests that this passage exemplifies the 'ethnic practice of interrogation [that] refuses to reduce the order of discourse to a single meaning, a single code or cultural model and prefers instead a strategy of perspectival ambiguity' (Boelhower 1989: 233). Yet this perspectival ambiguity does not spontaneously come about. It grows gradually out of experiences of migration and trials of identification that negotiate the different orders of discourse available to the immigrant. In the second poem, the speaker finds momentary comfort in joining the Italian–Canadian chorus that reprocesses Caboto's journey as part of the Canadian national heritage, as well as part of Italian–Canadian belonging:

> How many Italians took the boat
> with you? Today we are many, so many,
> and most of us are young,
> young and ambitious, like you,
> young and forced to emigrate, like you,
> to start a new life abroad, like you.
> You were the first to plant
> on the barren, wave-struck reef
> the Lion of St. Mark beside the Royal Jack.
> Today at the top of the sky-scrapers [*sic*]
> being built in this icy land
> by so many of your fellow countrymen,
> the tricolore flies
> beside the maple leaf.
>
> (Salvatore 1978)

The repeated likening of present-day Italian immigrants to Giovanni – the iteration of 'like you' – constructs a male immigrant subject, and reinstates the masculinist filiation from Caboto to his 'fellow countrymen', whose role as builders of the Canadian nation is asserted once again. However, the speaker questions the assumptions of filiation in light of the ignorance and indifference of his 'fellow countrymen' towards Caboto: 'Only few of them know you' (Salvatore 1978). The certainty of continuity is brought into question by considering what it means when people have forgotten: what is the meaning of historical memory if it does not relate to the daily life of those emigrants who 'speak about dollars/and houses to buy while they wait/ for the 79 bus at the terminal/and rub their noses'?

The distance, then, grows again. And in the third poem, in which the speaker returns to visit Caboto some months later to find him still gazing afar, oblivious to the 'warbles' of the couple of pigeons perched on his shoulders, the gap becomes unbridgeable. As he attempts to speak to Caboto, he finds he cannot: 'you are only a statue', he declares:

> you are a symbol. The life
> of your memory is as ethereal for me
> as this early morning-sun,
> as my lucidity ...
> People continue to come out [of the Metro],
> become a crowd that
> snakes me up, clogs me, carries me away.
>
> (Salvatore 1978)

The narrator's momentary alliance with Italian collective recollections, and his subsequent disconcerted realisation that Caboto is just a statue, questions the ethnic project behind the remembrances of past glories. If, as William Boelhower suggests, 'remembering itself is the ethnic project' (Boelhower 1989: 240), remembering, then, produces the very ethnicity that is said to be expressed by the recovery of the past. It follows that memories, indeed histories, are plural and subject to constant reprocessing. Salvatore's move away from Giovanni signals the refusal to engage further with it as a figure of identity, indeed as the father of the Italian presence in Canada.

His disengagement is additionally marked by the presence of 'an old drunkard' who appears at the end of the second poem (Salvatore 1978), and who is still there when the speaker revisits the statue in the third poem (Salvatore 1978). The old man is the French-speaking other – who 'gives me a shake and mumbles/in his whisky-stinking mouth, maudit' (Salvatore 1978) – and the loyal companion of Giovanni. His presence, his gesture of shaking the speaker, is a concrete manifestation of the 'scornful glances' encountered earlier. A reminder of 'what it means/to be an emigrant' (Salvatore 1978). This is a strange encounter between the emigrant who can no longer relate to Giovanni and a French–Canadian who has somehow appropriated the square where the statue stands. It is the drunkard, rather than the Italian immigrant, who seems to have made Caboto Square his 'base', his 'territory'. His drunkenness, in addition, signals the decline of Caboto as a figure of collective identification.

The poems end with uncertainty: the concluding image of the narrator being taken away by a wave-like movement of the crowd suggests an opening toward an indeterminate future. The distancing from some Italian memories in order to 'go with the flow', as it were, is what Salvatore views as the necessary step for the formation of a new cultural field that is no longer confined to, as he puts it in a interview with Fulvio Caccia, 'an ethnic vision' (Caccia 1985: 159). A new culture that emerges from the synthesis of two poles of reference, Italy and Canada, which is where an increasing number of Italian–Canadians feel at home (Caccia 1985: 158).

Unlike Italian officialdom in Canada, Salvatore's identity project is ongoing, always changing, subject to the movements of crowds or changes in the wind. Salvatore writes of an identity that is outside the conflation of history, territory and culture into one single timespace; it is rather an identity which lives through multiple histories, cultures and memories that circulate around him, and which he continually recombines in his own process of reinventing himself. Running through Salvatore's three poems are a number of entangled tensions that are woven through, and that gradually move beyond, the injunctions of national memory that dictate allegiance to and pride in the heroics of men from the past. By throwing open the meaning of memory, Salvatore challenges the question of legitimacy, of the right to belong by virtue of some historical past.

Revisiting the space(s) of diaspora

The quest for the ethnic patriarchal pioneer – which Salvatore gradually leaves behind – is part and parcel of a longing to belong that is provisionally solved through the reprocessing of the origins of the Italian presence in Canada. This cultural reprocessing is at once multilocal and grounded in the very history of migration, as well as constituting a way of rooting Italians in Canadian territory. Against the assumed isomorphism of diaspora cultures, the reconfigurations of home, origins and indigenousness invite us to interrogate the different ways in which migrant populations negotiate a place for themselves in relation to the place of residence.

First, with regard to the opposition between homeland and hostland, Avtar Brah offers a useful distinction between 'homing desire' and 'desire for the homeland' as a way of capturing the problematic of 'home' and 'belonging'. Brah introduces this differentiation because, she argues, 'not all diasporas sustain an ideology of "return"' (Brah 1996: 180). Indeed, many attempts to define diaspora have positioned the desire for the homeland as its central, if not sole, defining feature (Conner 1986; Safran 1991; Tölölyan 1996; Cohen 1997). In this context, Brah's distinction is pertinent for it draws our attention to how claims for 'home' may vary. The recent Italian historical narrative constructed around the figure of Caboto is about staking a claim to this land as belonging to Italians. It is about making Canada a second Italian homeland; it is about a desire for a homeland that is created through merging the homeland (Italy) with the new land of residence (Canada). This construction, in turn, results from the reconfiguration of the origins of Canada and its conflation with the voyage of an 'ancestor' of present-day Italian–Canadians.

Salvatore's narrative, in contrast, may be expressive of a homing desire, i.e. the desire to feel at home, without necessarily making a place his own. Indeed, in the conclusion of his three poems, his home appears to be diffuse – nowhere and everywhere at once. His poetic text emphasises the continual reconstruction of identity.

The reconstruction of the historical presence of Italians in Canada undoubtedly testifies to the malleability of the past and, more importantly, to the ways in which national belonging and origins may be contested. The narratives examined here operate from the standpoint of different relationships to home, in which Italy and Canada as 'homeland' or 'hostland' are redefined, indeed blurred. It is precisely this kind of 'entangled tension' that supports Clifford's appraisal of diaspora as the grounds for destabilising nationalisms. National narratives, based on common origins and gathered 'peoples', cannot easily accommodate groups that maintain important allegiances and connections with another 'homeland' or with communities dispersed elsewhere. The 'empowering paradox of diaspora', Clifford suggests, consists of challenging nationalisms' contentions about the congruence of territory and culture: 'dwelling *here* assumes a solidarity and connection *there*. But *there* is not necessarily a single place or an exclusivist nation' (Clifford 1994: 332; emphasis in the original).

But what the recovery of Giovanni Caboto reveals, however, is that the allegiance that Italians are trying to demonstrate is the allegiance to Canada while making it a (second) Italian homeland. Hence, questions arise as to where or what is 'there'? Is it necessarily *not* 'here'? Is it necessarily non-nationalist? Positing connections 'elsewhere' as a central defining feature of diaspora populations amounts to reproducing a nationalist contention that presumes, indeed that naturalises, people's allegiance to an *other* place. Diasporas are always already expected to maintain ties, emotional and practical, with their 'land' or 'culture of origin' (Safran 1991; Tölölyan 1996). So, too, are immigrants; until, that is, they gradually integrate in the 'host' society. I discuss the ambiguous distinction between immigrant and diaspora elsewhere (Fortier 2000). The point I wish to make here is that the very nationalism that Clifford seeks to discomfit with diaspora is reinstated within his theoretical discourse: the duality between here and there reinstates territory and geography as the key defining principles in definitions of diasporic subjects and cultures. Barbara Kirshenblatt-Gimblett suggests that such contentions may result from definitions of diaspora predicated on forced displacement, which 'still [assume] the primacy of an earlier placement' (Kirshenblatt-Gimblett 1994: 342). By establishing the defining moment of diaspora in its inception – the trauma of displacement – it is easy to reduce diaspora to its (dis)connection with a clearly bounded timespace, the 'homeland'.

In contrast, running through the appeals to Giovanni are processes of remembering – whether formalised as history or recounted as living memories – that continually displace territorial borders and redefine the confines of 'home'. Indeed, in the narratives discussed here, memory acts as the key vector through which spatiality is reconfigured. This is precisely what Paul Gilroy insists upon in his conception of diaspora: memory, rather than territory, is the principal ground of identity formation in diaspora cultures (Gilroy 1993, 1994). Remembering not only defeats the idea that the homeland is a constant and sole object of longing, but it is also tied to the very (re)construction of the identity of places; in this case, to the reconstruction of the identity of Canada. More locally, the calls to rename the Cabot Trail so it becomes the Caboto Trail (Harney 1989: 53), or the renaming of Caboto Square in Montreal in 1955 (Harney 1989: 52), consist of rendering an Italian identity to particular places, of investing them with an Italian memory. The act of remembering speaks of an enduring presence and 'roots' it within local territory. Speaking of migrant identity formation as a practice of remembering *places* disturbs fixed notions of spatiality and territory.

As stated earlier, the repeated appeals to Caboto's voyage paradoxically reinstate the migrant origins of Italians. The interesting twist of Salvatore's poems is that the speaker leaves the fixed and stayed figure behind to 'go with the flow', to 'return', ultimately, to his migranthood and make it his living ground. Certainly, many would not contest the migrant origins of Italians, and would even add the insipid declaration that 'we are all immigrants' in order to suggest a kind of pseudoequality between the 'founding peoples' and 'cultural communities' in Canada. Camillo Menchini joins this chorus in the preface of his book, where he asserts that natives too are immigrants, having migrated here through the Bering Strait in pre-Christian times. In so doing, Menchini adds an extra layer to his invalidation of autochthonous claims.

Far from wanting to defer to this proposition, my point is rather that claims of indigenousness are tied in with the migrant origins of the Italian presence in Canada. Which brings me to the third duality: indigenousness and migration. In her book on diasporas and identities, Avtar Brah introduces the notion of 'diaspora space', a social and political space that:

> is 'inhabited' not only by diasporic subjects but equally by those who are constructed and represented as 'indigenous'. As such, the concept of diaspora space foregrounds the entanglement of genealogies of dispersion with those of 'staying put'.
>
> (Brah 1996: 16)

This diaspora space is inhabited by subjects deemed separate and distinct: the diasporic and indigenous. As I suggest earlier, who is indigenous, when and for whom remains uncertain and inherently variable. Indeed, the polarisation of diaspora/dispersion and indigenousness/staying put becomes problematic when assessed in relation to the Italian–Canadian project of recovery and its deployment within a revised history of Canada's colonisation.

The construction of the Italian presence as both migrant and indigenous potentially disables the opposition between the terms. Moreover, it raises the issue of the significance of establishing connections with a land as a means of acquiring membership to the national body. In other words, indigenousness is woven with notions of 'staying put', of 'roots'.

Although some theorists suggest that we are in a transnational era which undermines any concern with roots, migrants are constantly negotiating their positions between nations, between 'where they're from', 'where they're at' (Gilroy 1991) and where they are going, and, in the process, creating identities that serve as momentary points of suture that stabilise the flow. As Barbara Kirshenblatt-Gimblett pointedly observes, 'staying put, which having been assumed as normative for so long, no longer seems to require explanation' (Kirshenblatt-Gimblett 1994: 342). Clearly, both narratives examined here are about seeking ways to 'settle'; rooting the Italian presence in Canada by tracing it back 500 years.

Interrogating migrant belongings, then, involves unpacking the social dynamics of rootings and routings, to paraphrase Paul Gilroy (1993, 1995) as grounds of collective identity. The Italian narratives on Giovanni Caboto speak of the ongoing attempts to create a place for Italians within the Canadian symbolic order. Routes and roots are deeply entangled here; they are not merely two intersecting but are distinct vectors. The nuance is perhaps thin, but it bears important implications for our understanding of diaspora as a space of mediation and tension between multiple poles of identification that people with different experiences of migration and (re)settlement have in common.

Notes

1   This is an abridged version of an article that was first published as 'Calling on Giovanni: Interrogating the nation through diasporic imaginations' in the *International Journal of Canadian Studies* no. 18, Fall 1998, pp. 31–49. Thank you to the *IJCS* for permission for reprint.
2   I wish to thank David Leahy and the two anonymous reviewers of the original draft, whose comments have been most useful.
3   I am thinking more specifically of the works of cultural critics such as Clifford (1994), Radhakrishnan (1996), Brah (1996), Gilroy (1993, 2000), Lavie and Swedenburg (1996), Cohen (1997) and Chow (1993).
4   It is worth noting that I do not include the work of Paul Gilroy among the texts I discuss critically here. Gilroy is commonly identified as a key precursor in the recirculation of diaspora within cultural criticism. In spite of this, however, few have taken on board Gilroy's critique of modernity and of nationalist conceptions of culture that cannot be dissociated from his conception of diaspora. I have argued elsewhere on the ways in which Gilroy's work avoids some of the traps discussed here precisely by considering the centrality of memory, rather than territory, in definitions of diaspora (see Fortier 2000).
5   The distinction between immigrant and ethnic is itself ambiguous; I shall return to this point in the concluding section of this paper.
6   I do not use the Canadian phrase 'cultural minority' because Italians occupy an ambivalent position of minority/majority within Canadian social and political

life. My analysis of narratives on Giovanni Caboto will hopefully highlight this ambivalence.

7 The distinction between scattering and displacement may be useful to differentiate two types of diasporisation. This distinction has been used at different times in Jewish history, including the present day, where diaspora, in Hebrew, means scattered, and is different from the word *Galut*, which means exile (Kirshenblatt-Gimblett 1994: 343n5; Tölölyan 1996: 11).

8 Agitation began in the years preceding the celebrations for the 400th anniversary of Jacques Cartier's first voyage to the Canadian coasts. For an account of the emergence of the propaganda and of the debates that opposed the Italian élite, and, alternately, the French–Canadian and the English–Canadian élites, see Perin (1982).

9 It is beyond the scope of this chapter to explore other forms of representation of the explorer, but it is worth noting that in the summer of 1997 the province of Newfoundland held a series of events around *John Cabot*. The ways in which these celebrations related to Newfoundland's own historical particularity within Canada would be worth scrutinising. Also, Amerindians contested the celebrations of what is to them a figure of colonisation, while Italian–Canadians made sure that the Venetian origins of Caboto were acknowledged. Hence, multiple layers of meanings were at play and recognised in various ways throughout the events marking the anniversary.

10 This is distinct from the claims of 'autochthony', founded on the 'natural' right to a land on the grounds that those who claim autochthony were never anywhere else (Boyarin and Boyarin 1993: 715).

11 From 17 September 1997 to mid-June 1998. Other Venetian explorers honoured in the exhibition include Amerigo Vespucci, Cristoforo Columbus and Giovanni da Verrazano and cartographer Vincenzo Coronelli.

8 Cieszyn Silesia

A transnational community under reconstruction[1]

Marian Kempny

Introduction

This chapter examines transnationalism as a form of collective identity being shaped under the conditions of globalization. All too often these days we hear about the effects that globalization might have on identity in terms of a 'post-national genre' or an 'in-between ethnicization' of identities – whereby identity becomes permeable, fluid and multiple. In sharp contrast, my focus in this chapter is on an apparently opposite process, that of constructing strong, local identities of a transnational character. This paradoxical twist can be explained in terms of the dialectics of globalization and localization that are omnipresent on a world scale. As described recently by Peter Kloos (2000: 281), globalization and localization are two processes seemingly pointing in opposite directions:

> ... in the realm of politics the national state is rapidly losing its glorified sovereignty in favour of transnational, continental, or even global regimes, while at the same time a number of substantive minorities are clamouring for more autonomy and political independence.

Consequently, it is necessary to distinguish at least three aspects of the phenomenon of transnationalism. In addition to its obvious political dimension it is often the economically driven flows that are referred to by various researchers in order to explain the rise of transnational communities. But even while looking at this phenomenon from the perspective of labour force migration, one puzzling feature is emphasized: the new types of migrants create communities that 'sit astride political borders' and that, as a very perceptive remark goes, are 'neither here nor there' (see Portes 2000: 254). In their pioneering work, Basch *et al.* (1994: 6) define transnationalism as follows:

> We define 'transnationalism' as the process by which immigrants forge and sustain multi-stranded social relations that links together their societies of origin and settlement. We call those processes transnationalism to emphasize that many immigrants today build social

fields that cross geographic, cultural, and political borders ... An essential element ... is the multiplicity of involvements that transmigrants sustain in both home and host societies.

As a result, such mobile communities have to be grounded in their sole fixed yet movable feature, i.e. the cultural identities of their immigrants themselves. It is for this reason that the national or local attachments and loyalties of their members should be taken into account while dealing with transnational communities.

The globalization–localization interplay

By globalization I mean the formation of a 'world society' in the widest sense of the term, accompanied by the simultaneous rise of localized identities based in particular localities and confined within state boundaries. Accordingly, we have to distinguish a separate level of identity that operates at the local level while it is also connected with transnational movements in space.

Indeed, these two levels are connected. The localization of identities fosters the production of identities trespassing or cutting across the boundaries of a particular nation-state. Usually, this happens in border regions where a minority settled within the boundaries of a neighbouring 'host' nation-state struggles for a correction of state borders so that it can become united (or reunited) with its co-patriots in the motherland. My discussion here aims to reveal the similar logic associated with a somewhat different process. Specifically, I enquire into the trigger that leads to transnational community formation. I argue that this trigger lies in the moment when a 'repressed' minority within the national territory starts to articulate its needs for cultural recognition, or puts forward claims of territorial autonomy stretching beyond the boundaries of a single nation-state. Simultaneously, the minority develops a view of its region as a homeland fenced off from the present political boundaries of nation-states.

Moreover, in today's global age it is possible to identify collectivities that do not even have to change their home addresses in order to assemble themselves into transnational communities. As Zygmunt Bauman (1998) puts it, ours is a world where there are no natural places left to occupy. In this contemporary shrinking world, the absence of mobility does not make much sense – in spite of the fact that individuals or communities seem to stay put. Whereas globalization makes all established borders permeable, communities often try to anchor their identities in something tangible, and tend to 'naturalize' the relationship between people and their 'proper' places. This tendency might lead to forging transnational communities of a different type from the one conventionally discussed in the literature on transnationalism. Such communities symbolically reclaim their place (or 'soil') irrespective of the political borders of national societies. For this symbolism to be effective communities remove their identities from the territorial imagery inherited in their past.

Consequently, the notion of 'deterritorialization' dominant in globalization discourse still remains somewhat problematic. For example, Lash and Urry's (1994: 323) vision of 'deterritorialization', according to which we have now all moved from place to 'flow, from spaces to streams, from organized hierarchies to disorganization', hardly gives a good rendition of globalization – and of transnational communities in particular. For it is fairly well known that different diasporic communities are enmeshed in long-distance nationalism, or are desperately trying to reproduce their homeland wherever they are. For immigrants and guest workers uprooted by global flows, deterritorialization is typically linked with reterritorialization. For most of them, the reassertion of their 'imagined communities' in new locations often seems to be a must. As Gupta and Ferguson (1992: 10–11; emphasis added) write:

> India and Pakistan apparently reappear in postcolonial simulation in London, prerevolutionary Teheran rises from the ashes in Los Angeles, and a thousand similar cultural dreams are played out in urban and rural settings all across the globe ... [While] *actual places and localities become ever more blurred and indeterminate, ideas of culturally and ethnically distinct places become perhaps even more salient ... as displaced peoples cluster around remembered and imagined homelands, places, or communities* in a world that seems increasingly to deny such firm territorialized anchors in their actuality.

This statement clearly indicates that the concept of 'transnational' community might be linked with the cultural construction of place and not with human territorial mobility alone. Under current conditions, I believe this assertion could be extended to encompass populations that have not experienced large-scale displacement. To my mind, such is the case of Cieszyn Silesians.

Consequently, while the following discussion refers to a single empirical case, my goal is to justify a broader theoretical claim. That is, under specific circumstances and in so far as the relationship between community and locality is understood according to the framework spelled out above (and in the introduction to this book), an otherwise typical 'sedentary' population can be viewed as an example of contemporary transnationalism. In developing this broader argument, I am relying upon Benedict Anderson's (1983) celebrated view of the nation as an 'imagined community'. However, while my discussion follows Anderson's interpretation of 'the nation' as a 'community without propinquity', I would like to stress that national (or any other cultural) boundaries are constructed rather than enduring forever as discrete, object-like phenomena confined to disconnected spaces. All these issues will be taken up in the empirical context of the collective identity shaping among the Cieszyn (Teschen) Silesians.[2]

The identity of Cieszyn Silesians

Poland is known as a stronghold of the Roman Catholic Church, and this is undoubtedly true. However, in certain regions of Poland, non-Catholics far outnumber the Roman Catholic population. This is evident in the Cieszyn region[3] known as Cieszyn Silesia. For centuries, Cieszyn Silesia, located at the present-day juncture of the Czech Republic, Poland and Slovakia, has been the home of a variety of peoples, languages and religions. Because of the frontier nature of the region, state borders have changed repeatedly. During the feudal disintegration of the Late Middle Ages and under the reign of the Silesian Piast dynasty (1290–1653), the region formed a separate Cieszyn Dukedom (*ducatus btessinensis*). Although the majority of the population was ethnically Polish (see Panic 1994) the region became a vassalage of the Bohemian crown (1327) and, subsequently, came under the reign of the Hapsburgs (1526). Finally, after World War I, during the disintegration of the Hapsburg empire, the region was divided into two parts that were incorporated into the resurrected Polish and Czechoslovak states respectively. Consequently, in the twentieth century alone, Zaolzie, the southern part of the district of Cieszyn Silesia, stretching along the western banks of the River Olza, was occupied by five different states: the Austrian Empire, Czechoslovakia, Poland, the Third Reich, Czechoslovakia again and, at present, the Czech Republic.

Language reflects these territorial changes. The dialect of Cieszyn Silesia is complex and reflects three different languages (Polish, Czech and Slovak). While different dialects and modern-day political borders in east–central Europe generally coincide, the linguistic borders are less precise in some areas. Such is the case in Cieszyn Silesia, which exhibits transitional and mixed dialects. Moreover, the contemporary linguistic situation has been greatly affected by the decision to partition Cieszyn Silesia between Poland and Czechoslovakia in 1920. The partition determined not only the political border of a previously united region, but also the fate of the region's spoken language. Since 1920, most of the new words in the Cieszyn Silesia lexicon (except for English ones) have come from Czech. This is the case even among the ethnic Poles in Zaolzie, across the Polish–Czech border (see Hannan 1996).

The language perplexities alone might account for the compound nature of the collective identities. Again, the contemporary situation is most complex in Zaolzie, now in the Czech Republic. Typically, there are only minor differences in language use between those who consider themselves Czech and those who consider themselves Polish. In fact, some ethnic Polish parents in Zaolzie have children who identify themselves as Czech. But, it is much more than language differences that should be taken into consideration.

In an insightful study, Kevin Hannan (1996) widely described the frequently ambiguous constructions of identity among Cieszyn Silesians. These constructions are based on 'subjective evaluations of shared geographical, historical, cultural, religious, social, linguistic, and biological relations'. It was the rise of ethnic consciousness among Cieszyn Silesians that had an impact upon the spread and development of language (mainly in the mid-nineteenth century). Moreover, it has been religious boundaries rather than political borders that have determined language and ethnic consciousness in the region. During past centuries, religion has been the main cause of differentiation among the mixed and internally diversified population of this region.

Therefore, in order to account for the large numbers of Lutherans in the region it is necessary to take a brief look at the region's historical circumstances. Protestant confessions set up their diasporas in Poland soon after the beginning of the Reformation in Europe. Yet, the dissemination of their beliefs was hampered by royal restrictions on the freedom of faith. In contrast, in the Cieszyn Dukedom, the impact of Martin Luther's teaching was initially promoted by the reigning family. Especially during the first half of the sixteenth century, the Dukes of Cieszyn supported the Lutheran faith. Subsequently, the Lutheran movement gained the upper hand over Catholicism among vast numbers of local peoples. As a result, until the second half of the sixteenth century the region's population was predominantly Lutheran (see Mach 1993: 225; Kubica-Heller 1996: 29ff.). However, after the Seven Years War, in 1526, when almost the whole of Silesia was taken over by Prussia, the Cieszyn region remained with Austria until the end of World War I.

The Counter-Reformation policy of the Hapsburgs led to the persecution of non-Catholic denominations and to subsequent changes in the population distribution of Catholics and Lutherans. Nevertheless, owing to the uneven territorial distribution of believers, some communities have continued to be predominantly Lutheran to this very day. Undoubtedly, under Hapsburg rule, it was resistance against political and cultural domination that fostered the development of a particular collective identity among the members of the mostly Polish Lutheran communities in Cieszyn Silesia. At the same time, the primary frame of reference for identity formation arose from belonging to a well-defined territorial site. Cieszyn Silesian Lutherans conceived of their homeland as the region occupied by the former Dukedom of Cieszyn. The Czechs and Germans were regarded as 'strangers' who were separated by a clear-cut language boundary as well as by religion. In contrast to the situation in the rest of Poland, in this region being a Catholic often meant being foreign, while Lutherans were usually Poles.[4]

Although the Cieszyn Lutherans were isolated in their homogeneous communities fighting against religious coercion, their collective identity reflected their self-ascription as the region's native population ('Cieszyn Silesians').[5] These religious and regional layers of identity interfered with the version of Polish identity that was promoted at the turn of the twentieth century by nationalist activists who were born and bred in the region.

The end of World War I brought the independence of Poland after 123 years of partition. It resulted, however, in a fifty–fifty partition of historical Cieszyn Silesia into a Polish part and a Czech part. When the partition took place, the local population was 434,000 (in 1920). Of these, only 55 per cent were of Polish descent, with 26 per cent of Czech descent and 16 per cent of German nationality.[6] In the Polish part of the now divided Silesia, religion very soon regained priority as the most important aspect of identity. This was especially true in the rural areas, where entire communities were inhabited mainly by Lutherans. In inter-war Poland, where the Roman Catholic Church enjoyed a privileged position, the main reference point for Cieszyn Lutherans' identity formation was their minority status *vis-à-vis* Poland's dominant Catholic majority. Both the Catholic clergy as well as popular political leaders and opinion-makers equated Lutheran faith with being a German rather than a Pole. This strengthened the tendency of the Lutherans to confine themselves to their communities and to remain apart from the Catholic inhabitants of the region. This isolation was particularly visible in the cases of closed religious-based communities, thus endorsing group endogamy – at least in terms of group ideology.[7]

Nevertheless, despite such transparent, clear-cut boundaries, the compound identities of Cieszyn Silesians were not necessarily based on an unambiguous inclusion/exclusion boundary, determined solely by confession. In addition to religious confession, social inclusion was also defined by feelings of belonging, of being rooted in a region wider than a particular municipality, a region inhabited by Cieszyn Silesians. Hannan (1996) provides numerous examples of this regional identity manifested in the distrust of outsiders, a separate folk culture, the dominant role of religion, the use of regional names and, last but not least, in the spatial imaginary of the territory and boundaries of Cieszyn Silesia.

In this region, World War II did not result in further changes in political boundaries. Nevertheless, as everywhere in post-World War II Poland, the local space was affected relative to the previous situation by the inflows and outflows of resettled populations and subsequently by migrants motivated by their search for work. The general trend towards the increase of space permeability in Cieszyn Silesia manifested itself in lifting the impenetrable barrier that used to divide local Catholics and Lutherans. Especially during the 1960s and 1970s, the massive Catholic immigration into the area accelerated this trend. It all went hand in hand with the region's greater urbanization and secularization. Needless to say, these processes led to a further plunge in the proportion of the region's Lutheran inhabitants. More specifically, in the 1970s, the region's so-called 'socialist industrialization' caused a serious disruption to the territorial ties typical for the *Geimeinschaft*-like confessional communities.

Just like many other areas in Poland, Cieszyn Silesia became an 'interstitial zone of displacement and de-territorialization' (Gupta and Ferguson 1992: 18). The flood of newcomers arriving mainly from what the locals considered to be 'very distant regions of Poland' led to the fragmentation of the localized religious-based communities and to a dramatic decline in the significance of religion as a factor for identity formation. Furthermore, under Communist rule, strict control was imposed upon the public articulation of religious identity. The removal of religion from the official public domain also resulted in a diminution of the sharp differences that had previously existed between religious communities. These differences used to be conspicuous in the pre-Communist period because of the public enactment of religious rituals.

As seen from the above, in Cieszyn Silesia's past, its basic minority – namely Lutheran inhabitants – tended to define their identity on the basis of religion and nationality symbolized by their Polish language and tradition. Later, when Poland regained its independence as a nation-state, regionalism overtook national identity in terms of its importance for the local society. Local identity has continued to be a defining factor until recently. People make a clear distinction between 'those who are rooted here' (*stela* – being native-born) and the newcomers who are regarded as 'uprooted' since they arrived from 'Poland' – the so-called 'recruits' (*werbusy*, which is a derogatory label for the guest workers used by the natives). Even for young people these two different forms of belonging still define the relation between 'us' and 'them'.[8]

The production of transnational locality

As soon as the Communist system collapsed in 1989, both religion and local identity re-emerged not only as vital elements of the political landscape but also as important markers used by individuals to classify themselves (i.e. the established) versus the 'newcomers'. Although local identity has never ceased to play an important role in Cieszyn Silesia, during the post-1989 period it gained in both importance and visibility. Consequently, examining Cieszyn Silesians' identity through reference to former historical borders allows one to grasp the region's transnational character. Furthermore, the nature and significance of imagined connections with the region is decisive for the manner in which Cieszyn Silesians conceive of their 'homeland' today.

The production of locality operates through the mapping of a 'delocalized' earlier group onto its 'proper' place. Specifically, Arjun Appadurai (1996a) tries to introduce a clear distinction between an (often territorially unbound) locality and a (territorially defined) community. His reflections concerning the 'production of locality' have been based precisely on an on-going debate about the future of the nation-state in the wake of 'transnational destabilization'. Finally, he draws a distinction between 'locality' and 'neighbourhood', which he suggests is relevant for all types of community 'in a world where locality seems to have lost its ontological moorings' (Appadurai 1996a: 178). From the point of view presented here, this distinction is relevant and applicable to the case of the Cieszyn Silesians. According to Appadurai (1996a: 178), locality is 'primarily relational and contextual' and owing to its 'complex phenomenological quality' it does not denote an actual place, site or locale. This is why, in his description, the key attribute of 'locality' becomes a structure of feeling produced by particular forms of intentional activity (Appadurai 1996a: 182). At the same time, Appadurai's notion of 'neighbourhood' has also been redefined to some extent. In effect, this term describes 'the actually existing social forms in which locality, as a dimension or value, is variably realized' (Appadurai 1996a: 185). Hence, locality, according to Appadurai, is inherently fragile and must be continuously reasserted. The case of Cieszyn Silesians seems to confirm that in such a ceaseless process 'the *spatial* production of locality' (Appadurai 1996a: 182) plays an even more important role under globalized conditions.

In addition, the history and evolution of the collective identities of the Cieszyn Silesians during the last several centuries provides the necessary background for understanding the recent tendency towards the reproduction of *transnational locality*. From this point of view, the really significant factor is the impact of the dramatic changes in the social context of collective life on the production of locality. Instead of focusing on territorially localized settings (i.e. neighbourhoods) the community of Cieszyn Silesians has started to generate a structure of shared feelings in a way that comes close to 'locality' in Appadurai's understanding of the term; its members have adopted a native construct of the 'local nature' of belonging which has been forged and reforged.

To recapitulate: despite the collapse of the real spatial boundaries that formerly enabled the Cieszyn Silesians to articulate their communal identity, locality – conceived as a contextually contingent symbolic construction – has overtaken national and subsequently religious frames of belonging in providing the substance for the different 'imagined communities'. Accordingly, the region's researcher is faced with the following predicament: today, the re-emergence of the Cieszyn Silesia community goes hand in hand with a wider process involving the reterritorialization of historical memory. In this reterritorialization of memory, the 'reinvention' of the former Cieszyn Dukedom's territorial integrity plays a crucial role.

This is why relying upon Appadurai's framework can also enable one to put forward a complementary interpretation of these developments. In other words, the proposition that what has recently happened in the region is the reterritorialization of a Cieszyn Silesian collective memory could find its validation in Anthony D. Smith's views on the significance of the territorial basis of collective identities nowadays. Indeed, and contrary to Appadurai (1990), Smith (1999) has used the term 'ethnoscape', coined by the former, in order to stress the importance of 'the process of territorialization of historical memory', which consists of a collective envisioning of national (subnational) 'sacred territories'. It seems clear that, in the Cieszyn Silesians' case, the formation of their regional entity illustrates the same social process through which people come to believe that their specific territory is unique and indispensable to the members of a community (Smith 1999: 16).

In this regard, and particularly telling, are the results of a survey indicating that among inhabitants of this region almost 95 per cent define themselves as Cieszyn Silesians and recognize themselves as inhabitants of a separate territorial entity (compared with Matykowski 1997). At the time of this research, the Polish part of the regions was incorporated (since 1975) into the larger administrative unit (*wojewodship*) of Bielsko-Bia. This unit was also perpetuated by the regional divisions introduced by the 'Solidarity' movement.

Within this broader unit, the so-called region of Beskidy Highlands (*Podbeskidzie*), a territorial subunit, is the area under study. In fact, the very name 'Cieszyn Dukedom' is not used frequently now. Nevertheless, the shared imaginings of the boundaries of this region are more or less co-extensive with the territory of the former historical entity. In particular, the findings of social geographers conclusively demonstrate that Cieszyn Silesia is still mostly envisioned in a historical, territorial and extended transnational manner.

One should recall that the territorial integrity of the former Dukedom was seriously circumscribed by its incorporation into the administrative grid of the Hapsburg Empire, where it remained for three centuries. The region was totally destroyed after World War I, and, hence, it is remarkable that, even today, a large portion of the region's population still recognizes several towns now located in the Czech Republic as important regional centres. These towns have not belonged to Poland since 1919.

Survey results confirm the principal role of the city of Cieszyn, traditionally identified as the region's 'capital' town, and a dominant feature of the region's spatial representations. Almost 92 per cent of respondents regard Cieszyn as the capital of the region,[9] whereas only 7 per cent mention Bielsko-Bia as the regional centre. This is all the more surprising because Bielsko-Bia (a former borderline town of the region) today dwarfs Cieszyn economically as well as with regard to population size.

It is therefore reasonable to suggest that the shared historical past has shaped the locals' collective imaginary. Transmitted through collective memory, the spatial referents of their collective's identity shaped their sense of a 'community without propinquity', located within the boundaries inherited from the Cieszyn Dukedom. For this particular case, Smith uses the term 'miniscapes' in order to describe the links of a local population to a territory much more circumscribed than the nation-state (Smith 1999: 16).

In fact, in this case, the circumscribed territory appears to be transnational. Somewhat unexpectedly, transnationalism, defined as 'clustering around remembered and imagined homelands' (Gupta and Ferguson 1992: 12), seems to induce here a 'localism' grounded in feelings of attachment to the soil and the experience of a sense of temporal and spatial continuity.[10] Since a portion of Cieszyn Silesians' original homeland was 'lost' to the former Czechoslovakia, historical memory operates at the level of ritual territorial reintegration. The most conspicuous examples of such feelings are connected with public events and folk festivals.

For example, in order to recast the Cieszyn Silesian community into a shared transnational space of belonging, the permanent element of boundary crossing was introduced. During the Communist period, this was especially visible in the city of Cieszyn itself during the May Day parades. The parades typically involved the uncontrolled crossing or 'trespassing' of the Czechoslovak–Polish state border by the Polish participants of the marches.

Needless to say, in an era of strict control of individual movement, such acts of trespassing had to be approved and orchestrated by the local municipality.

Furthermore, the municipality created public forums for events aiming to construct local 'sites of memory'. Their most important event was the annual commemoration of the erection of the town at the so-called Well of Three Brothers, a legendary meeting point of Cieszyn founders. In short, the central motif of these legends is that the town was built at the meeting point of three brothers who had left their previous homeland to conquer and master the surrounding lands, and who finally established the city in the place where they met once their toils were completed. In this context, the communal myths of the regional capital's foundation are supportive of the region's transnational imaginary. All these communal events survived the 1989 developments in Central Europe. Until recently, the regional ideology of Cieszyn Silesians called for the 'liberation' of Zaolzie from 'Czech rule'. But today, the regional setting is more influenced by the nationwide initiatives of Poland and the Czech Republic to integrate themselves into the European political structures. These general national priorities have pushed the knotty and thorny problem of Silesian irredentism to the margins.

Today, Cieszyn Silesians consider nation-state boundaries to be far less meaningful in so far as their territorial identities are concerned. In one of the responses to the question concerning which community the Cieszyn Silesians belonged to, the respondent stated openly that 'now [that] the state border is no longer [the] barrier ... it previously was, people often think about the Cieszyn region in its historical boundaries'. It is noteworthy that these attitudes are further fostered by the European Union's transnational economic integration and the total lack of restraints in transborder movement for the region's inhabitants.

Large-scale transborder petit-commodity trade takes place mainly in the Polish part of the region. More 'global' initiatives include the foundation of a transnational institution of regional cultural and economic cooperation called Cieszyn Silesia Euroregion. The very name of this 'Euroregion' reflects the coordinated efforts at self-governments by the Polish and Czech borderline districts. The local districts want to strengthen grass roots support for their transborder initiatives by making use of the region's historical memory.

This is an apt illustration of the 'localized' as well as transnational nature of the Cieszyn Silesian community. It is noteworthy that both Lutheran- and Catholic-born natives openly express their regionalism. According to them, Cieszyn Silesians remain socially distinct from the rest of Polish society in matters of religious life and child rearing as well as in the areas of high culture and the arts. As if deliberately engaging Max Weber's famous Protestant Ethic thesis, many Cieszyn Silesian Lutherans seem to believe that their work ethic, efficiency and organization are superior to those of the newcomers arriving from 'Poland'. However, in a twist directly clashing with Weber's thesis, they regard these virtues and assets as to some extent shared by the Catholic neighbours they regard as natives.

Thus, the most striking feature of Cieszyn Silesians' identity remains a tendency to rely on explicitly spatial markers defining the people's sense of belonging as well as a person's inclusion in, or exclusion from, a well-defined community of natives. This goes hand in hand with the vibrant character of associational life that is highly visible today, which also reflects the attempts of the religious groups in the region to articulate their interests at a collective corporate level. Clearly, although based on symbolic distinctions between the Cieszyn Silesians and outsiders, some activities in the local public sphere foster feelings of belonging to ethnic-driven networks. What should be stressed, however, is that numerous local initiatives, ranging from concerts of parish choirs to folk events to local political aliances,[11] encompass the entire population and contribute to the reconstruction of Cieszyn Silesia as an 'imagined community' envisioned this time in a transnational form.

Conclusion: a transnational community in reverse

From the perspective adopted in this essay, 'transnationalism' includes the construction of 'homelands' or localities in the world 'on the move'. I have discussed these mechanisms in the more empirically grounded context of the reterritorialization of collective identity among inhabitants of a borderline region of Poland, Slovakia and the Czech Republic known as Cieszyn Silesia. Cieszyn Silesia's complex transnational locality is an evident case of the interplay between globalization and localization.

Referring to the distinction between sociologically viable communal structures ('neighbourhoods') and the self-conscious production of locality, I have tried to stress reterritorialization as a factor of critical importance for a better understanding of cultural globalization.[12] The term 'Cieszyn Silesia' has mutated into a referent of belonging to an imaginary community of natives. Hence, Cieszyn Silesia is an example of a locality being produced in a deterritorialized fashion, not as a real but rather as a symbolic community.

To define this otherwise quite puzzling 'transnational community' it is necessary to incorporate the *production of locality* as a decisive factor in the globalization–localization interplay. In the case discussed in this chapter, this production has led to the construction of social loyalties and detachments shaped by an imagined ancestral land. Moreover, if an imagined community of the Cieszyn Silesians survived the destruction of their original place of residence it was partly thanks to their commitment to the historically shaped territorial notion of Cieszyn Silesia as their 'homeland'.

Seen in this light, globalization has had a significant impact on the social organization of Cieszyn Silesians' collective life. Post-World War II industrialization, in particular, led to significant inflows of people and resources into the region. Needless to say, these inflows have hardly ever been regarded as connected with globalization because they ended up having only a very local impact. However, these processes brought a total disruption of the territorial ties constitutive of former strongly religiously marked 'neighbourhoods'.

In effect, the leftovers of Cieszyn Silesian's 'own' land were 'invaded' by an 'alien' population over which they had no control and which has turned them into a kind of transnational community in reverse. But it is not until the political change in 1989 that this transnational nature of Cieszyn Silesia could be fully articulated. The situation is very different now, when a quest for more local autonomy can also be openly pronounced as an expression of fixed collective identities.

Consequently, despite the collapse of real spatial boundaries that formerly enabled the articulation of communal identities, locality as a contextually contingent symbolic construction has overtaken national and subsequently religious frames of belonging to the different 'imagined communities'. Paradoxically though, notwithstanding the annihilation of the territorially fixed entity of Cieszyn Silesia, recent social changes have facilitated the rebirth of a transnational community of meaning grounded in the spatial imagery of the bygone Cieszyn Silesia Dukedom.

Notes

1 This work was supported by the Research Support Scheme of the OSI/HESP, grant no. 1323/1997, and the State Committee for Scientific Research (KBN), grant no. 1HO1F 05611.

2 The empirical material discussed below comes partly from the survey research carried out in Cieszyn Silesia in 1998 (supported by the KBN grant) as well as from Jan Kubik's fieldwork in this region of Poland (Kubik 1994), and finally from my own recent intermittent fieldwork in the area.

3 During the historical boundaries of the Cieszyn Dukedom, this region covered approximately 2,300 km ^{2}, but nowadays it is divided by the state boundaries between Poland and the Czech Republic, and for decades there was no territorial equivalent of it in the grid of the administrative division of Poland. The territorial reform introduced in Poland in 1999, which brought back a three-tier structure of self-government, finally re-established a partial integrity of the former Dukedom in the shape of the district of Cieszyn (*powiat cieszynski*). One can estimate the population that inhabits the Polish part of the former Dukedom at 165,000, of whom 115,000 are Catholics and the rest are members of several other Christian churches. Within the twenty parishes of the Cieszyn Diocese, the largest one (the Polish Evangelical Church of the Augsburg Confession) includes over 48,000 Lutherans (more than half of its total membership, which is estimated at 87,000). The source of these data is the *Statistical Yearbook of the Republic of Poland* 2000, Central Statistical Office, Warsaw, Year IX.

4 In the memoirs of Jan Wantu, a bishop of the Polish Evangelical Church of Augsburg to which currently almost the whole Lutheran population of Cieszyn Silesia belongs, it was expressed thus: 'At the borderland, each Lutheran is a Pole, whereas each Catholic is a Czech' (ms, p. 79, cited in Kubica-Heller 1996: 53).

5 The ethnonim 'Cieszynioki' coined in the past is currently widely in use there.

6 Source: *Cesi a Polaci v minulosti*, Zacek, V. (ed.), Praha: Academia, 1967. According to Zdzis aw Mach (1993: 228), in 1923 the population of the whole region consisted of 76 per cent Poles and 23 per cent Germans (the remaining 1 per cent were of Jewish nationality).

7 This situation is well documented but a broader discussion is impossible within the confines of this chapter. The recent, thorough analyses of Grayna Kubica-

Heller (1996: see especially chapter 5) convincingly demonstrate that the Lutheran communities of the inter-war period were characterized by a social organization that permeated all crucial aspects of both individual and social life.

8   This thesis finds strong support in the light of the materials gathered as the outcome of the literary competition for the high-school youth on 'To be a Cieszyn Silesian – does it still mean something?' (materials deposited in Macierz Ziemii Cieszynskiej Library, Cieszyn).

9   The town itself has shared the fate of regional division, since 1919, into Polish and Czech parts.

10 As Marilyn Strathern holds: '"localism" conjures up several related images; being rooted in a place; the identity that comes from belonging; bounded social horizons; a sense of antiquity and continuity over time' (Strathern 1984: 185).

11 It is clearly seen in the domain of local politics. Swimming against the tide of national-level politics marked by a right-wing slogan – to be a Pole means to be a Catholic – the local politicians carefully avoided the danger of conflating politics and religion, and local 'ecumenical' alliances were able to win municipal elections in the two most important municipalities of the region in 1994 (their success has been partially repeated in the 1998 election).

12 In a more general vein, the discussion addressed the disembedding of identities and social relationships envisioned by the classical theories of modernity (Durkheim, Simmel, Weber) as well as by their contemporary heirs (Giddens, Mann). However, instead of the shift from concrete to abstract reference points for identity construction, we are witnessing a counter-movement that often leads to the redefinition of collective, communal identities and their relationship to particular regions, spaces or places.

9 Global industries and local agents

Becoming a world-class manager in the Mexico–USA border region[1]

Oscar Contreras and Martin Kenney

Introduction

The operations of multinational corporations (MNCs) in developing countries have attracted much interest and inflamed the passions of many. For critics these MNCs are seeking merely to improve their competitive position by exploiting inexpensive labor and weak government regulation. Defenders argue that there are significant benefits from hosting MNCs, including jobs and foreign exchange. Other literature has focused on understanding the reasons for globalizing production, examined corporate strategy, or studied the role of expatriate managers. The impacts on the host country and its citizens have been treated as side-effects.

In recent years there has been great interest in the transfer of knowledge through learning-by-doing, but studies of learning in MNC factories in Mexico have been almost entirely confined to studies of workers (Kenney *et al.* 1998; Contreras 2000). This chapter examines the transfer of knowledge and responsibility to Mexican managers and engineers working in MNC factories and through this process the emergence of an indigenous globalized managerial group in the Mexico–USA border region.

In this chapter we present a stylized version of the stages involved in the "localization" of the manufacturing and administrative knowledge derived initially from MNCs and with which Mexican professionals are increasingly entrusted until they eventually manage the local operations altogether. We also present a stylized schema of the career patterns of individual managers.

Despite the suspicion that the character of the maquiladoras (see below) was changing (González and Ramírez 1989) and that Mexican managers were taking a more important role in the factories, there have been no studies of their careers. This is consonant with other studies that treat indigenous managers as simple automaton-like agents of corporate headquarters. We argue that Mexican managers and engineers constitute a professional group engaged in establishing links between global industries and local society. In this process these managers and engineers are the social carriers of technological transfer and skill formation within the local society.

Managers and engineers in the maquiladoras

Maquiladoras is the name used in Mexico for factories that operate under a special law allowing the importation of foreign parts for assembly and re-export. The program was started in 1965 and by the late 1960s had only fifty small factories. But the maquiladora program grew rapidly in the 1970s as US firms accelerated the movement of production offshore. By 2000, there were approximately 3,500 maquiladoras employing 1.5 million people. For Mexico the maquiladoras have become Mexico's largest source of new employment creation and the second largest source of foreign exchange after oil.

Despite its importance to the economy the maquiladora program continues to be strongly criticized (Gambrill 1980; De la O Martínez 1997). Because of their emphasis upon the assembly of imported parts, the maquiladoras have not purchased many parts from Mexican vendors and local content averages only 3 percent (Kopinak 1996). The other criticism leveled at the maquiladoras revolves around the quality of the work. Put differently, critics charge that there is little training or investment in the workers (Reygadas 1992). The criticism of the quality of work continues to be debated. Some have argued that many of the electronic and auto-parts maquiladoras are examples of the so-called "second-generation" maquiladoras, which are technically more sophisticated and provide greater training and opportunities for worker improvement (Carrillo 1989; Gereffi 1994). The first generation of maquiladoras produced mainly clothing, assembled basic semiconductors and other light manufactures, and the objective was to reduce costs through the use of cheap labor.

The debate about the transfer of skills to Mexicans has, in large measure, focused upon Mexican workers, and the research results have been inconclusive. Although there seems to be some consensus that in the second-generation maquiladoras there has been greater training of Mexican technicians (Hualde 1995; Kenney *et al.* 1998), there remain many maquiladoras operating extremely simplified production processes for which little or no training is necessary (Contreras 2000). Still, there is little question that increasingly sophisticated manufacturing processes are being transferred to Mexico.

The emphasis on blue-collar workers has overshadowed another important group of workers in the maquiladoras – the Mexican managers and engineers. However, there is ample reason to believe that this is the class of Mexican workers that should have received the most training and investment. Given their relatively privileged positions they would be expected to have opportunities for more learning. In other words, a pool of capable Mexicans should be formed. These managers could remain within the corporations or transfer to Mexican firms, either already existing ones or as start-ups. In both cases, they participate in a transnational network of experts whose skills and values allow them to link the local environment to the global economy.

Regarding the creation of local companies, most previous research has focused primarily on production chains and development of suppliers (Wilson 1992). Authors have emphasized the problem of barriers to entrance (Gonzalez and Ramirez 1989), or the opportunities for US-based companies to supply the maquiladoras (Rosenfeldt and Ponthieu 1987).

Data collection and interviewee profile

We conducted semistructured interviews with sixty-four Mexican managers in Tijuana and Ciudad Juarez, which are the two largest cities in the Mexico–USA border region. The respondents were secured through a snowball sample in which each interviewee was asked to recommend other potential interview subjects. Each interview was conducted in Spanish and lasted for at least an hour. The interviews were taped and transcribed later. The interviews were conducted from late 1995 to early 1997.

All of the interviewees were Mexican: thirty-four of them were occupying the position of general manager of their plants (53.1 percent of the sample). As many as thirteen were in management in diverse areas of production (20.3 percent), fourteen in administrative areas (21.8 percent) and three more (4.7 percent) defined themselves as owners or associates of the company.

One characteristic of this group of managers was its relative youth since the average age was 41.5 years old, with a mode of 33. It is appropriate to underline the fact that the majority of the managers (53.1 percent) were natives of one or other Mexican border town, a figure linked to the phenomenon involving the substitution of the foreign management staff (mainly US citizens) by Mexican administrators born in Northern Mexico.

The most frequent career in the professional formation of these managers was engineering (71.4 percent), especially industrial engineering. A substantial proportion of these professionals (39.1 percent) completed their studies in local institutions (Tijuana and Ciudad Juarez).

The number of formal jobs performed by these managers along their professional trajectory yields an average of 4.4 jobs, with an average of 4.1 years per job and a total trajectory of 18 years of work. Current jobs had resulted in an average of 7.3 years of seniority. Most of the managers (68.8 percent) worked for a US-owned company, whereas 17.2 percent worked for a Mexican-owned firm and 14 percent for an Asian-owned company. The size of the plants employing the respondents varied widely: the mean number of employees was 964, with the largest factory employing 7,000 and the smallest employing only fifteen people. The age of the plants also varied, from less than 1 year old to 25 years old, with a mean age of 14 years.

Industrial maturation and professional upgrading

Tijuana and Ciudad Juarez are the two Mexican cities having the largest and oldest concentrations of maquiladoras in Mexico (Sklair 1993). From 1980 to 2000, about fifty new plants opened each year in both cities. This translates into roughly 300 new management positions each year. In the 1970s Tijuana and Ciudad Juarez were typical border towns both specializing in the services sector, with little industrial culture or experience. Any firm establishing a factory in either of these two areas had to supply its own management. In this environment there were few Mexican managers capable of higher level management tasks, so Mexican managers were confined to staff positions such as managing human resources and keeping administrative links with Mexican authorities. Incorporating Mexicans into line management and general management positions would require learning by Mexican managers.

By default the establishment of a factory in a region with no industrial infrastructure requires that the human resources necessary for many skilled activities be imported initially. The earliest factories in both regions were established to take advantage of low-cost unskilled labor. Of course, even an almost entirely enclave operation must interact with the local environment and local workers, so it is necessary to hire some local managers immediately to undertake these tasks. These staff positions can be largely segmented from the actual productive activities of the operation while the managerial skills required for such activities as human resources management are fairly general in character and are readily available in most local economies.

Any factory operation must draw in resources in the form of human beings. By creating a demand for these resources it will attract them either from the local economy or from outside. From either source, after attraction the resources become part of the local economy, except in the case of expatriates whose intention it is to return to their previous homes. Moreover, the expatriates are very expensive when compared with indigenous managers, so there will some pressure to replace them. Given that the number of maquiladoras has experienced almost uninterrupted growth since 1980, the demand for managers has also increased, drawing more Mexicans into managerial positions.

The Mexican managers inside the factories were learning-by-doing and the MNCs' operations were under constant pressure to lower costs. One obvious strategy for reducing costs was to cut back on expatriates, who were paid salaries commensurate with the conditions prevailing in developed countries. Whether the firms wanted to or not there was pressure to reduce costs. Of course, the substitution of Mexican managers would only be possible if the substitutes could adequately discharge the increased responsibilities. This could only occur if the Mexican managers were learning and improving their skills.

On the basis of our research we created a stylized model (Figure 9.1) of the various stages that an MNC operation might go through as it matured and became more highly integrated with the regional economy. Our model groups the managers into five functional groups that, as a whole, encompass all the functional activities of a manufacturing operation, but which we can also regard as a possible series of stages in the evolution of Mexican enterprises. Moreover, our model creates a hierarchy of localization, in that

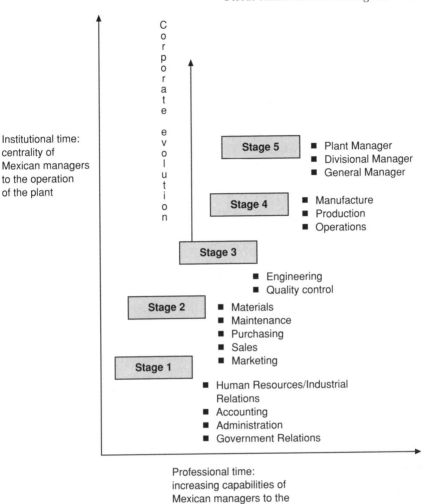

Figure 9.1 Evolution of the management functions in the maquiladoras.

as a typical factory matures indigenous managers occupy positions requiring higher skills. These stages are not necessarily deterministic in that one follows another inexorably or that the process inevitably follows one path. However, this does seem to be a generally consistent pattern. Finally, it is not necessarily the case – in fact, it seems unlikely – that one individual would advance through all these stages.

The first stage of functions is often referred to as "staff" positions and includes human resources, accounting, and administration. In this case, the tasks discharged are those of mediating between the foreign operation (the maquiladora) and the local social–institutional environment. Such managers manage the links to labor markets and local institutions, such as the government agencies. They are not involved in the value creation process within the operation. These managers concentrate on the administration of human resources and local administration such as payroll, administrative expense, fiscal obligations, and so on. The most simplified of these is the case in which an MNC contracts with a shelter-type company that essentially provides all of the services necessary to allow a foreign company to produce in Mexico. The MNC only needs to move its machines into the shelter company's building and begin producing. In essence, in stage 1 the Mexican managers provide fairly standardized and basic services to the MNC.

One human resources manager who began working in the maquiladoras industry in the 1970s described how he learned "the art of human resources" in this way:

> I developed a great intuition for managing people, because we had many discipline problems with these boys. In this situation what is necessary is to know how to control people, to the degree that when you put them in their place, when you scold them, they end up telling you thank you, thank you very much! That is a skill that they don't teach you in any school, and that is the key to success in this industry.

The administration of human resources and local accounting are certainly essential functions for the operation of the factory, as they establish the link with the local society. But their duties are peripheral to the manufacturing operations.

Stage 2 in our model is, in many ways, much more significant than stage 1 because it involves Mexican managers at the periphery of the actual production process. The materials managers are responsible for supervising inventories and the logistics of storing and delivering materials within the factory. The role of maintenance managers is to ensure that the equipment continues to operate well, and so requires technical training. The importance of these positions is that the incumbents learn about the actual operation of the factory, thus preparing them for movement to higher level and more responsible positions (equipment maintenance, process engineering, quality control, product engineering, and so on).

Stage 3 is where Mexican managers are hired as engineers. These technically trained Mexicans perform a wide variety of functions. Some are responsible for the organization of the lines of production, and some have control over the production process and/or the placement of equipment. Also, in some cases they have design responsibilities and oversee the development of new projects and instrumentation. This category also includes quality control managers responsible for developing quality control programs and inspection regimes. In some cases, they are also responsible for organizing quality control programs among suppliers. These positions are very important because they can be used by the individual as a step into management of the entire production process.

In any factory the most important line management position is the manager of manufacturing (in some plants this was called the operations or production manager). All the various functions such as quality control, engineering, and maintenance report to the manufacturing manager.

The highest position in the maquiladoras is the General Manager, with responsibility for the entire operation. Not only does the person in this position manage all the functions of the factory, he/she must also coordinate with headquarters. In effect, they are the on-site agents of the foreign corporate headquarters. This places them in the most powerful, yet most difficult, position because they must translate the policy of the foreign firm into an internal set of commands that all the other employees can perform. Simultaneously, they must manage production in Mexico while ensuring that corporate headquarters retains confidence in them.

This sequence can be described as a process of "transference" of management practices, as Beechler and Taylor (1994) put it, or else a "delegation" of authority, as Rosenfeldt and Ponthieu (1987) define it. This formulation of the process treats the indigenous managers as largely passive recipients, perhaps a useful way of thinking about it from a developed country perspective. However, from another perspective it can be seen as a learning process through which Mexican managers are absorbing and integrating foreign techniques into their management process.

Abo (1994), when discussing this, termed it a hybridization process. In this case, we are not claiming that the processes we are describing constitute "hybridization," as such, but we do feel that over time Mexican managers will acquire skills in management. Parenthetically, it should be noted that this process of appropriation is not entirely confined to individuals but also involves local organizations such as educational institutions and social–professional networks. Recent studies illustrate the crucial role played by local universities in providing education to managers and engineers (Hualde 1998; Vargas 1998). These institutions grew rapidly from 1980 and substantially adapted their career training programs in response to the maquiladoras and the demands for more professionals to undertake administrative and manufacturing tasks.

If the promotion of local management is conceived as a simple process of authority delegation, then it is made to appear as though headquarters always has the option of centralizing or decentralizing control functions. In this case, the dilemma is only one of deciding whether or not to send foreign managers or to contract local personnel. From this perspective, there are only calculations about contracting (or promoting) the local staff and the relative costs such as management salaries and the capacity to communicate with indigenous workers, which should be greater among the local managers.

From the host country perspective there should be a desire to accumulate technical, administrative, and management experience. From a societal perspective, the accumulated experience becomes a competitive factor in the professional labor market. For the locality, the maturation of a management layer and of a core of experienced engineers becomes a collective advantage that operates as a regional resource.

The formation of a local professional skill base depends upon an evolution in responsibility from the more peripheral administrative functions (administration of human resources and so on) to the more central functions located in production. The most direct and effective source in these industrial learning activities is, usually, the professional trajectory of the managers. In our interviews, three methods of learning that crystallized the managers' experiences were mentioned most frequently. The first was training received in other factories outside of Mexico. Another, even deeper, level of learning can come when the manager is actually involved in the transference of local operations in plants from the USA to Mexico. The general manager of a maquiladora manufacturing medical equipment described his experiences:

> In that company I learned a lot about the administrative process; precisely about planning, organizing, control. But after I had the opportunity to be involved in the initiation of an operation from its beginning, and from there I developed what is my strength, what has made me strong in the job I have right now. That experience was starting from zero ... from having an empty building nothing more and then coordinating the purchase of materials, coordinating the contractors, then the engineers, the installation of equipment, etc.
>
> You have to remember that the closing of 6 plants in the United States created this company and gradually the different operations were brought here to Tijuana. They put me in charge of the foremost part of the process, in order to transfer the operation from California. I worked with an U.S. manager for about 3 or 4 months, learning the basics of manufacturing their products and the policy of the company. Then I had the opportunity to qualify for the management of the plant and bring the operation to Tijuana. It was very hard but things went well, and when I showed them that the process was completely installed, functioning, and providing the level of production six months ahead of schedule, then they asked for the preparation of another assignment of the operation. They sent me to Chicago to learn all over again the operation of another plant. And we did the same thing: when the operation was ready another person stayed in charge of that department and they asked me to travel a third time, now to Wisconsin, to bring a third operation, a third line of products.
>
> The last one was the most difficult operation, because it was a question of transferring a complete manufacturing process. We were to start with the transformation of raw materials, from the entrance of the crude barrels of silicon, the mixture of the catalysts, the process of extrusion, three different types of dies for attaching manual assembly components, the different processes of inspection and testing, the washing, and down to the packaging of the finished product.

The final powerful learning process is the result of the very common interfirm mobility of managers. This allows the managers to learn about diverse productive processes, organizational structures, and corporate cultures. These varied experiences mean that Mexican managers also learn to be flexible and to adjust to different situations.

It is interesting to note that the history of the factories and that of the region are interdependent with the personal biographies of the managers. Without capable Mexican managers it is much more difficult to implement advanced manufacturing processes because they require personnel capable of managing them. Conversely, the formation of these capabilities in a particular region depends on the acquisition of more responsibility and experience that comes from managing ever greater portions of the entire set of skills required in manufacturing. In effect, if the process is working successfully, there is a virtuous circle of greater learning leading to more challenging activities, which creates more learning.

Work-force and especially managerial learning are very important for localization. However, this is not to assert that other factors are of no importance. Clearly, decisions to locate production in developing countries are driven by labor and other costs. But after the initial transfer and as long as costs do not rise quickly, there is a distinct possibility that the operation in the developing country can upgrade to higher value-added activities. Often, these upgrading effects can actually be the unintended and unforeseen consequences of earlier arrangements.

In effect, the formation of a group of competent indigenous managers introduces new components into the corporate and regional social dynamics. Inside the factory local personnel displace foreign managers sent from headquarters. Externally, in the region they use – and by using develop – their own local social network for recruiting technical, professional, and administrative personnel and, in some cases, even substitute local suppliers and contract services for imports. In the wider "social world" of the industry the local staff engages in a network whose skills and values are defined by a transnational community of experts. In so far as local managers are involved in core production and administrative tasks, their professional network is expanded far beyond the region and the country. An intense communication flow is established using telephone, fax, and especially the Internet, since these local managers must interact on a daily basis with their counterparts and superiors in the USA, in Asia, or in Europe. Sklair (2001) argues that these social processes are part of the mechanisms through which the global system is diffused, promoting the expansion of the global capitalist culture.

Starting new companies

The previous section approached this learning process at the structural level of different managerial functions in a firm. Another perspective is to consider the development of individual career trajectories. Figure 9.2 indicates that

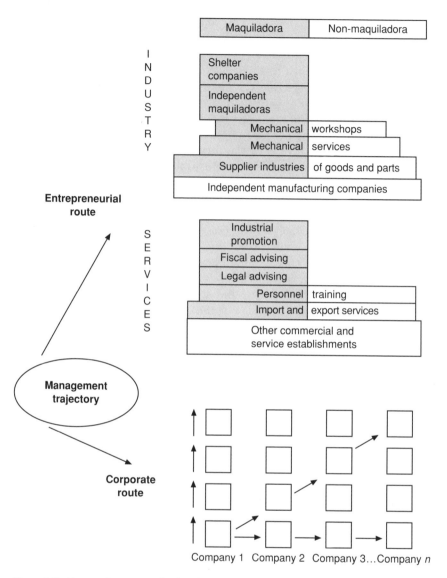

Figure 9.2 Alternative routes for local managers.

there are two potential trajectories for individuals. The first (the lower arrow) is for the manager to remain within a maquiladora and to try to ascend an internal job ladder, or to job-hop from firm to firm always improving his/her job position.

The other possibility is that the individual uses the accumulated learning process in order to establish a new firm. This is depicted in the upper part of the figure. It is clear that this level of utilization of the learning process involves moving more slowly than the promotion of Mexican managers to more responsible positions within actual MNCs. Nevertheless, our interviews show that there has been some movement on the part of Mexican managers to use the skills they learned in order to become entrepreneurs and especially to exploit the business opportunities opened up by the maquiladoras. Our data confirm the existence of a growing number of small and medium-size businesses emerging from the initiatives implemented by the managers and engineers of the maquiladoras. Some of these companies are also maquiladora plants that assemble or manufacture for foreign clients (in general, MNCs), established by ex-managers who acted to take advantage of their experience and their contacts in the maquiladoras.

Beyond shelter operations, there have been maquiladoras established by these managers that are usually small or medium-size factories dedicated to activities such as the assembly and subassembly of standardized parts or the remanufacture of electronic products. There are a few cases of firms that have been able to expand and diversify their client base. Interestingly, with the deepening investment, especially in the electrical and electronics assembly areas, some of the activities undertaken in the first phase of the maquiladora development have been abandoned by the MNCs. This has left niches to be filled, on a smaller scale, by these new local businesses.

The choice to become entrepreneurial was not always based on a rational, reasoned argument. In many cases it was a necessity forced upon the manager by the decline or the closure of the companies where they were working. One respondent described his decision:

> So it was that the operation left for China, and suddenly our programs faded, the factory continued working with about 15 operators, barely surviving. We [the engineers] had to leave to look for this type of idea, that is, to look for clients to establish our own operation. We had conversations with a Japanese company and with a North American one with whom we had had contact when we were making products for them. And it's that once you have learned the work, the structure, and the organization of a plant, and above all considering the team of engineers that we had there ... we could have done almost anything.

In other cases, the decision was more proactive as some of the new companies were the result of a plan developed over several years that was based on the managers' own expectations for their personal and professional development.

In addition to manufacturing operations, there is a wide range of what could be termed white-collar service activities that have been established by the local agents to provide various services to the foreign operations.

In the industrial area, in addition to the shelter-type companies and independent maquiladoras, activities such as the repairing of industrial machinery and supplying fixtures have developed. Although these activities have existed almost since the initiation of maquiladora operations, for some shops providing such services to the maquiladoras has became the main source of business. Ultimately, several of them have evolved into modern factories capable of producing original designs. Once the capacity to respond in terms of quality and punctual delivery is demonstrated, these companies are able to expand their market.

Industrial maintenance is another area in which Mexican suppliers have developed in response to the growth of the maquiladoras, although their activities are confined to peripheral areas. Given the complexity and high cost of machinery involved, the critical maintenance services are usually controlled by the machinery manufacturer.

In addition to traditional local producers (packaging, assembly materials) linked to the maquiladoras since the beginning of the operations, in recent years some high-technology, small and medium-size enterprises (SMEs) have appeared – dedicated, for example, to the design and manufacture of automation equipment, testing equipment, and industrial robots. Here again, the number of SMEs is small but increasing. At one of these companies, established by a young ex-manager of a television firm, we found that the plant employed more than thirty people (two-thirds of them engineers) and all its products were manufactured from original designs. Among the main clients of the firm was the young manager's previous employer, in addition to a number of the large television and auto-parts plants in the region.

Other start-ups have been established in areas such as plastic injection, molded parts, and the manufacture of electronic and electric equipment. However, the most frequent new start-ups have been established to provide a wide range of services such as industrial promotion, legal and fiscal advising, computer, cafeteria management, janitorial, import/export, and training services.

Conclusion

This exploratory study allows us to form some preliminary conclusions concerning the accumulation of capabilities by Mexican managers. The steady expansion of the maquiladoras has provided the environment in which a cadre of local managers experienced in managing factories has formed. On the basis of the interviews we developed an idealized stage model in which Mexican participation in management began in peripheral administrative areas largely linked to interfacing with the local environment. Later, the areas under the control of the local staff gradually expanded, and these staff gained responsibility for the more strategic functions related to engineering and production. This was the outcome of a process of learning-by-doing and it also fostered performance-based trust at headquarters. In this sense there was a double-loop learning process. While Mexican managers learned and broadened their understanding, headquarters also learned of what the Mexican managers were capable. In the process, the managers accreted more voice in the decisions made by headquarters. This enabled local managers and engineers to propose initiatives to headquarters and to develop a voice in corporate policy-making. Although this learning translated into transnational intrafirm capital at the national and global level, at the local level the skills and experiences of these managers provided the basis for an accumulation of valuable regional knowledge and skill capabilities. The ability to tap these intellectual resources became a positive externality in the environment and attracted yet other manufacturing operations. Put differently, their competence became an attribute of the locality or industrial region.

The relationship between MNCs and their local agents expresses itself in learning on three different levels. First, if the factory is successful, then it will undergo a gradual process of upgrading in which advanced manufacturing processes are introduced. This requires investment in management. Second, of special importance is the gradual transference of the direct line responsibilities from expatriates to indigenous engineers and managers. In a factory environment the production control is the critical issue. Third, providing that costs remain favorable, the availability of competent local staff (i.e. managerial resources) provides more incentive for the MNC to establish even more advanced and high value-added operations in the region. The creation of human resources capable of managing manufacturing operations and interfacing with the overseas headquarters' operations lowers the cost and risk of establishing yet other plants in the region. Thus, the emergence of a cadre of managers and engineers becomes an anchor indigenizing the industry.

The consolidation of a solid core of technical and organizational expertise in the local agents and their incorporation into the central functions of control at the plant level supposes an expansion of the decision space exercised locally. Through time, these managers can evolve from rather passive executors of directions given by expatriates and corporate headquarters to actors with some degrees of freedom and even an ability to affect the policy decisions at headquarters. This does not deny the fact that the reason for locating these plant in Mexico is predicated upon the global strategies of the MNCs. Certainly, if the economics of the operation changed dramatically, these processes would be vulnerable. However, in economic terms, the capable cadre of managerial employees created by the operation becomes an asset that lowers the cost of operations rather than seeking an entirely new location.

There was another more tentative process, which we observed anecdotally. This was the emergence of local Mexican-owned businesses incorporated into the supply chain of the MNCs. With respect to the Mexican maquiladoras this observation is novel, although it has occurred previously in various Asian countries, particularly Taiwan and Singapore and also, more recently, in Malaysia (for Taiwan, see Lam 1992; Kuo 1995; Kenney and Lowe 1999; for Singapore, see McKendrick *et al.* 2000; for Malaysia, see Rasiah 1995). The individuals most able to establish this linkage are the managers and engineers of the maquiladora plants, who, through their learning-by-doing in these factories, have a much clearer understanding of what is needed and – just as important – they have the connections in these operations to be able to secure contracts. In Mexico this process is still incipient and sporadic. Put differently, in contrast to some Asian countries, especially Taiwan, Mexico has not yet taken full advantage of the potential. Although this study did not directly examine the blockages to the formation of new firms in order to take advantage of the maquiladora investments by the MNCs, there is every indication that the institutional environment is not totally conducive to such venturing and so the important benefits it might bestow on the Mexican economy are incomplete.

This study was exploratory in nature, but there were significant results worthy of further study. First, we developed a stage model of the deepening of Mexican managerial responsibility and competence in the maquiladoras. Further research on the history of the devolution of managerial positions to Mexicans in firms would pay large dividends. Second, we identified the spectrum of functional opportunities that skilled Mexican managers have available for indigenization and entrepreneurial activities. Here again, there are substantial opportunities for further research. Third, we identified the local managers of foreign MNC operations as a class of actors worthy of study in their own right. For the most part, this class of employees has been ignored by the international development literature, by business studies interested in MNC investment, and, most important, by government policy-makers considering how to maximize the benefits of MNC production in their countries

Note

1 This chapter is based on a project funded by the Mexico–United States Foundation for Science. Oscar Contreras would like to thank the Center for US–Mexican Studies of the University of California, San Diego, for research support.

10 Punk and globalization

Mexico City and Toronto

Alan O'Connor

Most people know that there is a dispute about the origin of punk in the 1970s: about whether it started in New York or in London. But what about punk in places such as Mexico City and Toronto? What are the conduits by which punk and hardcore travel? Is it an example of cultural globalization or is punk itself shaped by Canadian and Mexican social structure, institutions and culture?

It's 1994 and I'm staying with my friend Pedro in his family's home in Ciudad Neza, a working-class extension of Mexico City. Pedro had just washed his hair under an outside tap. He hears a street vendor outside the courtyard and hits me up for 1 peso to buy a prepared jelly dessert in a tub. I think Pedro might be hungry because we hadn't yet eaten any breakfast. But no, he pulls back the foil lid on the little plastic tub, scoops out the contents and smears it into his hair. Soon his mohawk is standing straight up and Pedro is ready for the day. But when I meet him about a week later he had cut his hair. The police had stopped him at night near his home and harassed him. He took their threats seriously enough to trim back his long hair and hide the rest under a baseball hat.

About 10 years earlier, I'm in Larry's Hideaway, then the centre of the Toronto punk scene. I lean against the wall sipping a beer and watching the bands playing. The place is fairly full and there's a kind of feeling here that I like: the way people dress, the energy of the bands. I sense that people are checking me out. There are some occasional sideways glances, not unfriendly. Yet I'm very conscious of being gay here. It's hard to separate the ordinary hesitation to accept someone new from what might be homophobia. Later I read in *Maximum Rock'n'Roll* that the hardcore scene depends on participation. 'If you're reading this then you're part of it', the columnist said. I was grateful for the invitation, but it took me several years more to find a way of actually participating beyond occasionally buying records and zines (magazines).

How do we study culture in the global age? What I am suggesting here is a method based on multisite ethnography. That is, studying punk as it exists in the 1990s in both Mexico City and Toronto. And also recognizing that the movement exists not only in different sites but as a network of zines, do-it-yourself (DIY) record labels and venues: a shifting network exemplified by the band on tour. Ethnography, as I understand it, means creating relationships with people, relationships filled with all of the ordinary ambiguities, difficulties and pleasures of friendships. The difficulty is: how to write about such relationships. It is not only a matter of research ethics and sensitivity to political situations. The hard part is to find a way of writing. This is not only a matter of being responsible to people, but also a matter of situating relationships, scenes and cities in a global context. No anthropologist imagines that people live in isolated villages. All communities exist in complex relationships with larger systems and these world historical connections are not directly knowable (Marcus and Fischer 1986: 77–110). Social science and statistics can give some sense of the larger system. But ultimately there is a need for theory, for ideas about complex global systems in which communities and scenes are to be located by the ethnographer. And theory is never certain, not least because the future is never fully predictable.

El Tianguis del Chopo and Who's Emma

Every Saturday huge crowds of kids descend on an open-air market near the railway station in Mexico City. There's nothing unusual about that. Street markets are a ubiquitous part of life in Mexico, places to buy everything from freshly squeezed orange juice to a new pair of shoes. But El Tianguis del Chopo is the place to come for music: heavy metal, reggae, punk, but above all for rock music. 'We have rock in English and rock in Spanish', says a sign in one booth. The crowded street is packed with two aisles of stalls covered in bright-blue plastic and each displays tapes, CDs, posters, magazines, T-shirts, patches, bracelets and necklaces. It is also a place to come to meet your friends, hang out and listen to the latest gossip. Skater kids rub shoulders with *heavies* (heavy rock fans) and the punk kids gather in large groups on the steps near the railway station, talking and kidding around.[1]

The *tianguis* is an institution that dates back to the period before the Spanish conquest in the sixteenth century. It is a temporary market (in this case weekly) but also an important social institution. There is something uniquely Mexican about El Chopo. The anthropologist Guillermo Bonfil describes this as the *México profundo* (the hidden or deep Mexico) and he argues (Bonfil 1996) that it is to be found in the cities as well as in rural communities. Bonfil helped to establish the Museum of Popular Culture in Mexico City, which has explored the idea of a *México profundo* in food (maize, chilli), popular speech (with influences from indigenous languages), music, popular dancing, wrestling, comic books and a traditional working-class neighbourhood in Mexico City. As one of Mexico's most respected anthropologists, Bonfil is well aware of regional and ethnic differences in Mexico. The *México profundo* is not an argument for a primordial culture or identity. It is an intervention in political debates about the Mexican nation. Against the official 'imagined community' of Mexico as a developing nation, against the values of global capitalism and NAFTA (the free trade agreement with the USA and Canada that came into effect in 1994), Bonfil makes a case for an indigenous social ecology. The case for a *México profundo* is a political intervention against the development project of Mexico's ruling élite. Bonfil argues that municipalities should have the political freedom to choose which foreign elements to adopt and which to reject.

The Tianguis del Chopo has been a site of struggle. It started at El Chopo Museum, which is operated by UNAM (Mexico's largest university), in a working-class shopping area of downtown Mexico City. The small museum with its modernist cast-iron exterior had been famous with generations of Mexican children for its dinosaur skeleton. Starting in the early 1980s the museum changed its focus and new staff were hired to organize art shows, courses and other cultural events. As the punks tell the story, while the museum staged a punk-related exhibit in 1980, vendors set up in the street outside. There were punk shows inside the museum itself. Local residents and businesses complained and the market was moved, eventually ending up at its present site on a quiet street near the railway station. In the early years the market was frequently raided by police on the pretext that they were looking for drugs. The Mexican state is nervous about rock music and concerts are heavily policed. But the *tianguis* also had to struggle with commercialization. After 20 years of existence it is well organized (with its own security) and punk is only a very small part of its activities. It is even listed in hip travel guides such as the Berkeley students' handbook *Mexico on the Loose* (Tyler and Miller 1994: 86). Nonetheless it is still an important social space for punks. They arrive in late afternoon when the market is beginning to die down and visit the small number of punk booths for information on shows. They may share *pulque* or beer in one of the small bars on the street or leave in groups for a show in some remote *barrio*. These kinds of struggles over public culture are typical of Mexican political culture today.

Who's Emma opened in Toronto in the summer of 1996. The punk volunteer-run storefront is located on a side street in Kensington Market and sells records, zines and books. You can also get coffee and vegan cakes. The picnic table outside is a popular place to hang out. The store is run by a volunteer collective and is named after the anarchist Emma Goldman, who lived on a nearby street in the 1920s and 1930s after she lost her US citizenship (Donegan 1985: 124). At that time, the market was a working-class Jewish neighbourhood. Today, the synagogues are almost empty. The next wave of emigrants were from Portugal and the area became a fruit and vegetable market with bars and restaurants and other stores catering for hard-working Portuguese immigrant families. Chinatown is edging into the market and some of the fruit and vegetable shops are now operated by Asian–Canadian families. Newer waves of immigrants operating small businesses are here too: West Indian, Mexican and Iranian. In many ways, the market is a microcosm of Canadian society: the indigenous presence pushed aside and a history of layers of immigrants. Kensington Market has also been home to Toronto punks since the 1980s.

I was one of the people who started Who's Emma (O'Connor 1999). The volunteer structure was very much based on my experience as a gay activist in the 1980s. It was an open collective: anyone was free to join. As well as doing a weekly shift of 4 hours in the store, volunteers could choose to join working groups that ordered records, books or zines. Other groups took care of finances and educational workshops. Each of the working groups was accountable to a monthly general meeting. Decisions were taken by consensus, with the role of facilitator rotating among the group and every second general meeting was facilitated by a woman. Although based in 1990s punk and hardcore, Who's Emma attempted to welcome people who didn't have much knowledge about bands. We also had feminist books, posters and women's bands on special display and from the beginning the store was operated only by women on Mondays.

As the project emerged in the first year the practical working activities fell into place quite nicely. The store was open 7 days a week and people did their shifts conscientiously. Books and records were ordered and we seemed to be selling enough material to cover the store expenses (but nothing else). We had workshops on silk-screening, operating a sound system at a club, promoting a show and political topics such as MOVE (the Black-American movement). Our library and infoshop never really got going, although our notice-boards were always full and leaflets left in the window were invariably picked up by people. The difficulties with Who's Emma had to do with the tension between hardcore kids who were mainly interested in music and others who had anarchist and feminist politics. When it came to practical decisions such as whether to increase the mark-up on records we had no problem in taking decisions. But on political matters it proved impossible to reach a consensus. The group would split on predictable lines between punks and anarchists. The most difficult issue during the first year was whether to stock straight edge bands that are in opposition to abortion. Many women and the anarchist punks didn't want to sell these records. But less political punks saw this as an attack on punk music and freedom of expression. The major problem during the first year of Who's Emma was that we were completely unable to reach a consensus on this issue.

La tocada/the show

In both cities, the show (*la tocada*) is the central collective expression of hardcore culture. To be a punk means to go to shows – and in Mexico to participate in *el slam*. In Toronto and Mexico City the entrance charge is low and commercialization of the scene is energetically resisted. Bands that demand guarantees and seek to make money from the scene are strongly disliked. Promoters are expected to cover their costs but not to profit personally from putting on shows. Bands and promoters gain respect and popularity for their efforts. It is a system of mutual aid that has as its aim the creation of a strong scene.

It's July 1994 and there is a show in a well-established but poor *barrio* built on hills to the south of Mexico City. I go by the metro and then by bus with a 16-year-old Mexican punk kid who is presently living on the streets. The show is on a flat piece of ground, like a small basketball court, beside a house. It has an earth floor, and a tarpaulin (tarp) protects the equipment and part of the audience from the afternoon rain. There are about 150 punks at this show and the entrance fee is N$12 (about US$3.50). It is collected at a narrow entrance. Bands receive food and travel money only. The public address (PA) system is good. At shows like this all the bands usually share the same equipment. There's one drum kit, one bass amplifier (amp) and one guitar amp. Most bands even share the same electric guitar and bass. Among the bands Desviados are very popular. They make me think of punk in London in 1977 – they even have a 'No future' song: 'No hay futuro, no hay solución'. I like Ley Rota (broken law), who are crazy punks and play good fast songs. Vomito Nuclear and Estrudo play fast generic hardcore (punk music played fast and loud). There are lots of political statements and lyrics. Songs are about school, unemployment, the police and the military – there is even one funny song about Christmas.

This show is in a very remote *barrio*. Some people pool their money and buy industrial alcohol, which they dilute with bottled fruit drinks. Others stick to beer, also bought in a nearby general shop. There is quite a bit of glue sniffing. A young punk woman reads out a letter about somebody who was attacked last week. Many people sign. She asks me to sign even though I'm not Mexican. Luis approaches me and we have a conversation about punk in Mexico and in Canada. He a bit older than most people here, plays in his own band and takes courses in social science and politics at the university, where there are no tuition fees. Then he takes me around and introduces me to a lot of people. One is an Afro-Caribbean man who lived for a while in Montreal and who speaks perfect English. 'Now you know everyone', Luis says. This would never happen at a show in Canada. Mexican punks don't applaud but make an energetic pit or *el slam* (part of the stage where everyone dances together) for bands they like. As the show builds up steam, a vigorous pit happens with bodies and elbows flying. It goes in a circle and speeds up and increases force with the pace of the song. No women participate and neither do I. Luis teases me about this. 'Are you a punk or not?' he says. Canadian punks don't often make pits like this anymore. This is like California in the mid-1980s. The late afternoon turns into early evening and I look out from under the tarp at the flickering lights of the small houses built on the surrounding hills.

Many shows in Toronto take place in the suburbs, where the scene is contemporary hardcore. Shows in downtown Toronto are usually in clubs or restaurants and the scene is more punk: people have weird hair, dress in black with spikes or patches. It is more of a drinking scene. A hardcore show in the suburbs is held in a rented hall, a gym at the YMCA (Young Men's Christian Association) or the basement of the United Church. These spaces have to be negotiated (having parents on the church committee helps) and the rent of $250 for the evening is not cheap. In addition, you need a PA system. Either the space has one or you rent it or acquire it through benefit shows. This is a temporary space, negotiated and supervised. No drinking or smoking is allowed. The space can easily be lost because of graffiti in the washroom or if someone is caught smoking a joint outside. But in general this is a young and non-drinking crowd. Many are straight edge. The style is more skater than classic punk. Most people dress in loose pants and oversized T-shirts with underground band logos or a political message (often vegan). Sometimes people wear service job shirts (not their own). There are a lot of wallet chains, some stylishly long. Hair is usually short, sometimes bleached, rarely dyed. Jeans, leather boots, mohawk hair and T-shirts for bands like the Sex Pistols are not what this scene is about.

At the entrance there is a table staffed by friends of the kid who is putting on the show. You pay and get your hand marked. It's usually $5 unless there is a justifiable reason (such as several touring bands to pay). Promoters are not allowed to make money from shows. Local bands might expect $50–100 and touring bands $100–200 from a successful show. Sometimes bands get a lot less. There are no agreed fees or guarantees and no written contracts. The system works on trust. Around the hall there are tables where bands sell their tapes and records. They might have home- made silk-screened T-shirts and patches. The T-shirts are often recycled, bought by the pound from goodwill stores. There might be an animal rights table or an Anti Racist Action information table. Sometimes, Who's Emma will set up a table with records and books from its storefront. A big black Who's Emma banner is taped to the wall.

There are five bands to play. They are almost all boys, aged 17–23 years and mainly white. The audience is mostly white too. Some of the bands have expensive electronic equipment: drum kits costing $3,000 are not unheard of. Between sets each band takes down and sets up its own equipment. Occasionally, a band will lend another a bass amp or drum kit, but this is something that results in special thanks: 'We'd like to thank Ian for putting on the show and Shotmaker for letting us use their drums'. Broken strings during a performance do result in mutual aid. 'Does anybody have a spare string? This will just be a minute'. A successful show requires popular local bands. Touring bands do not draw a crowd unless they are very well known but they get paid more to cover their travel costs. The audience mostly consists of boys (perhaps 80 per cent) and they are very young. There is only a handful of people over 25 years old. The band plays on the floor right in front of the audience and is expected to mix with people before and after their set. Mostly the audience stands still, moving their bodies a little to the music. Sometimes there may be a small pit of faster dancers but 'moshing' (mass dancing) is looked down on. That's what people do in music videos or at commercial rock concerts. There is a high value on safety and respecting other people's space. Everyone has the right to enjoy himself or herself. The scene turns over rapidly.

After two or three years one suburban school crowd replaces another. The faces change.

Bands play quite loud. Quite a few band members and some of the crowd use brightly coloured earplugs to reduce the decibel damage. Bands tend to sound fairly similar, following a limited number of styles. At any show there may be one or two good bands out of five or six. Bands may have limited musicianship, with not enough practice behind them or they be too similar to others. Lyrics are most often poetic and vague. This is the land of Emo, a subgenre initiated by bands such as Rites of Spring and Fugazi in Washington, DC. Where lyrics are political they usually work along well-worn themes: animal rights, against rape, against violence. Shows are sometimes benefits, e.g. for a women's shelter (probably the most popular cause), animal rights, anti-racism, a community centre or Food Not Bombs. However, most never move beyond this to engage with a more explicit kind of politics. There are never benefits in support of striking workers, political prisoners or socialist or anarchist organizations. Friends often hug on meeting each other. This includes boys and so there is a fairly conscious progressive gender politics at work here. But there are few queer boys who are out and they almost never find boyfriends in this scene. The hugs and greetings have an emotional importance. Sometimes one hears of an absent emotional life at home: divorced or busy parents, lack of communication and understanding or hurtful remarks from siblings.

Two recordings: Massacre and Shotmaker

In North American hardcore today a band will typically release a 7" record. They either do it themselves or a tiny label, often run by a friend, puts it out. The records are sold at $3 each, mainly at shows but also through mail order and swaps with other small labels. The label pays the band in terms of records, which they can then sell at shows. A first pressing usually consists of 1,000 copies and it is not difficult to sell this number of records in the underground. A second pressing makes more money. Bands do sometimes issue demonstration tapes, but a 7" record followed eventually by a 12" album is the typical pattern. In Mexico this is not possible. Bands usually issue cassettes.

The Mexican band Massacre has a cassette issued by the Mexico City record store Rock and Rollo Circus. The dedication reads:

> This disc is dedicated to all the victims who fell on 2nd of October 1968 in the Plaza of Three Cultures. To all persons who are disappeared, who are tortured for their libertarian principles. To prisoners of conscience who are imprisoned under false pretexts. To workers and campesinos who day after day are exploited. To the students ... and all those who seek liberty.

The song titles are equally political:

Side 1	*Side 2*
One day in Peking	We do not agree
So many days, so many years	Victims of vice
Rotten system	Corrupt police
National army	Misery
Capitalist crime	Elections
Tortures	Them or us
Massacre 68	Damned candidates

Massacre's sound is fast hardcore. The drums beat a rapid steady rhythm, with some changes in tempo. Guitars and bass are simple and fast. The voice is slightly grating but the lyrics are clearly audible. The sound is straightforward and enjoyable: quite typical of what one hears at punk shows in Mexico City. Here are the lyrics to one of their songs – 'Corrupt police':

> (No more police, no more repression)
>
> Corrupt police
> Thieves and assassins
> They believe they have the right
> To abuse my person
> They are nothing more than ignorant
> And have their dreams of grandeur
>
> No to corrupt police!
>
> They are really dirty and repugnant
> Loathsome like a rat
> With their shitty corporation
> Controlled by the state
> They disperse the people
> Who demonstrate against 'the government'
>
> No to corrupt police
>
> (No more police, no more repression)

Not all Mexican bands are this political. Not all sound exactly like this. But it is fair to take this as a typical example of Mexican City hardcore.

Meanwhile in North America and Canada punk has developed into several different musical subgenres and scenes (O'Hara 1995; Lahickey 1997; Profane Existence 1997). With the influence of bands such as Fugazi, some bands have slowed down, have become more musically complex and write vague personal lyrics. Perhaps the distinctive characteristic of Emo is that songs have several different tempos. Slow parts suddenly crash into fast and heavy rhythms. While the gender politics of mainly boys singing about emotions (hence the name Emo) is interesting, women have said that their personal issues are seldom expressed in this scene. Another subgenre is straight edge (a musical genre and lifestyle which rejects such temptations as alcohol and drugs). The sound is often influenced by heavy metal and the rhythms are composed to encourage vigorous mosh pits. These are sometimes quite violent. Most people in this scene are vegetarian and vegan and support animal rights. But this can result in an emphasis on purity. Straight edge bands can be conservative and nationalistic. Some are opposed to abortion. An important minority of those associated with this scene is involved in the Hare Krishna movement. Punk in North America has changed and evolved both musically and in terms of its politics. One cannot assume that it is articulated with respect to radical or anarchist positions. Many bands support animal rights. Some try to have feminist positions. Many subscribe to DIY ethics, but others have no problem with major labels. In general, punk has difficulty moving beyond lifestyle politics.

It is more difficult to choose a single Toronto band as typical of the scene. The scene is more diverse than in Mexico City where punks have great difficulty understanding what Emo is about. The band that I have chosen is not strictly from Toronto. It was based in Belleville and Ottawa but had very close links to the Toronto scene. This usefully introduces the idea of a network that is not based in only one locality. The band Shotmaker had many friends in Toronto and played there often. Its first 7" record was put out by someone in Toronto who played an important role in the punk scene in the city. Shotmaker is Emo. The sound has moved away from Massacre's fast, straight-ahead hardcore. Songs are complex and layered. There are changes in tempo from slow and melodic to fast and driving. The band was a threesome with the musical direction coming more from the guitarist, who mainly played chords, but melodic lines were also evident in some slower sections of songs. The drum parts were solid rock drumming at a fast tempo with the almost continual use of cymbals to create a drum wall of sound. Slower sections often have a simple rhythm on the high hat. The bass provides melodic lines and is almost buried in the recorded sound mix. The vocals usually involve a single young male voice – a distressed shout. There are occasional back-up vocals from the drummer. The recorded sound is tight – too rough to be indie rock – but some of the songs are quite melodic. Here are the lyrics of one song ('Security') from their album *The Crayon Club*, issued on vinyl by a small but well-organized punk label in Ottawa.

> I know for what reason. i know for what
> reason. it's not a matter of black or white.
> it's only shades of grey. i know, i know. i
> see, i see. we all need security.

The allusive lyrics seem to refer to some unstated emotional issues: 'it's not a matter of black or white: we all need security'. This is clearly quite different from the public and political subject matter of Massacre. In fact, a song like this is quite unimaginable in Mexican hardcore.

Global networks: Los Crudos on tour

It is not clear that postmodern theories of global flows (Appadurai 1996a) are needed in order to explain how punk travels around the globe. Punk is an international movement and the conduits are fairly obvious. Zines such as *Profane Existence* almost always have articles on scenes in various countries and lists of contact addresses. Records and tapes are sent in the mail. Punks are great letter writers and travellers. Visitors are generally welcomed and often helped with meals and places to stay. There are occasional international gatherings such as the 'Encuentro Punk' in Uruguay in January 1998 that attracted participants from Mexico and the USA. But probably the most important contacts are through bands on tour.

The Chicago-based band Los Crudos toured Mexico in 1994. The band is very popular in both the 'crusty' and Emo/straight edge scenes in North America. They play fast energetic hardcore and their lyrics are all in Spanish. The singer is a Latin American teacher and photographer and the bass player and guitarist are Mexican. In part, because the songs are in Spanish, the singer developed a breathless style of speaking after every few songs in order to explain what the songs are about. Their best-known song is 'Asesinos', which speaks about the disappearances of radical youth during military dictatorships in Latin America. Los Crudos's first show in Mexico City was on 12 July 1994 and was advertised by a very small number of posters in El Chopo and by word of mouth. The show was on the outskirts of the city, a long bus ride from the La Paz metro station. It was organized by anarchist punks and was a benefit for the Zapatista convention in Chiapas to be held in August. Most people paid in bags of rice and bars of soap for the convention. The show was in a basketball court and the entrance was only opened wide enough for one person to squeeze in at a time. There was a quick body check. Once inside, there were several large anarchist banners on the walls and an information table. One woman had a questionnaire for youth enquiring about what issues concerned this group with respect to the Zapatista convention (for example, the issues of compulsory military service). There were about 100 punks at 4.30 p.m., and later about 250. It rained as usual in the afternoon and a large tarp kept the PA system and guitar amplifiers dry. It seemed to be an open stage for whatever bands wanted to play. Unlike North American shows, all the bands shared the same equipment and drum kit. Everyone used the same electric guitar and bass. The audience stood expressionless for the Mexican bands but started a vigorous pit when Los Crudos performed. Mexican punks do this for bands they like. They knew the words of the songs from the first 7" record. Musically, Los Crudos were noticeably tighter than the local bands, which were mainly straight-ahead fast hardcore. All the bands were highly political in their introductions and their songs. However, some people in the audience were restless with the Los Crudos singer's political monologues. They wanted to dance. Overall this was a well-organized show and political event. The young organizers had arranged not only the space and the equipment but also political information, leaflets and vegetarian food. Many people left after Los Crudos finished. It was getting late and was about to rain again. Many people faced a long journey home across the city.

Los Crudos was enormously popular in Mexico. Its largest show was organized by a Mexican promoter and advertised by huge posters pasted on the walls of the El Chopo market. There was some controversy because the admission was N$30 (about US$9), whereas the usual admission to punk shows was N$10. Many kids could not afford the 30 pesos. When Los Crudos realized what was happening they negotiated with the promoter to lower the price. The show was on a Sunday afternoon in the large ex-Olympic swimming pool building and required a fairly large PA system. Many of the bands playing had been around for many years and some were criticized for attempting to make money from the scene. What happened on the day of the show was that at the start people were charged N$30. But after about 300 people had paid that price and several bands had played, the price was lowered to N$20 and at about 3:30 p.m. to N$10. A large group of more political punks held out on principle until it reached N$10 and only then entered. Then we heard Desviados and my friend Pedro jumped up on stage and sang into the microphone for their song 'No hay futuro, no hay solución'. The next band was unpopular because it was too commercial. The criticism was less about its sound than that it was trying to make money from punk. A very cool anarchist punk band played with an energetic but rudimentary sound. When Los Crudos finally played, the band didn't go over as well as at the small shows it had done. There was barely a murmur for an encore and fewer than half of those present participated in the slam. There was the usual impatience from some people with the singer's political statements and a broken string interrupted the show until it was replaced. Many people here at this big show wanted fast music and a good time. Los Crudos was paid almost nothing for playing. It would seem that the promoter made quite a bit.

Punk in the 1990s: local scenes and global networks

Punk exists in the from of local 'scenes' in different cities and as networks that extend beyond the local.[2] Writing about global cities, Eade *et al*. (1997a) stress that community extends beyond locality. For example, people who live in Toronto may have significant links with the Caribbean. In turn, Toronto hosts a major Caribbean music festival each year that attracts tens of thousands of visitors from the islands. This type of space–time compression is certainly the case for punk with international conduits formed by zines, record distribution, letters, travel and touring bands. Most parts of the punk scene (but not all) have little interest in the nation-state and welcome contacts with punks in different parts of the world. The contemporary hardcore scene is a good example of a global movement.

But the different aspects of globalization do not mean the erasure of the social. The multisite ethnography proposed here examines contemporary punk and finds that it is articulated differently in Mexico City and in Toronto. Each scene is not self-contained locally. The band Shotmaker does not strictly speaking come from Toronto. Los Crudos is a good example of the cultural dimensions of globalization, both in Chicago and on tour in Mexico. Yet at the same time the scenes in Toronto and Mexico City are articulated according to social and political patterns that need to be theorized differently. Punk in Mexico City is obviously not a matter of US cultural imperialism. The argument made here for the Mexican scene is that proposed by Bonfil (1996) in *México Profundo*. There may be an element of romanticism in this, but it is not in any way an appeal to a primordial Mexican identity. Bonfil's work is clearly a political intervention into debates about Mexico as imagined community. He argues strongly against the image of Mexico as a 'developed' nation, against the political and economic project of the Mexican élite. His invented phrase is now used quite widely in Mexico. However paradoxical it may seem, my argument is that Mexican punk patterns itself after the *México Profundo*. The ethnographic evidence clearly shows a politics that is against the state and its development project and that demonstrates strong support for the issues raised by the Zapatista uprising in 1994. It would be reductionist to argue that practices such as low admission charges and shared equipment at shows are explained only by poverty and a lack of resources. Mutual aid and disapproval of personal gain are central to the subculture.

Whereas punk in Mexico City is involved (in complex ways) with the Tianguis del Chopo, in Toronto we find an example of a North American and European punk infoshop. Who's Emma locates itself in anarchist history (near to the street where Emma Goldman lived) but is also situated in a market area shaped by generations of different immigrants to Canada. To some extent, Who's Emma had to negotiate its space within a declining Portuguese neighbourhood. The politics of Mexican punk is explicitly against the state and the ruling political party. Even bands that have little actual political motivation sing songs about police brutality. The politics of the punk scene in Toronto is much more ambiguous. Only a minority of the Toronto hardcore scene is anarchist. Issues of identity politics (such as feminism and access to abortion) are not completely absent from the Mexican scene, but tend to be the central issues in Canada and the USA.

In the North the punk scene has evolved both musically and in terms of different subscenes: especially the difference between 'crusty' punks, who drink and so on and who may be involved in the street, and the more suburban Emo and straight edge scenes. In Mexico City this kind of evolution has not happened. Mexican punks simply cannot understand the Emo phenomenon. For them punk has to be musically fast, heavy and straightforward. Their style of dress is more 'classic' punk with black jeans and jackets covered in silk-screened patches. And the Mexican *slam* would have been typical of California in 1985: fast, aggressive with elbows and bodies flying. This type of dance is frowned upon in many (but not all) parts of the North American punk scene. It is a matter of intense debate, but in Toronto the Mexican slam would be regarded by many punks as inauthentic (copying the 'mosh pits' in commercial music videos) and as macho, and as an unsafe space for women.

We do not need to adhere to outdated notions of local culture in order to find evidence of social structure and political struggles. Punk scenes reach out to globalizing networks but also have their own patterns. Los Crudos on tour in Mexico offers an excellent image of these networks. Yet another band (for example, one singing in English rather than in Spanish) would not have had the same reception. And however popular Los Crudos is in Mexico, it also had to negotiate its relationship with the scene there. The consequences of globalization call for new ways of thinking about musical scenes, new ways of doing ethnography. Although this remains worth doing, such attempts need to resist the generalizing versions of modernity and globalization that are often found in cultural studies if they are to provide a genuine ethnography of hidden musical worlds.

Notes

1 There is an interesting description of El Chopo in Martínez (1992: 148–64), although the scene he describes is Mexican indie rock and not punk. For the history of El Chopo, see Pantoja (1996).

2 In his study of youth gangs in Tijuana, Valenzuela (1988) argues that punks are much less tied to their local *barrio* than *cholo* youth. Nonetheless, many punks do live with their families, much harassment from police happens near home, shows depend on local contacts to secure a hall or basketball court and there is a large punk scene in Ciudad Neza, an extension of Mexico City with high youth unemployment. The punk use of space in Mexico City goes against the grain of the pattern described by Canclini and Piccini (1993), in which because of economic crisis and pressures of life in a big city many people retreat to their home, television, radio and recorded music.

11 Navigations

Visual identities and the Pacific cultural subject

Elizabeth Grierson

Part of our cultural survival is doing our art. If we don't, then we are lost. We are lost in another country, without an identity.

(Feu'u 1999)

Visual images, objects and artefacts have a significant role in the constitution and shaping of cultural identities. This essay engages with the politics of signification in visual practices of colonial and post-colonial discourses in Pacific locations. The speaking position of Pacific Islands' artists in a recent Auckland art event, Navigating Pacific Art in the Present – Testing Traditions: Pacific Sculpture Symposium (3–13 March 1998), is juxtaposed against an analysis of representations of Pacific 'otherness' in conditions of modernity. Two discourses are situated – one *ao fo'ou ta* (new time), the other *ao taf ta* (time of light or colonial time)[1] – in which the practices of art and education prescribe and confirm value. At this time of the millennium when pasts and futures become the topic for concerned reflection, it seems appropriate that visual significations of the 'Pacific cultural subject' might be appraised in terms of new political formations of place and identity.

Navigating Pacific Art in the Present – Testing Traditions: Pacific Sculpture Symposium was hosted by the Bachelor of Visual Arts degree students and staff at Auckland University of Technology (AUT; then Auckland Institute of Technology),[2] Aotearoa/New Zealand[3] and Tautai Contemporary Pacific Arts Trust, and was sponsored by Creative New Zealand.[4] The stated objectives of Tautai Pacific Arts Trust, which was founded in 1995 by Auckland-based Samoan artist Fatu Feu'u, are: 'to help establish the mana [status, prestige] of contemporary Pacific art; to promote contemporary Pacific art in New Zealand and abroad; to help with the education and support of emerging contemporary Pacific artists' (Tautai Contemporary Pacific Arts Trust 1998). With these objectives in mind the symposium was positioned within several institutional sites: the 'artworld' of an undergraduate degree programme; in the more formally prescribed institutional practices of New Zealand's largest Institute of Technology; and in the rhetorically inscribed 'global village' as a conceptualised space of cultural identity for institutional purpose and practice.

The aim of Navigating Pacific Art in the Present was to bring together Pacific Islands' artists, to 'test tradition' in Pacific art practices and to explore possibilities of new alignments of *Pasifika*[5] artist and educational communities.

Transnationalism marked the nature of cultural engagement in the symposium, with artists coming from a range of independent Pacific Islands and New Zealand territories and from countries such as Japan and Papua New Guinea, which reinforces the post-war identification of 'Pacific Rim' as a geopolitical entity. The heterogeneous mix drew attention to the many facets of Pacific arts and cultural forms and also enabled emergent possibilities of identity and community in the contexts of the migration of people, ideas and aesthetic practices across national and island borders.

The symposium called attention to an active dialogue between notions of 'traditional' and 'contemporary', with each artist linking past and present understandings of 'what it means to be a Pacific Islander living in New Zealand' (Tautai Contemporary Pacific Arts Trust 1998). The issue at stake here is one of reconceptualising and actively intervening in the notion of Pacific as unified 'other', a region framed and represented through dominant speaking positions of colonial discourse. New alignments today reframe the region through political and economic interests, particularly following the Korean and Vietnam wars and the events in East Timor, all of which reinforce Asia-Pacific's 'emergence as a security community', as discussed by Lim and Dissanayake (1999: 2). The symposium coincided with renewed attention being paid to place and identity of the Asia-Pacific region in major exhibitions such as Beyond the Future: The Third Asia-Pacific Triennial of Contemporary Art held at Queensland Art Gallery, Brisbane (9 September 1999 to 26 January 2000), and Bright Paradise: the 1st Auckland Triennial at New Gallery, Artspace, and The Kenneth Myers Centre, Auckland (3 March to 29 April 2001). The aim at such events is to re-identify the 'Pacific cultural subject' through contemporary art practices, marking the immense political and economic dislocations and realignments of the past decade in the Asia-Pacific region, whereby transnational encounters played out a kind of geopolitical identifying procedure.

New alignments

Symbolic narratives from *ao taf ta* (time of light) and *ao fo'ou ta* (new time) offer two different modalities of thought (see Hereniko 1994: 410–18). *Ao taf ta*, a colonial procedure, which defines identity as an essential formation of racial and cultural subjectivity; *ao fo'ou ta* engages cultural difference via the deconstruction of hierarchical categorising devices through opening the terrain of subjectivity to spaces of hybrid formation. The former practice depends upon binary significations of 'otherness' for its purchase whereby cultural identity is deemed to be a matter of original form, devoid of social or political contexts. The latter engages the politics of difference whereby ethnicity may be understood via a politic of location and enunciation. In conditions of globalisation the contemporary Pacific subject extends frontiers of identity to generate a kind of intersubjective hybridity (see Bhabha 1995) through transnational navigations of inventive practice.

A genealogy of representational practices in colonial discourses of art and literature discloses the constant repetition of the idea of navigation in the eighteenth and nineteenth centuries. Framing devices of the Empire's sustaining ideology were based in epistemological systems which the Empire itself canonised and instituted through political and social action as a watertight and normalised system of knowledge formation. Indigenous peoples were marked and measured through binary categorising devices and were rendered voiceless by unlocatable power operations whose parameters are always elsewhere, 'offshore' from 'here'. In that site of nowhere, their 'otherness' was cemented in a space beyond the frontiers of progressive positivism.

By contrast, an exciting, if sometimes uneasy, amalgam was created of institutional and non-institutional expectations at the Pacific Sculpture Symposium – which was a first for the Auckland Institute of Technology. In 1997, the Bachelor of Visual Arts programme, resources, students and staff moved across Auckland from the suburb of Ponsonby to the main institutional campus in the centre of Auckland city, interjecting contemporary art practices into the larger institutional setting. Visible, material, noisy, colourful, the Pacific Symposium could be interpreted as the first public announcement of the arrival of the Bachelor of Visual Arts on the Wellesley campus. In a rationally ordered world of institutional practices, contemporary arts may be deemed incommensurable with other forms of educational praxis such as studies in science and health or commerce and business, in that the latter are historically more predictable in a disciplinary sense. However, no longer were visual arts practices secreted in garrets of old buildings across town where, out of sight, they might gaze upon their own historical discourses. Now they were the stuff of public display, on the grassed and paved quadrangle fronting the main administration building, in the centre of Auckland's busiest business, cultural and university district.

Sites of conversation and interrogation offered a challenge to the notion of Pacific art as consumable tradition or stereotypical display. Negotiated settlements were reached as pragmatic needs rubbed against creative practices. AUT sculpture lecturer James Charlton (1998) explained that through the symposium art educators aimed to provide opportunities for art and design students 'to observe and participate in the evolution and revolution of Pacific Art forms' through which students could 'test their own traditions'. Institutional managers played out identifiable expectations for economic opportunities which might translate into competitive advantage while pressures to conform to disciplinary order were evident with 'noise disturbance ... the greatest source of complaint from within the institute' (White in Grierson 1999). Some academic managers were positive: 'The best thing we have ever seen here!' said one (personal comment, 1998), while others were less impressed: 'How will we ever return this grass to normal?' bemoaned the property division (personal comment, 1998). Beyond pragmatic considerations, equity was high on the political agenda of institutional rhetoric. It could be said that the university faced an instant historical transformation at the intersection of institutional and cultural practices with 'bits of log and chunks from huge, one tonne stones ... flying at AIT' (Auckland Institute of Technology 1998).

If the concept of a Pacific cultural event reinforces the popular idea of a unified Pacific stereotype as a geopolitical and cultural region, then the participating artists ensured that they moved well beyond such traditional stereotypes and laden myths – of either the 'noble savage' with his 'primitive carvings' or 'the happy islander' with her flowers and *lei*. The artists demanded that viewers engaged rather than gazed. Competing and contradictory voices oscillated in the artistic disruptions as the politics of difference played out their inscribing potential in the institutional setting. Bhabha (1995: 2) points to the contingent nature of such a procedure when he writes of the representation of difference, which 'must not be hastily read as the reflection of *pre-given* ethnic or cultural traits set in the fixed tablet of tradition'.

Throughout the symposium, theoretical issues surrounding the politics of construction and representation became more evident as inventive procedures materialised. The voices and practices of Pacific Islands' artists energised the institutional environment with diverse and creative expectations. Within the concept of one 'Pacific', many 'Pacifics' speak when Pacific arts and visual cultures are rescued from foundationalist accounts of modernity.

In a deliberate move away from 'the fixed tablet of tradition' (Tautai Contemporary Pacific Arts Trust 1998) the dedication of the *Tautai Trust* to siting Pacific Islands' art within mainstream spaces was played out in order to generate further awareness of contemporary Pacific artists in Aotearoa, while strengthening networks and ties of Pacific artists in the wider region. As a range of *Pasifika* artists worked on site, Pacific Islands' art practices constructed a central presence within the mainstream space of an educational institution and urban community.

Samoan artist Fatu Feu'u, founder of *Tautai Trust* and co-organiser of the Pacific Sculpture Symposium, anticipated the event as 'a watershed for Pacific Island art'. Feu'u acknowledged tensions between traditional and contemporary approaches to issues of identity and art practice when he noted, 'Bridges will be built and some will be burnt. Anything different has been hard for some to accept, but attitudes are changing, new ideas are empowering and energising our people' (Feu'u 1998).

Six per cent of New Zealand's 3.8 million population are Pacific Island immigrants, predominantly from Western Samoa, Tonga, Niue, Tokelau and the Cook Islands. In the transnational context of Pacific identities, Feu'u (1999) suggests that the site of Pacific Islands' arts is not without its struggle and contention. For centuries, colonisers inscribed their modernist modes of thought and action. The political practices of modernity involved a search for the 'original' in terms of what was 'new' (for example, the original discovery of lands, or original ideas in artworks, or original inventions in science and industry or the origins of meaning and truth). On the other hand, classical and romantic idealism re-made the old by searching for origins (the original moment or source) while compounding a reverence for tradition and the replication of so-called original cultural formations. Privilege of origin holds sway in each of these modes through which the eyes of modernity locate Western ontology and epistemologies to the detriment of those 'others' outside the norms of Western civilisation.

Too easily, when it comes to the Pacific, identification procedures may articulate ideals of cultural unity; a 'plurality of voices' approach, a unifying rhetoric which simply reinforces Pacific as 'other' and serves the purpose of consumption by the cultural norm. Moreover, the economy of tourism promotes the idea of the Pacific as the 'exotic other' by posing its timeless potential for pleasure as a binary opposite to the world of work and urban pressures. 'Far from being unitary or monolithic or autonomous things, cultures actually assume more "foreign" elements, alterities, differences, than they consciously exclude', claims Said (1994: 15). This being so, then the discourse of identity demands a theoretical and conceptual space of understanding beyond reductively unifying concepts – what Clifford (1988: 5) calls 'endangered authenticities' in which difference is rendered ontological rather than contingent and contextual.

Navigations

Tautai is 'navigator', Samoan, an expert in all things relating to the sea (Vercoe 1999). The metaphor of 'navigation' evokes transit in space, time and epistemologies. Both across and beyond the Pacific, the metaphor is an evidential as well as poetic space. Navigation speaks of conceptual and physical migrations and networks, as well as calling forth hybridised cultural practices and languages. Then why did homogeneous ideas of identity become currency in an economy of cultural authority?

In addressing this question, examples from educational experiences in post-war Auckland show that multiple narratives of Pacific identity were minimised; and when spoken they were marked through fearful tales of 'otherness' in order to reinforce the reigning narrative of progressive civilisation. One thousand years ago skilled navigator Kupe set sail from the Polynesian homeland Hawaiki, across vast oceans in the south. The space of articulation was oral and unheeded by written authority. Kupe's navigations by wind, stars and sea currents led to the discovery of long narrow islands in the southwest, shrouded in white cloud as far as the eye could see. So the land was thus named Aotearoa, Land of the Long White Cloud. Other tales were told of the founding of Aotearoa. One day in time and space, Maaui-Tikitiki-a-Taranga caught a great fish from the South Pacific seas, but Maaui's brothers hacked at the big fish, sliced its smooth back, hurling fragments across the Pacific Ocean. And there they settled into the jagged mountains and valleys of the North Island Te Ika a Maaui – the fish of Maaui – and the South Island Te Waka a Maaui – Maaui's canoe. A new land had been cast across the south-west Pacific Ocean, a land that would later be named in European history as New Zealand. Maaui is said to have fished up other islands such as Tonga, and Mangaia in the Cook Islands, but that narrative trace did not even make the story books.

As a child growing up in New Zealand in the 1950s, I read the myths of Maaui at home in my *Maoriland Fairy Tales* (Howes 1950), written and illustrated through the universalising eyes of Empire. My Auckland primary school did not talk of variegated voices or Pacific narratives. Maori language had been beaten out of existence, quite literally, through the education system, and Pacific languages were other to the otherness of Maori; thus they were unlocatable territories. 'History' began categorically with Abel Tasman's sighting of New Zealand in 1642 and the Great Age of Exploration. Pacific Islands were barely mentioned except in relation to Captain James Cook, circumnavigating and charting the coasts of New Zealand,[6] exploring the East Coast of Australia, which he claimed for Britain, and his untimely death in Hawaii in 1779. The name of the Hawaiian chief Kalei'opu'u, who resisted going aboard the *Resolution* as prisoner, was never spoken; that Captain Cook was clubbed from behind, by 'savages', was. For epistemic systems of universal success laden with valour and moral worth, the names *Endeavour* and *Resolution* were synonymous. One could be reminded: 'There is no neutral place in teaching. Here, for example, is not an indifferent place' (Derrida, 1990, cited in Egéa-Kuehne 1996).

The politics of signification

When cultural practices and identities are examined the politics of signification underlie questions of representation. As Edward Said confirms (1994: 22):

> One significant contemporary debate about the residue of imperialism – the matter of how 'natives' are represented in the Western media – illustrates the persistence of such interdependence and overlapping, not only in the debate's content but in its form, not only in what is said but also in how it is said, by whom, where, and for whom.

Classical historians appealed to grand narratives of Enlightenment epistemology and ontology. Their Pacific was a whole 'other' entity, albeit a void, awaiting enlightened naming devices. Through recognition and disavowal, binary oppositional categories defined the world in terms of presence–void, white–black, north–south, known–unknown, civilised–barbarian. In each case the Pacific was the secondary or negative term. The establishment of 'barbarian' was deemed necessary for the substantiation of subjectivity as presence. Thus, the indigenous and its habitat was displaced, disavowed and re-imagined through stereotypical signifying systems. Values implicit within civilising ideologies of Empire framed the Pacific through visual, literary and scientific accounts of naval heroes navigating and mapping the southern void, with Kupe or Kalei'opu'u violated via omission or stereotypical portrayal.

The Pacific account was thus represented through signifying practices of social order circulating in educational sites in Auckland schools and other public institutions. Intercultural relationships between Pacific Islands' neighbours were omitted. Written history was cemented for the New Zealand pre- and post-war child through accounts of the 1840 Treaty of Waitangi, ceding Maori sovereignty to the Queen of England and Empire, 1907 Dominion status, and independence within the Commonwealth in 1931. The Repeal of the British Corn Laws was taught; local history was not. What any of this might signify at the time was unreachable for a small New Zealand girl, with a mother of Scottish lineage and a London-born father who wore a McDonald tartan kilt even though New Zealand was 12,000 miles away from his Scottish mother's home.[7]

A child's world is quickly normalised. Local community and national interests alike shared the assumptions of the educators. That a tattooed eagle from the Royal Navy was inscribed across my father's chest was never languaged in terms of *moko* or *tatau* (tattoo). The Great War was the authorising agent for such body adornment – which war, if ever mentioned, was uttered through the language of valour, making it wholly justifiable. Maori and Pacific Island cultural adornments and material practices resided in ethnographic accounts of an unassailable otherness. They became the miscreants of museums and anthropologists, carefully contained.

Art museums were effulgent with grand paintings about indigenous peoples and Pacific localities in the 'time of light'. On the walls of the Auckland Art Gallery hangs *The Arrival of the Maoris in New Zealand* (1898), a large, classical, history painting, after Géricault's *The Raft of the Medusa* (1819, The Louvre). Painted in academic style by New Zealand's best-known, European-born, academically trained painter of Maori portraits, Charles F. Goldie, in collaboration with L. J. Steele, the painting was acclaimed by local critics for the supposed 'accuracy' with which it depicted this historical moment of the Polynesian migrations. In truth *The Arrival* testifies to the ways 'the Pacific void' as a primitive site was considered, constructed and confirmed through centuries of signifying practices.

In 1898, *The New Zealand Graphic* (cited in Blackley 1997: 12–13) claimed the painting as a triumph, making specific reference to the painting's content. The critic, writing of the Pacific through nineteenth century familiar rhetoric, referred to the abject Polynesians as 'the starving voyagers from far Hawaiki at the moment when, hopeless and desperate, they catch a glimpse of land through a break in the storm' – quite overlooking the Polynesian mastery of navigation. The Pacific Ocean was a 'lowering sky and dark weary waste of the waters over which the weather-battered canoe is making its way' and tales of shipwrecks were reflected in 'the idea of utter loneliness' and 'exhausted watchers in the canoe' (ibid.). Then, consistent with the repulsion and compulsion towards the 'noble savage', *The Graphic* (ibid.) states that 'there is a terrible attraction in these naked emaciated figures huddled in all different postures of agony and despair in the canoe'. The painting was and is a potent image. As Leonard Bell points out in *Colonial Constructs*, 'visual representations do not necessarily just reflect prevailing views and attitudes, but can actively contribute to their formation' (Bell 1992: 259).

Maori leaders and revisionist historians alike agree that the painting was more a representation of Western Enlightenment ideologies – enunciating the civilising desires of British settler culture and acclaiming art academy's methods and meanings – than of actual Polynesian migrations. The painting represents a language of empiricist historiography in which such reality is deemed to be universally valid and understandable as a totality of knowledge, represented as fact through assimilated symbolic forms. To decode the painting is an exercise which decodes cultural assumptions embedded in truth regimes of colonial settler culture, classical art history and Western academic training. Through an artwork which occupies the presence of a civilising, didactic *tour de force*, the Polynesian navigators are cast into the role of barbarians.

'Expectations of wholeness, continuity, and essence have long been built into the linked Western ideas of culture and art', writes Clifford (1988: 233). The discourse I have disclosed is one of power relations, which continue to be intervened and displaced through the work of contemporary Pacific artists. Although the Polynesians depicted by Goldie and Steele are generalised as 'Maori', the visual signifying system is one that is specifically reserved for the generic indigenous 'other', be they Maori or Pacific Islanders. The painting speaks of the way that navigations happened, as though by chance, devoid of skill or traditional knowledge in the Pacific seas.

Reclaiming the space: the symposium

Having traced a landscape of colonial representational practices in the Auckland Pacific setting, the task remaining now is to focus on *ao fo'ou ta* (new time), where 'the local posits the terrain of disjunctive global/local cultural flows ... [and] where indigenous imagination might achieve renewed social agency' (Wilson and Dissanayake 1996: 8). A range of *Pasifika* artists worked at the symposium. Transnational encounters are evidenced in the names and genealogies of participating artists. Diverse backgrounds represent some sort of shared regional heritage of Pacific Islands' birth, parentage, locale or practice. As the Tautai Contemporary Pacific Arts Trust details (2001), some artists are New Zealand-born Pacific Islanders whose parents or grandparents emigrated to New Zealand in the early 1960s with the promise of unskilled work in the burgeoning industrial sector. Issues of place and identity, disenfranchisement or dislocation frequently find voice in their work. For others born in island nations such as Tonga, Samoa or Cook Islands, 'memories of "home", legends, cultural practices and traditional icons are often a feature of their art' (ibid.). Others share Pacific Islands' ancestry with European or Maori parentage.

Threaded through the creative practices at the symposium were genealogies of nationhood, lineage, language and material practices. Artist Albert McCarthy (of Maori, Samoan, English and Irish descent) worked with Dion Hitchings (Chinese, Maori and English descent). Such identifications typify the hybrid nature of cultural groupings, latticed networks and conceptual circuits. Inia Taylor (English and Maori, of *Ngati Rakawa, Ngati Toa Rangatira, Koroki, Te Atiawa* – tribal affiliations – most famous for his tattoos in the film *Once Were Warriors*) worked with Te Rangi Tu Netena (Maori of *Nga Puhi* tribal affiliation) and English artist Adrian Bennett. When Pacific communities are drawn together with a common aim, art practice inscribes a forum for exchange and a potent site of knowledge generation through such encounters.

Pacific Rim identifications were evident in the work of Toegamau Sefo, from the Melanesian Solomon Islands, Gickmai Kundun, from Papua New Guinea, and Hisao Kameyama and Toshiaki Izumi, guest artists from Japan. Meanwhile, Stephen Gwaliasi from Solomon Islands worked on the bridging of nationalities and histories through combining traditional and contemporary forms. His 'Melanesian Kiwi' drew attention to the hybridised nature of a Solomon Islander living in 'Kiwiland' (New Zealand):

> When people look at my work for the symposium, I want them to say 'Wow, look at the size of those lips and that nose.' I want it to be obviously a Melanesian face I'm creating. I see the whole theme of this symposium questioning 'what is tradition?' Contemporary is a bridge between its past and the present.
> (Gwaliasi cited in Tautai Contemporary Pacific Arts Trust 1998)

The symposium provided space for generative networks to challenge and interrogate the idea of 'Pacific' anew across that 'bridge' identified by Gwaliasi. Artists contested the educational community's assumptions concerning specious notions of 'Pacific identity' as an 'ontologically given and eternally determined stability, or uniqueness, or irreducible character, or privileged status as something total and complete in and of itself' (Said 1994: 382).

For some island-based artists it was their first visit away from their island home. Dick Ukewed and Kiki Poma (Kanak or Melanesian guest artists from French New Caledonia) re-engaged with tradition in the Auckland environment. Ukewed and Poma took their Melanesian designs from Kiki's region in the north of New Caledonia, working with traditional tools in wood. The ideas explored tribal life, 'the clan and the small chiefs. The gecko represents New Caledonia – a god in our culture. It's also a totem of some of the clans' (Tautai Contemporary Pacific Arts Trust 1998).

'Life is a zig-zag', said Filipe Tohi, who in 1978 migrated to New Zealand from his birthplace, the independent kingdom of Tonga. In Tohi's work a unique mix of Tongan and Maori iconography utilises New Zealand wood and stone combined often with industrial materials. He speaks of 'the lashing between the stones [as] a bridge – the link between cultures and lifestyles' (ibid.). Such concepts imaginatively worked through the material practices of sculptural forms speak of transnational and transaesthetic practices, mapping the social spaces of Auckland's Pacific communities.

Iosefa Leo, John Ioane and Johnny Penisula are Samoan. John Ioane, a New Zealand-born Samoan, works as a multimedia artist synthesising sculpture, installation, performance and sound, in keeping with the major rituals and celebrations of Polynesian culture. His is a 'living' artform, which practises art as living and living as art. Ioane made work 'about an artful way of living. During the week, I'll be carving wood and stones, which will be turned into an umu (hangi) fire on the final night of the Symposium. The wood sculptures will fuel the fire and heat the rocks, which in turn will cook mussels. Cooking is artful – and art and life are one and the same' (ibid.).

Contemporary urban and migrant experiences are inscribed through the work of Richard Cooper (Cook Islands and Maori of *Nga Puhi*, tribal affiliations) and Samoan-born Iosefa Leo, who migrated to New Zealand in 1987. Cooper: 'The piece I'm working on for the symposium has to do with Awhina mai – support for our young people – represented by the interlocking pieces' (ibid.). Also mindful of concern for the next generation is Iosefa Leo, who works in Mt Somers Limestone from New Zealand's South Island. Throughout the week he carved and created the weighty figure of a man carrying a load of coconuts on his back (purchased by AUT and sited in the Wellesley library). 'In some ways it's the "load" – the knowledge and culture – that's carried by Samoans when they come to live in other countries', says Leo (ibid.). Leo's figurative works reference *Fa'a Samoa*, the Samoan way, spiritual teachings from the Bible and ethical and family relationships. *Alofa*, the love of culture, family and God and the teachings of the *matai* (chiefs) mark the strength of his figures, which carry the earthly and spiritual weight of knowledge and social responsibility within them.

References to locational sources, media and method mark the work of Auckland-based artist Jim Vivieaere (Rarotongan), who frequently intervenes in the notion of tradition in the contemporary space of urban imagination. He speaks of 'surfaces and pigmentation' through his exploration of media. 'A plank of pine has been planed and sanded, and stained with Tongan tapa ink, then French polished. The East Coast driftwood has been imbibed with Dutch pastels used by British artist David Tremlett, whose art deals with composition and textures' (ibid.).

Another intervention by the female artists disrupted the gendered activities of traditional practice. 'One of the most successful aspects of this symposium was the inclusion of young women artists who had not previously participated in the more traditional male dominated stone symposiums', said Deborah White (cited in Grierson 1999). Veronica Vaevae, identifying herself as Rorotongan, contested two stereotypical notions – that Pacific Islands' sculpture is carved wood or stone, and that men make sculpture and women do something else. 'The installation I'm doing is a play of light and glass. Working in this medium challenges the idea of what is usually considered sculpture in Pacific Island art', said Vaevae (Tautai Contemporary Pacific Arts Trust 1998).

Niki Hastings-McFall is a contemporary Auckland-based artist whose genealogy traces Samoan, Irish, German and English interconnections. Her work combines notions of contemporary jewellery with traditional forms of adornment such as mother-of-pearl shell, *lei* and *kapkap* (a form of pendant from north-west Pacific which denotes specific meanings and status). The potent mix of traditional with urban materials, such as computer discs, aluminium, or plastic fishing line, brings new meanings to what it means to be a Pacific Islander in an urban location. Hers was 'a playful piece about the great chief who developed the fishing net ... [incorporating] plastic fish you get with sushi, filled with food colouring and nylon and plastic, but using colour and repetition in a very Pacific Island way' (ibid.).

Lily Laita (Samoan Maori of *Ngati Raukawa*, tribal affiliation) worked on a 'large clay sculpture of a woman preparing ava (kava) ... I'm making four clay coconuts which represent the four main familial lines in Samoa; a ring mat, representing the ava bowl, and a tuiga suspended in mid air to represent Nafanua, the goddess of war' (ibid.). Laita's work often challenges the stereotypical portrayals of Pacific Island peoples and of the Pacific as a unified region, calling attention to the different ways that cultures communicate and record knowledge. Combining images with text, Laita's space of enunciation incorporates Maori, Samoan and English – through which the veiling of cultural knowledge is encoded. She explores the complexities of mixed cultural heritage, offering her viewers the idea that hidden knowledge binds us in cultural communities (see Tautai Contemporary Pacific Arts Trust 2001).

National borders and boundaries were criss-crossed by various genealogies and artistic practices. The transmigration of enunciative and aesthetic practices made the symposium unique as the whole idea of 'the Pacific' as a unified region was revisited through the politics of difference. As well as those already identified, there were many family and community supporters, assistants and friends. Languages included Samoan, Rarotongan (Cook Islands), Maori, English, Pidgin, French, Japanese and local dialects of Solomon Islands and Papua New Guinea. Some worked in traditional ways and others intersected with tradition to make forms anew and to weave contemporary concerns.

At public lectures artists talked of their work. Interrogations flowed into discussions and debates with art students in university art and design studios.

These events were enlivened by community sharing of food, music and company. Where difference may be celebrated as it plays out a defining principle of identity formation, artistic practices and social networks coursed through the veins of modernity and peppered the ubiquitous demands of cultural tourism. For Pacific students on campus one of the long-lasting and most positive effects has been the affirmation of place, a strengthening form of empowerment for minority students in a dominant *palangi* (European) environment. 'Such events lift the *mana* of the Pacific students on campus', said Isabella Rasch of AUT Pasifika Liaison (Rasch 2001). A reminder of the value of the event is the permanent display of the two significant sculptural works purchased by the university, the establishment of further equity scholarships, including an annual *Pasifika* scholarship within the School of Art and Design and continuing improvement in Pacific student enrolments (increased from less than 6 per cent in 1998 to 7 per cent in 2001). The institutional challenge remains to continue the project of affirmation and to ensure the retention rates of Pacific students continue to improve along with enrolment figures.

Destination

Art is such a potent form of expression, so visible. The Pacific Sculpture Symposium offered a site for interrogating issues of place, identity and subjectivity. For a week, the university was transformed as visual and aural practices, languages and music disturbed what Bhabha (1995: 162) calls 'the calculation of power and knowledge' and disrupted the norm of modernity's inscribed 'other'.

The symposium succeeded in bringing difference into the cultural and political spotlight, so initiating 'new signs of identity, and innovative sites of collaboration, and contestation, in the act of defining the idea of society itself' (ibid.: 1–2). It also provided a space for the exploration of 'tradition' and the 'contemporary' through shifting boundaries of material and poetic realities.

This discussion has shown how intercultural and intersubjective hybridities may reveal new signs of identity through visual practice when pared away from teleological input and rationalised categories of colonial discourse. New forms of 'local' may emerge when transnational encounters disrupt historical discourses and re-examine the false expectations of 'global village' rhetoric.

Testing tradition through Navigating Pacific Art in the Present, Pacific stereotypes are displaced as contemporary Pacific Islands' concerns are expressed, narrated, celebrated and, above all, made visible and viable. Pacific identities are thus rescued from colonial inscriptions of 'otherness' to be reinscribed in the present and reidentified with candour in contemporary educational practices through a revitalisation of the 'local' in a transnational context.

Notes

1 See the further discussion of Rotuman or islander perspectives of time in Vilsoni Hereniko (1994).

2 At the time of the symposium (March 1998), Auckland Institute of Technology was the largest polytechnic institute in New Zealand. Founded over 100 years ago, the Institute became Auckland University of Technology on 1 January 2000, according to the definitions of the New Zealand Education Act, 1989, and its Amendments, 1990. New Zealand's eighth university, it is globally the first university of the new millennium. The Institute is abbreviated to AIT and the University to AUT.

3 The name Aotearoa is beginning to come into general use, although it 'was not a name commonly applied by the many Maori tribes who colonised New Zealand in successive voyages from their mythical homeland of Hawaiiki' (Burke 1995: 15).

4 Creative New Zealand is the public art's organisation distributing contestable grants for arts projects. The Pacific Islands Arts Committee granted NZ$20,000 for the symposium.

5 Pasifika: Pacific.

6 Captain James Cook's first voyage took place during 1768–71 in *H.M. Barque Endeavour*; the second voyage took place from 1772 to 1775 in *Resolution* and *Adventure*; the third voyage was from 1776 to 1779 in *Resolution*.

7 Hugh McDonald Botting was born in Middlesex in 1889, of Scottish and English parents. He joined the Royal Navy in 1915, fought in the Battle of Jutland (31 May 1916), was the recipient of a tattoo while in the Royal Navy at the age of 16 years, he married in New Zealand in 1930 and died at Auckland in 1961.

12 Home away from home?

Transnationalism and the Canadian citizenship regime

Lloyd L. Wong

Introduction

Contemporary international migrations and movements of people have led to the emergence of transnationalism, transnational communities and deterritorialization. While complex transnational communities are emerging throughout the world, they, along with other forms of human migration and circulation, are also threatening the normative charter of the modern nation-state (Appadurai 1996a: 191). Thus, there is a crisis of nationalism and the nation-state in the current global system, where the nation is losing its privilege as the site of mediation between the local and the global. However, with respect to control of human migration and citizenship, the nation-state continues to be a powerful site, albeit with somewhat diminishing authority. The social processes of globalization have produced a disjuncture between how people are politically organized – such as traditional states based on nations, regions and cities – *and* many of their familial, cultural, economic and physical activities that are transnational and globalized. Herein lies the paradox: transnational communities operate in opposition to politically bounded nation-states, yet it is precisely these same nation-states that attempt to control their transnational geographies and spaces. Thus, increasing globalization, 'diasporization', transnationalization and deterritorialization have produced contested meanings of the notion of 'home' at the individual level and of the notion of citizenship at the nation-state level.

Essentially, the concept of 'home' has been viewed as a singular framework. In the migration literature, binary oppositions around this theme include such pairs as 'origin' and 'destination'; 'sending' and 'receiving' country; immigrant and native; and push and pull. The concept of 'home' has been contrasted with the notion of being 'away'. At another level the notion of a homeland has been contrasted with that of a host country. Currently, the meaning of home is undergoing transformation, with scholars reassessing it in the light of transnational communities and transmigration (Al-Ali 2000). With increasing transnationalization it is possible to recast the binary way of thinking of home and to conceptualize it as being plural and evolving. That is, it is possible to have a 'home', or several 'homes', away from 'home'. In other words, the traditional notion of 'home' being associated with a single country of origin or birth does not necessarily always apply. Rather, 'home' becomes trans- or multilocal. Moreover, the concept of home is always evolving and under construction. Werbner (1997: 12) has defined transnationals as people who create collective 'homes' around themselves. Historically, it was only the élite global capitalist class who had collective 'homes away from home' while others were merely sojourners. But the nation-building projects in the New World, in countries such as the USA, Canada and Australia, operated through massive immigration. Consequently, these 'new nations' are among the many multiple sites of 'home' for those in transnational ethnic communities. Therefore, emerging transnationalism has modified the traditional historical experience of past ages. Today, many ordinary people in transnational ethnic communities have similar cultural practices and identities.

Unlike other chapters in this volume, this one does not examine a specific transnational community. Instead, this chapter begins with a general discussion of transnationalism and deterritorialization followed by some evidence on the operation of transnationalism in the Canadian context – including the different means employed, especially two that are important to many transmigrants, namely financial transfers and ethnic media.

It is argued then that, with increasing transnationalism in Canada, citizenship policy is now poised to shift in the direction of reclaiming authority and control via reterritorialization and demands of greater loyalty to the nation-state. An examination of newly proposed citizenship legislation illustrates this point. Compared with other countries Canada has had relatively high rates of immigration over the past forty years; leading to the creation of well-established transnational communities whose members straddle the oceans. People in these communities have dual or multiple loyalties, homes and citizenships.

Transnationalism and deterritorialization

Globalization and transnationalism facilitate deep attachments to more than one 'home'. Thus, it is necessary to conceptualize these dual or multiple loyalties as sincere, legitimate and natural rather than disingenuous, illicit and artificial. Transmigrants maintain multiple linkages to their 'homeland' and increasingly have multiple interconnections that cut across international borders; while their public identities are configured in relationship to more than one nation-state (Basch *et al.* 1994: 7; Schiller *et al.* 1995: 48). At the behavioural and structural levels transmigrants' actions and identities are embedded in transnational social networks. Such networks stand in sharp contrast to the older traditional notion of sojourning – where migrants became incorporated into the economy and political institutions, localities and patterns of daily life of the country where they resided. By definition, transmigrants are engaged *elsewhere* in the sense that they maintain connections, build institutions, conduct transactions and influence local and national events in their countries of emigration (Schiller *et al.* 1995: 48). Scholars now face the challenge of reassessing the traditional notions of territorially based communities and singular societies and cultures.

As Albrow (1996: 156) has argued, social activities that transpire in a given locale also contribute to social worlds that may extend beyond the local and the national level. These levels include obvious economic linkages, but equally the kin-based, friendship and special interest relationships. These linkages have been affected by space–time compression (Harvey 1989: 241) and time–space distanciation (Giddens 1984: 377). Deterritorialization occurs when production, consumption, community, politics and identities become detached from local places (Kearney 1995: 552). However, deterritorialization must be contextualized in relation to specific processes and to different levels of analysis.

Transmigrants have multiple identities which are grounded in more than one society and thus, in effect, they have a hybridized transnational identity. This identity simultaneously connects them to several nations. In a deterritorialized context, the conventional one-to-one relationship between state and territory is increasingly questioned and challenged. Appadurai (1996b: 48) points out that, as a result of the increasing population movements, states are attempting to monopolize the idea of territory as the diacritic of sovereignty. In the newly developed global 'market for loyalties' (Price, as cited in Appadurai 1996b: 48), states do not compete very well:

> ... the global competition for allegiances now involves all sorts of nonstate actors and organizations and various forms of diasporic or multilocal allegiance ... . Where states could once be seen as legitimate guarantors of the territorial organization of markets, livelihoods, identities, and histories, they are now, to a very large extent, arbiters (among other arbiters) of various forms of global flow. So territorial integrity becomes crucial to state-sponsored ideas of sovereignty, which, on close inspection, may be in the interest of no other organization than the state apparatus itself. In short, states are the only major players in the global scene that really need the idea of territorially based sovereignty.
>
> (Appadurai 1996b: 48–9)

The deterritorialization and the delinking of community and identity from place opens up the possibility of new theoretical developments. At the same time, however, it is important to insist on recognizing the importance of place, or, in some other cases at least, the significance of a geographic contextualization of the transnational discourse (Mitchell 1997). The attachment to 'place' is critically important for identity formation and is gaining sociological importance (Gieryn 2000). Thus, deterritorialization should not be conceived as excluding or negating local 'place' or territory but rather of relativizing or decentring it. The terms 'translocalities' (Appadurai 1996a: 192) and 'multi-locationality' (Brah 1996: 197) are used to indicate a local embeddedness or 'rootedness' to transnational processes. In other words, these are culturally heterogeneous places that are largely divorced from their national contexts and that straddle formal political borders (Hyndman 1997: 153). Thus, transnational identity formation illustrates the claim that identity is always plural and is always in process (Brah 1996: 197).

Historically, the nation has been an imagined community. When that imagination moves beyond borders, transnational communities are also imagined communities. However, these are also very much encountered communities and at an empirical level their transnationalism can also be measured. Van Hear's (1998: 242–4) suggested empirical measurements of transnationalism incorporate the notion of a community's commitment to place of origin and current place of residence. More specifically, he suggests that the level of transactions with the place of origin (such as financial transfers, social exchanges, remittances, maintenance of property and so on) can measure 'commitment' to transnationalism.

Transnationalism in Canada: financial transfers and ethnic media

This section briefly demonstrates how transnationalism is practised in Canada by examining two types of transactions with places of origin: financial transfers and the ethnic media. There are many transnational communities that geographically intersect with Canada. Of them, the Chinese and Indian communities are two very large transnational communities. The 1996 Canadian Census enumerated nearly 1 million Chinese and 0.75 million South Asians. Canada's largest cities are among the most multicultural in the world, where immigrants, most of whom are Asians, make up 42 per cent of Toronto's population, 35 per cent of Vancouver's, 20 per cent of Calgary's and 18 per cent of Montreal's (Statistics Canada 2000). While past evidence suggests that transnationalism is more likely to be manifested among the first immigrant generation, this situation may be changing. For example, research has shown that immigrant youth in Canada is more likely than Canadian-born youth to hold on to traditional culture (Tonks and Paranjpe 1999) and hence to have a transnational identity. Yet, recent research by Heibert (2000) in Vancouver also suggests that even among the second-generation Chinese–Canadian youth has taken place an emergence of hybrid identities, cultural reflection and re-evaluation, as the number of Chinese immigrants to the city has increased and as the degree of transnationalism has deepened. While the demographic data point to the likelihood of the existence of transnational identities, a closer examination of transnational practices via financial transfers and ethnic media is warranted.

The level of financial transactions within transnational networks can provide a useful indication or measure of transnationalism. In Canada, financial transfers (including the sending of remittances) have been practised by sojourners and migrants for centuries. Currently, there are extensive financial transactions in terms of remittances by individuals in transnational communities as well as by small and medium transnational ethnic businesses.

Unfortunately, data on financial remittances from Canada are not available. However, Vertovec (2000) has shown that recent annual remittances from the USA are in the tens of billions of dollars (US$29.6 billion in 1996). Vertovec has argued that remittances 'transnationalize' social, cultural, economic and political life within transnational communities by affecting such matters as household decision-making, family life courses and strategies, cultural institutions, community development and so on. It is safe to estimate that remittances from Canada are also quite considerable (and amount to billions of Canadian dollars) and that, on a per capita basis, they are higher than the USA as Canada's annual immigration rate is much higher than that of the USA. In terms of ethnic businesses, recent research by Wong and Ng (1998) found that approximately 50 per cent of Chinese immigrant entrepreneurs in the Vancouver area resort to businesses that are organizationally transnational. This organizational transnationalism often relies on family networks and extensive transmigration. For example, Chan's (1997) recent work suggests that a paradoxical rational family decision is often made that involves dispersing the Chinese matrilineal family in order to preserve and strengthen the family in a resourceful and resilient way. He notes that 'families split in order to be together translocally' and cites the Hong Kong 'astronaut families' as a model. Moreover, Chan argues that these spatially dispersed families constitute strategic nodes and linkages of an ever-expanding transnational field of an emerging Chinese identity (Chan 1997: 195). Over the past decade or so a new Chinese diaspora has emerged with transmigrants attaining 'hypermobility' through transnational networks (Chan 1994: 320). They operate in transnational social networks which allow them to flow from one part of the system to another, depending on conditions of economic boom or recession and the political liberalization or repression that pertains in any part of that system (Skeldon 1995: 72). While Chan's and Wong and Ng's work focused on Hong Kong-based transnational entrepreneurs in the mid-1990s, recent Canadian immigration from the People's Republic of China has undergone a major shift. Since 1998, China has become the leading country of immigration to Canada, a status attributed to China's rapid industrialization and burgeoning population. Thus, Chinese transnational communities and Chinese transnational entrepreneurs are likely to be sustained in the coming years.

Ethnic media is pervasive in the large cities of Canada. They include films, videos, television, newspapers and radio and provide a nexus for instant transnational communication sustaining transnational communities. Karim (1998) points out the connection between the globalization of ethnic media and their function of providing communication networks for diasporic and transnational communities. For example, Canadian ethnic media for the Indian and Chinese transnational communities include: 'Bollywood' (India's transnationally distributed film industry based in Bombay); a multitude of satellite television stations (Chinese Television Network and Chinese Communication Channel); several Chinese radio stations in Toronto and Vancouver; and dozens of Chinese and Indian newspapers available online and in hard copy (*Sing Tao Daily* and *Ming Pao*).

While the above examples pertain to Asian transnational communities alone, it should be noted that these media are also very significant for many non-Asian transnational communities. For example, satellite television is also popular among European communities (Karim 1998: 9). With regard to the ethnic press, Grescoe (1995, cited in Karim 1998) has noted that in Vancouver, Canada, the total circulation of the forty-six ethnic newspapers is larger than the combined circulation of the two main English-language newspapers. Thus, the cultural and social flows of the Canadian ethnic media provide for a high level of contact and exposure to the 'other' home for news and entertainment. Moreover, this interaction can extend beyond the country of origin. A recent study of the transnational social fields of the Youraba in Toronto found that, through ethnic media, they reached out not only to their 'home' country but also to their fellow countrymen in other societies of settlement around the world (Adeyanju 2000: 10).

Social processes and institutions, such as financial transactions and ethnic media, constantly facilitate and negotiate the changing conceptions of home and of citizenship for those in transnational communities. As Faist (2000: 212) has recently suggested, interlocutors and new media help to forge new symbolic ties to putative ancestors abroad and to reinforce transnational networks. In addition, cultural forces, such as religion and food, provide the avenues for central links to flourish between those living in transnational communities. While the discussion thus far has primarily used Chinese and Indian examples, there is growing documentation concerning the transnationalism of other groups – such as Caribbean, Greek, Italian, Croatian and Burmese communities.

In summary, the transnational practices and deterritorialized social identities of transmigrants provide a challenge for nation-states. Globalization involves a relativization and destabilization of old identities and the creation of new hybrid entities (Albrow 1996: 93). The deterritorialization of social identity challenges the nation-state's claim of making exclusive citizenship a defining focus of allegiance and fidelity, in contrast to the reality of overlapping, permeable and multiple forms of identity (Cohen 1997: 157). Can the nation-state remain as the basis and reference point of citizenship?

Changing conceptions of citizenship

The foundation of the nation-state was based on sovereignty over territory. Today, territory is the site of the crisis of sovereignty in our transnational world (Appadurai 1996b: 41, 57). The deterritorialization of identity within transnational communities threatens the modern nation-state. With economic and cultural globalization the relationship between territorial nation-states and citizenship must be re-examined as deterritorialization increases social ties and fosters membership in transnational communities.

The notion of citizenship has recently re-emerged as a prime area of investigation (see, for example, Turner 1990, 1993; Kymlicka and Norman 1994; Roche 1995; Bader 1997). Current debates regarding the definition and content of citizenship now include the question of how citizens view and fulfil their responsibilities and roles as citizens in the light of competing forms of national, regional, ethnic or religious identities. Turner's (1993: 2) conception of citizenship has highlighted the notion of 'citizenship as social membership'. Accordingly, citizenship consists of formal obligations, which are legally defined, as well as informal practices. Both formal and informal dimensions constitute the sphere of civil society. Thus, theories and models of contemporary citizenship incorporate both dimensions, i.e. citizenship-as-legal-status and citizenship-as-desirable-activity – although the two are sometimes conflated (Kymlicka and Norman 1994: 353). Citizenship is not only a legal concept but is a normative one as well. Transmigrants are *de facto* citizens of more than one nation-state although not necessarily *de jure* ones. The traditional concept of citizenship as a singular loyalty is fading as the moral tie between land and people becomes attenuated with the decline of national civil society and the weakening of territorial identities (Jacobson 1997: 125).

Roche (1995: 726) reminds us that citizenship is not reducible to the 'national citizenship' of the modern nation-state. Historically, citizenship has been defined in many ways outside the modern nation-state (from city states to empires) with dual or plural structures of membership, legal identity and rights. Hence, citizenship is definable in terms of the existence of a political community, civil society and public sphere. It is not coterminous with a nation-state. This line of argument has led to the 'post-national problematic', in which the study of citizenship, with its emphasis on social formations of rights, obligations, membership and identity, could not be comprehensive or credible if it restricts itself to the assumptions of the nation-state-based framework of analysis (Roche 1995: 717). The post-national citizenship literature is most developed in the case of the European Union.

The European case: a post-national citizenship?

The existence of millions of denizens in Europe, combined with the European Union's decision to allow member citizens freedom of movement, has contributed to the beginnings of a redefinition of citizenship and national identity to one of a European context. The need to develop a post-national perspective on citizenship was recognized in the early 1990s, and the theme of the 'deterritorialization of citizenship' in Europe from national boundaries has been adopted by many scholars (see, for example, Weale 1991; Meehan 1993; Soysal 1994; Roche 1995; Jacobson 1996; Oommen 1997b).

Soysal (1994) challenges the traditional assumption that national citizenship is a precondition of membership in a polity and proposes a model based more on human rights than on territorial considerations. She attempts to reconcile the emergence of the post-national model with the persistence of the nation-state system, particularly where the source of legitimacy in the post-national model is the transnational community. Further, she points to the growing number of dual-nationality acquisitions as a formalization of the fluidity of post-national membership and the multiplicity of memberships (Soysal 1994: 141). In his recent work, Kastoryano (1998) concludes that European Union (EU) citizenship is 'extraterritorial'. He (Kastoryano 1998: 2) points out that according to Article 8 of the Maastricht Treaty, any individual who holds the nationality of a member state is a 'citizen of the Union', which is a projection of citizenship in relation to nationality, worked out within the framework of nation-states. For Kastoryano the empirical evidence in Europe is still one that shows nation-states remaining as the driving force of the EU in spite of the fact that they have submitted to supranational norms. Thus, while there is an absence of a European identity at this point in time, the possibility of such an (pan-European) identity cannot be ruled out and could be socially constructed as a European identity project (Castells 1998a: 333). This may begin to happen if, and when, the euro becomes the common currency of the (currently expanding) EU.

In summary, the post-national model presents a conceptualization running counter to the national citizenship model. Transnational structures in Europe are viewed as having transcended the power and influence of individual nation-states. To that effect, EU citizenship has at least the potential to be a new institution that delinks citizenship from nationality and territory and is inclusive of transnational communities. While to some degree this new model represents aspects of the social reality of transnational communities, it, nevertheless, must still account for the continued influence of the nation-state. While nation-states no longer have the monopoly of power within the politics of globalization (Holton 1998: 107) they will attempt to re-establish the integrity of national citizenship. This is precisely the case of the Canadian national state.

Canadian citizenship regime: towards reterritorialization and reaffirmation of loyalty to the nation-state

Nation-states have attempted to make exclusive citizenship a *sine qua non*; however, as Cohen (1997: 174–5) notes:

> The world is simply not like that any more; the scope for multiple affiliations and associations that has opened up outside and beyond the nation-state has also allowed a diasporic allegiance to become both more open and acceptable. There is no longer any stability in the points of origin, no finality in the points of destination and no necessary coincidence

between social and national identities. What nineteenth-century nationalists wanted was a 'space' for each 'race', a territorialization of each social identity. What they have got instead is a chain of cosmopolitan cities and an increasing proliferation of subnational and transnational identities that cannot easily be contained in the nation-state system.

The Canadian State cannot contain the increasing proliferation of subnational and transnational identities among its population. This is due to Canada's historical and contemporary reliance on immigration for nation building and economic growth. However, the state certainly governs and intervenes through its immigration and citizenship policies.

Citizenship in Canada is currently being redefined as the process of globalization is applying pressure for a reconfiguration of responsibilities among the triangular relationship of states, markets and communities (Jenson 1997: 628). This occurs within a 'citizenship regime', which includes the institutional arrangements, rules and understandings that guide and shape state policy (Jenson 1997: 631). While a citizenship regime, by definition, does not change quickly or easily, we shall see that the Canadian state has attempted to reverse its diminishing authority over citizenship using reterritorialization and the imposition of a pan-Canadian citizenship regime in its newly proposed citizenship legislation.

Prior to 1947 there was no such thing as a Canadian citizen, but rather British subjects living in Canada. On 1 January, 1947, the first Canadian Citizenship Act came into effect and lasted thirty years until 1977, when it was revised. These revisions reflected a growing and changing society with access to new technologies, improved communications and increased personal freedom. Twenty-two years later, in 1999, another major revision to the Citizenship Act was proposed in the form of Bill C-63. This bill was debated and subsequently revised. However, it did not pass before the Canadian Parliament was dissolved to make way for the November 2000 general federal election. At the time of writing, the re-elected Liberal government is planning to reintroduce Bill C-63 later this year (2001). Given its large majority in Parliament, the bill is likely be enacted.

The Canadian Government's rationale for revising the current Citizenship Act (Bill C-29) is that the act contains inconsistencies, and some of its core provisions are vague and open to interpretation by the courts. Additionally, the act is perceived to be open to 'abuse' from people seeking Canadian citizenship (Citizenship of Canada Act 1998: 2). The government feels that the newly proposed act (Bill C-63) will not only correct these inconsistencies and clarify ambiguous provisions, but, more importantly, it will strengthen the value and integrity of Canadian citizenship under a new act and legislative framework. In effect, Bill C-63 engages in a reterritorialization and a reaffirmation of loyalty to the Canadian nation-state. This is an attempt by the Canadian State to reconstitute territorial and social integrity in an era of globalization and transnationalism.

Reterritorialization

The evidence of the Canadian State's focus on reterritorialization is most evident in Bill C-63's proposed residency requirements for citizenship. Currently, a permanent resident must have at least three years of residence in Canada within a four-year period preceding his or her application for citizenship. However, the courts have engaged in diverse interpretations of what constitutes 'residence' in Canada. Many judges believe that it is the 'quality of attachment to Canada' which determines residency and not just the number of days a person is physically present in the country. For example, Federal Court Judge Jean-Eudes Dube recently wrote: 'Residency in Canada for the purposes of citizenship does not imply full-time physical presence' (Duffy 1999). Rather, the quality of attachment to Canada has been measured by ownership of a home in Canada, having a home address, having a Canadian bank account, payment of Canadian taxes and having family members in Canada. This current interpretation of residency entails a decentring or relativizing of 'place' or territory. In contrast, Bill C-63 represents a process of reterritorialization and the centring of 'place'. It stipulates that a permanent resident must have accumulated at least three years (1095 days) of actual physical residence in Canada (feet on the soil) within a six-year period preceding application for citizenship. While the three-year time period remains the same and the base period increases from four to six years, it is the strict and narrow interpretation of permanent residence, as being physically present and residing in Canada, which is the major change. The government has stipulated that applicants will be responsible for proving their physical presence in Canada using official documents such as school records for students, affidavits or letters from employers, landlords, neighbours and stamps in passports.

This proposed requirement also reflects the Canadian state's desire for potential citizens to demonstrate their attachment to Canada (CIC 1998a) by making Canada their residence or home with the assumption that 'home' is where one must spend most of one's time. This begs several questions in light of the previous discussions of transnationalism. Why does one need to spend most of one's time at home? Can one not make Canada one of one's homes and also have a 'home away from home'? Another rationale expressed by the Canadian state is: 'the intent is that individuals should be familiar with the Canadian way of life before they're admitted as citizens. And the only way to do that is to be here' (Laghi 1998). This begs the question: 'What is the Canadian way of life?'

This proposed 'physical presence' residency requirement will land-lock people into Canada in an age of globalization. It is contrary to the trend of transnationalism and will have an impact on immigrant entrepreneurs who have transnational small or large businesses. It will also affect young immigrant students whose career paths take them abroad for work, study and travel. The current policy, which has a more flexible, discretionary and interpretative residency requirement, is much more suited to the realities of globality than the proposed one that is rigid, narrow and physically restrictive. When Canada's proposed residency requirements are compared with other countries, the three-year 'feet on soil' requirement is longer than the requirements of Australia, the USA and Great Britain.

Another form of reterritorialization in Bill C-63 is the proposed limitation on the transmission of citizenship. Currently, children born abroad, of a Canadian parent, automatically acquire Canadian citizenship at birth and this is a form of *jus sanguinis*. All generations, beyond the first, of Canadians born abroad also acquire Canadian citizenship at birth but lose their citizenship status at age 28 unless they apply to retain it. In order to qualify for retention, there is a requirement of one-year residence in Canada prior to application. In Bill C-63 there is no change for the first generation of children born abroad to a Canadian parent. However, for the second generation born abroad, upon application by age 28, the new residency requirement is that they must be 'physically present' in Canada during at least *three* of the five years preceding the application before age 28. This is a tripling of the current residency requirement, coupled with the strict definition of physical presence in Canada mentioned earlier. Moreover, the third generation and beyond will no longer have a claim to Canadian citizenship, thus limiting its transmission to the second generation. This proposed limitation further reflects the Canadian State's desire for reterritorialization in its restriction of citizenship and is a reaction against emergent transnational intergenerational networks of Canadian citizens in transnational communities.

In another realm, Canada has allowed dual/multiple citizenship since 1977 and has made it possible to have two or more citizenships for an indefinite time. Bill C-63 continues to allow for indefinite dual/multiple citizenship, however, in 1997, the Canadian Government floated a proposal to eliminate dual/multiple citizenship. This proposal has been interpreted by some as a reminder on the part of the federal government to the Province of Quebec concerning the possible cost of sovereignty. The government literature on dual/multiple citizenship devotes minuscule space to the advantages of dual/multiple citizenship and large amounts of space warning about its hazards and disadvantages. Hence, it is clear that dual/multiple citizenship is something that is discouraged by the Canadian state (CIC 1998b), reflecting its ideological position of preferred reterritorialization. Dual/multiple citizenship reflects the reality of hybrid identities, and this has implications for national allegiances. Thus, it is not surprising that the Canadian State has considered the elimination of dual/multiple citizenship.

While the Canadian State's citizenship policy is generally moving towards reterritorialization in the areas mentioned above, there has been contradictory deliberation regarding birthright and territory. While there is no change in Bill C-63 in this regard – i.e. children born in Canada acquire automatic citizenship (*jus soli*) – there was serious disagreement among government cabinet ministers and backbenchers as to whether Canada should continue automatically to give citizenship to everyone born in the country. This debate occurred during the spring of 1998 while Bill C-63 was being drafted (Thompson 1998). Former Citizenship and Immigration Minister Lucienne Robillard floated a proposal that Canada should consider eliminating birthright. This was a reaction to an Ontario court decision quashing deportation of a non-Canadian Toronto mother on the grounds that it violated the rights of her two Canadian-born children. In the final analysis, Minister Robillard decided against ending an automatic right of citizenship for children born to parents without status in the country. This would have meant putting the children in a situation of being stateless in Canada, which she was not prepared to do after giving the matter serious consideration. It is clear that as transnational communities become established there will be increasing legal and illegal movements of people between countries for purposes of work and leisure. Thus citizenship, via birthright, should not be viewed in a negative light, which was the impetus for the Canadian government's consideration of this issue.

Reaffirmation of loyalty to the nation-state

Current policy requires potential citizens to demonstrate an adequate knowledge of Canada and of the responsibilities and privileges of citizenship through a formal test of knowledge. Explicitly, this knowledge reflects how a person understands Canada, and implicitly it reflects commitment and loyalty. Since many immigrants have a mother tongue other than English and French, their knowledge can be demonstrated through the use of an interpreter. Bill C-63 also requires a demonstration of knowledge but it has to be communicated in English or French *without* an interpreter. This new language requirement is also a form of reterritorialization that establishes a cultural criterion of language to citizenship. Those migrants from English- and French-speaking nations will have a citizenship advantage. In one sense this requirement imposes compliance to language as a requirement for citizenship in a contemporary democratic society. In another sense it is an issue of governmentality or a way of framing governance mediated by the notion of an imagined Canadian community, which speaks exclusively English or French. That is, you are not really Canadian if you do not speak English or French. While some scholars may refer to this as a racist policy, it is more appropriately viewed as a form of cultural fundamentalism.

The newly proposed oath in Bill C-63 retains allegiance to the British monarchy and has allegiance to Canada as a priority. For many people living in Canada – such as the Québecois, First Nations and those in transnational diaspora communities – the swearing of allegiance to the Queen has been problematic. While the swearing of loyalty and allegiance to a queen living in another country may seem strange and confusing for some transmigrants, this irony perhaps illustrates transnationalism itself. At a symbolic level, the oath is a statement created by the state to reflect a commitment to shared values and loyalty to the nation. The oath combined with the test on 'knowledge of Canada' are really referents to values. As a popular Quebec journalist recently questioned:

> Ms Robillard wants the future citizens to 'know Canada, share its values and develop a sense of belonging' … . What do private feelings have to do with citizenship? We should require future citizens to obey our laws, follow our main social codes and support themselves. Period. … As for the 'values' well, the fact is that Canadians don't share common values. Some don't even believe in democracy, which is okay in a democracy. And what are Canadian values?
>
> (Gagnon 1998)

In summary, a couple of the proposed policies in Bill C-63 remain compatible with the trends of deterritorialization and emergent transnational and diaspora communities. These include the continuation of birthright and dual/multiple citizenship, although these policies have recently undergone much debate engendered by the Canadian state. However, most of the changes in Bill C-63 demonstrate the Canadian State's move towards re-establishing authority via reterritorialization and reaffirmation of loyalty. These include: (1) strict physical residency requirements; (2) the limitation of the transmission of citizenship to the second generation; (3) knowledge of Canada as demonstrated through English or French language proficiency; and (4) the Oath. These changes illustrate the Canadian state's attempt to reverse its diminishing authority over citizenship and in many ways these proposed changes illustrate a fear of diversity and a fixation with space in an attempt to homogenize Canada's political body.

Conclusion

Globalization and emergent transnational communities have contributed to the deterritorialization of social identity and changing conceptions of citizenship. The social forces of globalization and transnationalism now, more than ever before, challenge the Canadian State as a definer of citizenship. The Canadian State's proposed policy, as exemplified in Bill C-63, is a response to these global forces. The citizenship regime in Canada is shifting to an exclusive one focusing on the soil, allegiance and loyalty. It is an attempt to counter transnationalism and transnational communities with a citizenship policy that focuses on reterritorialization and reaffirmation of commitment to the nation. Potentially, these restrictive policies may lead to critical losses of economic and entrepreneurial skill to the Canadian economy. In addition, this citizenship regime fails to recognize the realities of deterritorialized transnational and diaspora communities and their participants' inherent multiple and transnational identities and their changing conceptions of citizenship.

Bibliography

Abo, T. (1994) *Hybrid Factories*. New York: Oxford University Press.

Abu-Lughod, L. (1991) 'Writing against culture', in *Recapturing Anthropology: Working in the Present*. Fox, R.G. (ed.), Santa Fe, NM: School of American Research Press, pp. 137–62.

Adeyanju, C.T. (2000) *Transnational Social Fields of the Yoruba in Toronto*. Available online at: http://ceris.metropolis.net/virtual%20library/other/adeyanju1.html.

Al-Ali, N. (2000) *New Approaches to Migration: Transnational Communities and the Transformation of Home*. Available online at: http://isim.leidenuniv.nl/newsletter/4/conference/1.html.

Albrow, M. (1996 and 1997) *The Global Age*. Cambridge: Polity Press (1996), and Stanford, CA: Stanford University Press (1997).

van Amersfoort, H. (1978) 'Minority as a sociological concept', *Ethnic and Racial Studies* 1, 218–34.

van Amersfoort, H. (1993) 'International migration and population in the Netherlands', *Tijdschrift voor economische en sociale geografie* xxxiv, 65–74.

van Amersfoort, H. (1995) 'From workers to immigrants: Turks and Moroccans in the Netherlands, 1965–1992', in *The Cambridge Survey of World Migration*. Cohen, R. (ed.), Cambridge: Cambridge University Press, pp. 308–12.

van Amersfoort, H. (1999) 'Migration control and minority policy: the case of the Netherlands', in *Mechanisms of Immigration Control. A Comparative Analysis of European Regulation Policies*. Brochmann, G. and Hammar, T. (eds), Oxford: Berg, pp. 135–67.

van Amersfoort, H. (2001) 'Transnationalisme, moderne diaspora's en sociale cohesie', paper presented at the conference 'Sociale cohesie', Amsterdam: Institut voor Migratie – en Etnische Studies (IMES), Universiteit van Amsterdam.

Anderson, B.L. (1983 and 1991) *Imagined Communities: Reflections on the Origin and Spread of Nationalism*. London: Verso (revised 1991).

Anderson, B.L. (1993) 'The new world disorder', *New Left Review* 193, May/June, 3–14.

Anderson, J., Brook, C. and Cochrane, A. (1995) 'Introduction', in *The Global World: Re-ordering Political Space*. Anderson, J., Brook, C. and Cochrane, A. (eds), Milton Keynes/Oxford: Open University/Oxford University Press.

Anthias, F. (1998) 'Evaluating "Diaspora": beyond ethnicity?', *Sociology* 32, 557–80.

Anzaldúa, G. (1987) *Borderlands/La Frontera. The New Mestiza*. San Francisco, CA: Aunt Lute.

Appadurai, A. (1990) 'Disjuncture and difference in the global cultural economy', in *Global Culture: Nationalism, Globalization and Modernity*. Featherstone, M. (ed.),

London: Sage Publications, pp. 295–310; also published as 'Disjuncture and difference in the global cultural economy', *Theory, Culture and Society* 7, 295–310.

Appadurai, A. (1991) 'Global ethnoscapes: notes and queries for a transnational anthropology', in *Recapturing Anthropology: Working in the Present*. Fox, R. (ed.), Santa Fe, NM: School of American Research Press, pp. 191–210.

Appadurai, A. (1995) 'The production of locality', in *Counterworks: Managing the Diversity of Knowledge*. Fardon, R. (ed.), London: Routledge, pp. 204–25.

Appadurai, A. (1996a) *Modernity at Large: Cultural Dimensions of Globalization*. Minneapolis, MN: University of Minnesota Press.

Appadurai, A. (1996b) 'Sovereignty without territoriality', in *The Geography of Identity*. Yeager, P. (ed.), Ann Arbor, MI: The University of Michigan Press.

Auckland Institute of Technology (1998) 'Pacific Island artists test traditions in AIT symposium', in *Portrait*. Auckland: Auckland Institute of Technology, *Te Whare Takiura O Tamaki Makau Rau*, Autumn.

Bader, V. (1997) 'The cultural conditions of transnational citizenship', *Political Theory* 25, 717–813.

Bakhtin, M.M. (1968) *Rabelois and his World*, Cambridge, MA: MIT Press.

Bakhtin, M.M. (1990) 'Author and hero in aesthetic activity', in *Art and Answerability: Early Philosophical Essays by M.M Bakhtin*. Holquist, M. and Liapunov, V. (eds); Liapunov, V. (trans. and notes), Austin, TX: University of Texas Press.

Balibar, E. (1988) 'The vacillation of ideology', in *Marxism and the Interpretation of Culture*. Nelson, G. and Grossberg, L. (eds), Urbana, IL: University of Illinois Press.

Balibar, E. (1994) 'What is a politics of the rights of man?', in *Masses, Classes, Ideas*. London: Routledge.

Balibar, E. and Wallerstein, I. (eds) (1992) *Race, Nation, Class: Ambiguous Identities*. London: Verso.

Barthes, R. (1977) *Image, Music, Text*. London: Fontana.

Basch, L., Glick Schiller, N. and Szanton Blanc, C. (1994 and 1995) *Nations Unbound: Transnational Projects, Postcolonial Predicaments and Deterritorialized Nation-States*. New York: Gordon & Breach (reprinted Basel 1995).

Baudrillard, J. (1983) *Simulations*. New York: Semiotext(e).

Bauman, Z. (1998) *Globalization. The Human Consequences*. Cambridge: Polity Press.

Beck, U. (1992) *Risk Society*. London: Sage.

Beck, U. (1994) 'The reinvention of politics: towards a theory of reflexive modernization', in *Reflexive Modernization: Politics, Tradition and Aesthetics in the Modern Social Order*. Beck, U., Giddens, A. and Lash, S. (eds), Cambridge: Polity Press, pp.1–55.

Beck, U. (2000a) *The Brave New World of Work*. Malden, MA: Polity Press.

Beck, U. (2000b) *What is Globalization?* Oxford: Polity Press.

Beechler, S. and Taylor, S. (1994) 'The transfer of human resource management systems overseas', in *Japanese Multinationals: Strategies and Management in the Global Kaisha*. Campbell, N. and Burton, F. (eds), London: Routledge.

Bell, L. (1992) *Colonial Constructs: European Images of the Maori 1840–1914*. Auckland: Auckland University Press.

Bendix, R, (1967) 'Tradition and modernity reconsidered', *Comparative Studies in Society and History* 9, April, 292–346.

Bennett, T. (1986) 'Hegemony, ideology, pleasure: Blackpool', in *Popular Culture and Social Relations*. Bennett, T., Mercer, C. and Woollacolt, J. (eds), Milton Keynes: Open University Press.

Bessant, J. and Watts, R. (1998) *Sociology Australia*. St Leonards, NSW: Allen and Unwin.

Bhabha, H. (1994) 'Between identities', in *A Special Edition of International Yearbook of Oral History and Life Stories*. Vol. III. *Migration and Identity*. Benmayor, R. and Skotnes, A. (eds), Oxford: Oxford University Press, pp. 183–99.

Bhabha, H.K. (1995) *The Location of Culture*. London: Routledge.

Bhachu, P. (1996) 'The multiple landscapes of transnational Asian women in the diaspora', in *Re-Situating Identities: The Politics of Race Ethnicity Culture*. Amit-Talai, V. and Knowles, C. (eds), Peterborough: Broadview Press.

Bhatt, C. (1997) *Liberation and Purity: Race, New Religious Movements and the Ethics of Postmodernity*, London, UCL Press.

Bill C-63 (1998) *An Act Respecting Canadian Citizenship*, first reading 7 December.

Blackley, R. (1997) *Goldie*. Auckland: Auckland Art Gallery, *Toi O Tamaki*, in association with David Bateman.

Böcker, A. (1992) 'Gevestigde migranten als bruggenhoofden en grenswachten. Kettingmigratie over juridisch gesloten grenzen', *Migrantenstudies* 8 (4), 61–78.

Böcker, A. (1994) *Turkse migranten en sociale zekerheid: van onderlinge zorg naar overheidszorg?* Amsterdam: Amsterdam University Press.

Boelhower, W. (1989) 'Italo-Canadian poetry and ethnic semiosis in the postmodern context', in *Arrangiarsi. The Italian Experience in Canada*. Perin, R. and Sturino, F. (eds), Montreal: Guernica: pp. 229–44.

Boli, J. and Thomas, G.M. (eds) (1999) *Constructing World Culture: International Nongovernmental Organizations Since 1875*. Stanford, CA: Stanford University Press.

Boli, J., Loya, T.A. and Loftin, T. (1999) 'National participation in world-polity organization', in *Constructing World Culture: International Nongovernmental Organizations Since 1875*. Boli, J. and Thomas, G.M. (eds), Stanford, CA: Stanford University Press, pp. 50–77.

Bonfil Batalla, G. (1996) *México Profundo: Reclaiming A Civilization*. Dennis, P.A. (trans.), Austin, TX: University of Texas.

Bottomley, J. (1992) *From Another Place*. Cambridge: Cambridge University Press.

Bourdieu, P. (1984) *Distinction: A Social Critique of the Judgement of Taste*. Cambridge: Harvard University Press.

Bourdieu, P. (1990) 'Programme for a sociology of sport', in *In Other Words: Essays Towards a Reflexive Sociology*. Bourdieu, P. (ed.), Cambridge: Polity Press.

Bovenkerk, F., Eijken, A. and Bovenkerk-Teerink, W. (1983) *Italiaans IJs: de opmerkelijke historie van de Italiaanse ijsbereiders in Nederland*. Meppel: Boom.

Boyarin, D. and Boyarin, J. (1993) 'Diaspora: generation and the ground of Jewish identity', *Critical Inquiry* 19, 693–725.

Brah, A. (1996) *Cartographies of Diaspora. Contesting Identities*. London: Routledge.

Brouwer, L., Lalmahomed, B. and Josias, H. (1992) *Andere tijden, andere meiden: een onderzoek naar het weglopen van Marokkaanse, Turkse, Hindostaanse en Creoolse meisjes*. Utrecht: Jan van Arkel.

Buchanan, S.H. (1977) 'Language and identity: Haitians in New York City', *International Migration Review* 13, 298–313.

Burke, G. (1995) *Cultural Safety: Contemporary Art from New Zealand*. Wellington: City Gallery, *Te Whare Toi*, and Frankfurt: Frankfurter Kunstverein.

Caccia, F. (1985) 'Filippo Salvatore', in *Sous le signe du Phénix. Entretiens avec 15 créateurs italo-québécois*. Montreal: Guernica, pp. 150–65.

Caillois, R. (1988/1939) 'Festival', in *The College of Sociology 1937–39*. Hollier, D. (ed.), Minneapolis, MI: University of Minnesota Press.

Canclini, N.G. and Piccini, M. (1993) 'Culturas de la ciudad de México: símbolos colectivos y usos del espacio urbana', in *El Consumo Cultural en México*. Canclini, N.G. (ed.), San Ángel, Mexico: Consejo Nacional para la Cultura y las Artes.

Carrillo, J. (1989) 'Transformaciones en la industria maquiladora de exportación', in *Los Maquiladoras: Ajuste estructural y Desarrolo Regional*. Barajas, R. and González-Arechiga, B. (eds), Tijuana: El Colegio da la Frontera Norte, pp. 37–54.

Castles, S. and Miller, M.J. (1993) *The Age of Migration: International Population Movements in the Modern World*. London: The Macmillan Press.

Castells, M. (1996) *The Rise of the Network Society*. Oxford: Blackwell.

Castells, M. (1998a) *End of Millennium*. Oxford: Blackwell Publishers.

Castells, M. (1998b) 'Information technology, globalization and social development', paper prepared for the UNRISD Conference on Information Technologies and Social Development, Palais des Nations, Geneva, 22–24 June. Available online at: http://www.unrisd.org/infotech/conferen/castelp1.html.

Caves, R. (1971) 'International corporations: the industrial economics of foreign investment', *Economica* 38, 1–27.

CBS (2000), *Allochtonen in Nederland*. Voorburg: Centraal bureau voor de Statistiek (Statistics Netherlands).

Chaliand, G. and Rageau, J.-P. (1995) *The Penguin Atlas of Diasporas*. New York: Viking.

Chan, K.B. (1994) 'The ethnicity paradox: Hong Kong immigrants in Singapore', in *Reluctant Exiles?* Skeldon, R. (ed.), Armonk, NY: M. E. Sharpe.

Chan, K.B. (1997) 'A family affair: migration, dispersal, and the emergent identity of the Chinese cosmopolitan', *Diaspora* 6, 195–213.

Charlton, J. (1998) 'Comment', in *Pacific Island Artists Testing Traditions in AIT Symposium*. Media Release: Auckland Institute of Technology, *Te Whare Takiura O Tamaki Makau Rau*, 27 February.

Chow, R. (1993) *Writing Diaspora. Tactics of Intervention in Contemporary Cultural Studies*. Bloomington, IN: Indiana University Press.

CIC (1998a) 'Criteria for obtaining citizenship: residency requirements and knowledge of one's new country', news release 3, 7 December.

CIC (1998b) *Dual Citizenship*. Available online at: http://cicnet.ci.gc.ca/english/citizen/dualci_e.html.

Citizenship of Canada Act Ottawa (1998) Citizenship of Canada Act, Ottawa. Available online at: http://cicnet.ci.gc.ca/english/about/policy/citact_e.html.

Clapp, J. (1997) 'Threats to the environment in an era of globalization: an end to state sovereignty?', in *Surviving Globalism*. Schrecker, T. (ed.), Basingstoke: Macmillan, pp. 123–40.

Clifford, J. (1988) *The Predicament of Culture: Twentieth Century Ethnography, Literature and Art*. Cambridge, MA: Harvard University Press.

Clifford, J. (1992) 'Travelling cultures', in *Cultural Studies*. Grossberg, L., Nelson, C. and Treichler, P.A. (eds), London: Routledge and New York: Chapman Hall, pp. 96–116.

Clifford, J. (1994) 'Diasporas', *Cultural Anthropology* 9, 302–38.

Cohen, A.P. (1985) *The Symbolic Construction of Community*. Chichester: Ellis Horwood and London: Tavistock Publications.

Cohen, R. (1997) *Global Diasporas. An Introduction*. Seattle, WA: University of Washington Press.

Collins, J. (1988 and 1991) *Migrant Hands in a Distant Land: Australia's Post-war Immigration*. Leichardt, NSW: Pluto Press Australia (updated 2nd edn, London: Pluto Press, 1991).

Conner, W. (1986) 'The impact of homelands upon diasporas', in *Modern Diasporas in International Politics*. Sheffer, G. (ed.), New York: St Martin's Press, pp. 16–46.

Constantakos, C.M. (1982) 'Ethnic language as a variable in subcultural continuity', in *The Greek American Community in Transition*. Psomiades, H.J. and Scourby, A. (eds), New York: Pella, pp. 137–70.

Constantinu, S.T. (1989) 'Dominant themes and intergenerational differences in ethnicity: the Greek Americans', *Sociological Focus* 22, May, 65–77.

Contreras, O. (2000) *Empresas globales, actores locales. Producción Flexible y Aprendizaje Industrial en las Maquiladoras*. Mexico: El Colegio de México.

Daftary, F. (1998) *A Short History of the Ismailis*. Edinburgh: Edinburgh University Press.

Danforth, L. (1995) *The Macedonian Conflict: Ethnic Nationalism in a Transnational World*. Princeton, NJ: Princeton University Press.

Danforth, L. (2000) 'Ecclesiastical nationalism and the Macedonian question in the Australian diaspora', in *The Macedonian Question: Culture, Historiography, Politics*. Roudometof, V. (ed.), Boulder, CO: East European Monographs, distributed by Columbia University Press, pp. 25–54.

Debord, G. (1995) *The Society of the Spectacle*. New York: Zone Books.

De la O Martínez, E. (1997) *Y por eso se llaman maquilas. La configuración de las relaciones laborales en la modernización. Cuatro estudios de plantas electrónicas en Ciudad Juarez, Chihuahua*. Mexico: El Colegio de México. Tesis de doctorado.

Demografski i prostorni ... (1968) *Demografski i ekonomski aspekti prostorne pokretljivosti stanovnistva u Jugoslaviji posle Drugog svetskog rata* (*Demographic and Economic Aspects of the Spatial Mobility of the Population of Yugoslavia after World War II*). Beograd: Institut drustvenih nauka, Centar za demografska istrazivanja.

Denich, B.S. (1970) 'Migration and network manipulation in Yugoslavia', in *Migration and Anthropology, Proceedings of the 1970 Annual Spring Meeting of the American Ethnological Society*. Spencer, R.F. (ed.), Seattle, WA: University of Washington Press.

Dickson, P. (1991) 'The Greek pilgrims: Tsakonas and the Tsintzinians', in *New Directions of Greek American Studies*. Georgakas, D. and Moskos, C.C. (eds), New York: Pella Publishing, pp. 35–54.

Dinnerstein, L. and Reimers, D.M. (1982) *Ethnic Americans: A History of Immigration and Assimilation*. New York: Harper and Row.

Dolan, J.P. (1985) *The American Catholic Experience: A History from Colonial Times to the Present*. New York: Doubleday.

Dominguez, V. (1998) 'Asserting (trans)nationalism and the social conditions of its possibility', *Communal/Plural* 6, 139–56.

Donegan, R. (1985) *Spadina Avenue*. Vancouver: Douglas and McIntyre.

Doomernik, J. (1991) *Turkse moskeeën en maatschappelijke participatie: De institutionalisering van de Turkse Islam in Nederland en de Duitse Bondsrepubliek*. Nederlands Geografische Studies, 129. Amsterdam: K.N.A.G./Instituut voor Sociale Geografie.

Doomernik, J. (1998) *The Effectiveness of Integration Policies Towards Immigrants and their Descendants in France, Germany and The Netherlands*. Geneva: ILO (International Migration Papers No. 27).

Drucker, S.J. and Gumpert, G. (1990) 'Public space and media, the metamorphosis of Greek social life: from Greece to New York', in *Eurospace Symposia Proceedings*, vol. V. Mazis, A. and Karaletsou, C. (eds), Thessaloniki: Aristotle University of Thessaloniki, pp. 234–52.

Drucker, S.J. and Gumpert, G. (1991) 'Public space and communication: the zoning of public interaction', *Communication Theory* 1, 84–100.

Duffy, A. (1999) 'Citizenship rulings a "sorry mess," lawyer says: Contradictory judgements', *Southam News* (Canada), 9 April.

Durkheim, E. (1971) *Selected Writings*. Giddens, A. (ed.), Cambridge: Cambridge University Press.

Durrschmidt, J. (1997) 'The delinking of locale and milieu: on the situatedness of extended milieux in a global environment', in *Living the Global City: Globalization as Local Process*. Eade, J. (ed.), London: Routledge, pp. 56–72.

Dyker, D. (1977) 'Yugoslavia: unity out of diversity?', in *Political Culture and Political Change in Communist States*. Gray, J. and Brown, A. (eds), London: Macmillan.

Eade, J. (ed.) (1997a) *Living The Global City: Globalization as a Local Process*. London: Routledge.

Eade, J. (1997b) 'Identity, nation and religion: educated young Banlgladeshis in London's East End', in *Living the Global City: Globalization as Local Process*. Eade, J. (ed.), London: Routledge, pp. 142–62.

Egéa-Kuehne, D. (1996) 'Neutrality in education and derrida's call for "double duty"', in *Philosophy of Education 1996*. Available online at: http://www.mii.kurume-u.ac.jp/~leuers/derrida.htm.

Elias, N. and Scotson, J.L. (1965) *The Established and the Outsiders: a Sociological Enquiry into Community Problems*. London: F. Cass.

Epitropoulos, M.F.G. and Roudometof, V. (eds) (1998) *American Culture in Europe: Interdisciplinary Perspectives*. Westport, CN: Praeger.

Erlich, V. (1966) *Family in Transition: A Study of 300 Yugoslav Villages*. Princeton, NJ: Princeton University Press.

Ethnic and Racial Studies (1999) Special issue on transnationalism. *Ethnic and Racial Studies* 22, 2.

Evans, M.D.R. (1984) 'Immigrant women in Australia: resources, family and work', *International Migration Review* 18, 4.

Faist, T. (1999) 'Transnationalism in international migration: implications for the study of citizenship and culture', working paper series for the ESRC Transnational Communities Programme at Oxford University, pp. 1–42.

Faist, T. (2000) 'Transnationalization in international migration: implications for the study of citizenship and culture', *Racial and Ethnic Studies* 23, 189–222.

Fanon, F. (1968) *Black Skin White Masks*. London: Paladin.

Fanon, F. (1968) *The Wretched of the World*, translated by C. Farrington. New York: Grove Press.

Featherstone, M. (1997) 'Travel, migration, and images of social life', in *Global History and Migrations*. Gungwu, W. (ed.), Boulder, CO: Westview, pp. 239–78.

Featherstone, M. and Lash, S. (eds) (1999) *Spaces of Culture: City–Nation–World*. Sage, London.

Feu'u, F. (1998) *Pacific Island Artists Testing Traditions in AIT Symposium*. Media release. Auckland: Auckland Institute of Technology, 27 February.

Feu'u, F. (1999) 'Comment' in *Tautai Contemporary Pacific Arts Trust* Available online at: http://www.vicnet.net.au/~acaf/024.htm.

Fitzgerald, T. (1995) *The Orthodox Church*. Westport, CN: Greenwood.

Fortier, A.-M. (2000) *Migrant Belongings. Memory, Space, Identity*. Oxford: Berg.

Forum (1989) *Newsletter of the Orthodox Christian Laity*, vol. 2 (2) Summer.

Forum (1990) *Newsletter of the Orthodox Christian Laity*, vol. 3 (2) Spring.

Friberg, M. and Hettne, B. (1988) 'Local mobilization and world system politics', *International Journal of Social Science* 40, 117, 341–60.

Friese H. and Wagner, P. (1999) 'Not all that is solid melts into air: modernity and contingency', in *Spaces of Culture: City–Nation–World*. Featherstone, M. and Lash, S. (eds), London: Sage, pp. 101–15.

Gagnon, L. (1998) 'Citizenship rules for homebodies', *Globe and Mail* 19 December, D3.

Gambrill, M.-C. (1980) 'La Fuerza de Trabajo en las maquiladoras. Resultados de una Encuesta y Algunas Hipótesis Interpretativas', in *Maquiladoras*. Centro de Estudios Económicos y Sociales del Tercer Mundo (ed.), Mexico: CEESTEM.

Gans, H. (1979) 'Symbolic ethnicity: the future of ethnic groups and cultures in America', *Ethnic and Racial Studies* 2, 1–20.

Geertz, C. (1973) 'Deep play: notes on the Balinese cockfight', in *The Interpretation of Cultures*. London: Fontana Press, pp. 412–54.

Gellner, E. (1983) *Nations and Nationalism*. Oxford: Blackwell.

Gereffi, G. (1994) 'Mexico's maquiladoras in the context of economic globalization', paper presented at the conference on *The Maquiladoras in Mexico, Present and Future Prospects of Industrial Development*. Tijuana: El Colegio de la Frontera Norte.

Giddens, A. (1984) *The Constitution of Society: Outline of the Theory of Structuration*. Cambridge: Polity Press.

Giddens, A. (1990) *The Consequences of Modernity*. Cambridge: Polity Press.

Giddens, A. (1994) 'Living in a post-traditional society' and 'Risk, trust and reflexivity', in *Reflexive Modernization: Politics, Tradition and Aesthetics in the Modern Social Order*. Beck, U., Giddens, A. and Lash, S. (eds), Cambridge: Polity Press, pp. 56–109 and 184–97.

Gieryn, T. (2000) 'A space for place in sociology', *Annual Review of Sociology* 26: 463–96.

Gilroy, P. (1991) 'It ain't where you're from, its where you're at ... the dialectics of diasporic identification', *Third Text* 13, 3–16.

Gilroy, P. (1993) *The Black Atlantic. Modernity and Double Consciousness*. London: Verso.

Gilroy, P. (1994) 'Diaspora', *Paragraph* 17, 207–12.

Gilroy, P. (1995) 'Roots and routes: black identity as an outernational project', in *Racial and Ethnic Identity. Psychological Development and Creative Expression*. Harris, H.W., Blue, H.C. and Griffith, E.E.H. (eds), London: Routledge, pp. 15–30.

Gilroy, P. (2000) *Between Camps. Nations, Cultures and the Allure of Race*. London: Allen Lane–The Penguin Press.

Glick Schiller, N., Basch, L. and Szanton Blanc, C. (1995) 'From immigrant to transmigrant: theorizing transnational migration', *Anthropological Quarterly* 68, 48–63.

Goldring, L. (1998) 'The power of status in transnational social fields', in *Transnationalism From Below. Vol. 6. Comparative Urban and Community Research*. Smith, M.P. and Guarnizo, L.E. (eds), New Brunswick, NJ: Transaction Publishers, pp. 165–95.

Gómez-Peña, G. (1996) *The New World Border*. San Francisco, CA: City Lights.

González, B. and Ramírez, J.C. (1989) 'Productividad Sin Distribución. Cambio Technológico en la Maquiladora Mexicana', *Frontera Norte* 1, 97–124.

Gouldner, A. (1989) 'Cosmopolitans and locals: toward an analysis of latent social roles', in *Classic Readings in Organisational Behaviour*. Ott, S.J. (ed.), Pacific Grove, CA: Cole Publishing Company.

Gramsci, A. (1971) *Selection from the Prison Notebooks*. London: Lawrence & Wishart.

Granfield, R. (1991) 'Making it by faking it: working-class students in an elite academic environment', *Journal of Contemporary Ethnography* 20, October, 71–83.

Grierson, E.M. (1999) 'Pacific sculpture symposium questionnaire', unpublished research document. University of Brighton.

Guarnizo, L.E. and Smith, M.P. (1998) 'The locations of transnationalism', in *Transnationalism From Below*. Smith, M.P. and Guarnizo, L.E. (eds), Rutgers, NJ: Transaction Publishers, pp. 3–34.

Gupta, A. and Ferguson, J. (1992) 'Beyond "culture": space, identity, and the politics of difference', *Cultural Anthropology* 7, 6–23.

Habermas, J. (1989) *The Structural Transformation of the Public Sphere: An Inquiry into a Category of Bourgeois Society*. Cambridge: Polity Press.

Hall, S. (1991) 'Old and new identities', in *Culture, Globalization and the World, System Contemporary Conditions for the Representation of Identity*. King, A.D. (ed.), Binghampton: Department of Art and Art History.

Hall, S. (1992) 'The question of cultural identity', in *Modernity and its Futures*. Hall, S. Held, D. and McGrew, T. (eds), Cambridge: Polity, Blackwell and Open University Press, pp. 273–316.

Hall, S. (1998) 'New cultures for old', in *A Place in the World*. Massey, D.B. and Jess, P.M. (eds), Oxford: Oxford University Press and Open University, pp.174–214.

Hall, S. and Sakai, N. (1998) 'A Tokyo dialogue on marxism, identity formation and cultural studies', in *Trajectories: Inter Asia Cultural Studies*. Kuan-Hsing, C. (ed.), London: Routledge.

Hanagan, M. (1998) 'Irish transnational social movements, deterritorialized migrants, and the state system: the last one hundred and forty years', *Mobilization* 3, 107–26.

Hannan, K. (1996) *Borders of Language and Identity in Teschen Silesia*. New York: Peter Lang.

Hannerz, U. (1992) *Cultural Complexity: Studies in the Social Organization of Meaning*. New York: Columbia University Press.

Hannerz, U. (1996) *Transnational Connections: Culture, People, Places*. Routledge, London.

Harney, R.F. (1989) 'Caboto and other *Parentela*: The Uses of the Italian–Canadian Past', in *Arrangiarsi. The Italian Experience in Canada*. Perin, R. and Sturino, F. (eds), Montreal: Guernica, pp. 37–61.

Harvey, D. (1989) *The Condition of Postmodernity*. Oxford: Blackwell.

Harvey, D. (1995) 'Globalization in question', *Rethinking Marxism* 8, 4, 1–17.

Harvey, S. (1997) 'Ethnic communities', in *Social Self, Global Culture*. Kellehear, A. (ed.), Melbourne: Oxford University Press.

Hasiotis, I.K. (1993) *Overview of the History of the Modern Greek Diaspora*, Thessaloniki: Vanias (in Greek).

Hastrup, K. and Fog Olwig, K. (1997) 'Introduction', in *Sitting Culture: The Shifting of the Anthropological Object*. Fog Olwig, K. and Hastrup, K. (eds), London: Routledge.

Hayashida, M. (1994) 'Entrepreneurship in Taiwan and Korea: a comparison', *Asia-Pacific Review* 1, 59–82.

Hedetoft, U. (1999) 'The nation-state meets the world: national identities in the context of transnationality and cultural globalization', *European Journal of Social Theory* 2, 71–94.

Hegedus, Z. (1989) 'Social movements and social change in self-creative society: new civil initiatives in the international arena', *International Sociology* 4, 19–36.

Heibert, D. (2000) 'Cosmopolitanism at the local level: immigrant settlement and the development of transnational neighbourhoods', working paper series no. 00–15. Vancouver: Vancouver Centre of Excellence – Research on Immigration and Integration in the Metropolis.

Held, D., McGrew, A., Goldblatt, D. and Perraton, J. (1999) *Global Transformations: Politics, Economics, and Culture*. Stanford, CA: Stanford University Press.

Hereniko, V. (1994) 'Representations of cultural identities', in *Tides of History: The Pacific Islands in the 20ᵗʰ Century*. Howe, K.R., Kiste, R.C. and Lal, B.V. (eds), St Leonards, NSW: Allen & Unwin, pp. 406–34.

Hicks, S. and Couloumbis, T. (1980) 'Greek Americans and the Turkish Aid Issue, 1974–75', in *Sourcebook on the New Immigration: Implications for the United States and the International Community*. Bryce-Laporte, R.S. (ed.), New Brunswick, NJ: Transaction, pp. 151–5.

Hoben, A. and Hefner, T. (1991) 'The integrative revolution revisited', *World Development* 19, 3, 17–30.

Hobsbawm, E.J. (1990), *Nations and Nationalism since 1780*. Cambridge: Cambridge University Press.

Holjevac, V. (1967) *Hrvati izvan domovine (Croatians Outside homeland)*. Zagreb: Matica Hrvatska.

Holton, R. (1998) *Globalization and the Nation-state*. New York: St Martin's Press.

Hooghiemstra, E. (2000) 'Gemengd huwen en transnationaal huwen in Nederland: enkele feiten', *Migrantenstudies* 16, 198–208.

Howes, E. (1950) *Maoriland Fairy Tales*. London: Ward, Lock & Co.

Hualde, A. (1995) 'Técnicos e Ingenieros en la Maquiladora Fronteriza de México: Su Rol Como Agentes Innovadores', in *La Fromación Para el Trabajo en el Final del Siglo*. Gallart, M.A. (ed.), Buenos Aires: Red Latinoamericana de Educación y Trabajo, Lecturas de Educación y Trabajo, no. 4.

Hualde, A. (1998) *La articulación entre el sistema educativo y el sistema productivo en la frontera norte de México: un estudio en Tijuana y Ciudad Juárez*. México: Universidad Nacional Autónoma de México, Facultad de Ciencias Políticas y Sociales, Tesis de doctorado.

Hughson, J. (1997), 'Football, folk dancing and fascism: diversity and difference in multicultural Australia', *ANZJS* 33, 2.

Humphrey, J. (1993) 'Japanese production management and labour relations in Brazil', *Journal of Development Studies* 30, 92–114.

Humphrey, J. (1995) 'The adoption of Japanese management techniques in Brazilian industry', *Journal of Management Studies* 32, 767–87.

Hyndman, J. (1997) 'Border Crossings', *Antipode* 29, 149–76.

Ianucci, S. (1989) 'Contemporary Italo-Canadian Literature', in *Arrangiarsi. The Italian Experience in Canada*. Perin, R. and Sturino, F. (eds), Montreal: Guernica, pp. 209–27.

Jacobson, D. (1996) *Rights Across Borders: Immigration and the Decline of Citizenship*. Baltimore, MD: JHU Press.

Jacobson, D. (1997) 'New frontiers: territory, social spaces, and the state', *Sociological Forum* 12, 121–33.

Jacobson, M.F. (1995) *Special Sorrows. The Diasporic Imagination of Irish, Polish, and Jewish Immigrants in the United States*. Cambridge, MA: Harvard University Press.

Jenson, J. (1997) 'Fated to live in interesting times: Canada's changing citizenship regimes', *Canadian Journal of Political Science* XXX, 4, 627–44.

Jusdanis, G. (1991) 'Greek Americans and the Diaspora', *Diaspora* 1, 209–23.

Kaplan, C. (1996) *Questions of Travel. Postmodern Discourses of Displacements*. Durham: Duke University Press.

Kaplinsky, R. (1994) *Easternization: The Spread of Japanese Management Techniques to LDCs*. London: Frank Cass.

Kaplinsky, R. (1995) 'Technique and system: the spread of Japanese management techniques to developing countries', *World Development* 23, 57–72.

Karakasidou, A. (1994) 'Sacred scholars, profane advocates: intellectuals molding national consciousness in Greece', *Identities* 1, 35–61.

Karim, K.H. (1998) *From Ethnic Media to Global Media: Transnational Communication Networks among Diasporic Communities*. Transnational Communities Working Paper Series. Available online at: http:www.transcomm.ox.ac.uk/working_papers.htm.

Karpathakis, A. (1993) 'Sojourners and settlers: Greek immigrants of Astoria', unpublished Ph.D. dissertation, Columbia University.

Karpathakis, A. (1994) '"Whose church is it anyway?" Greek immigrants of Astoria, New York and their church', *Journal of the Hellenic Diaspora* 20, 97–122.

Karpathakis, A. (1999) 'Home society politics and immigrant political incorporation: the case of Greek immigrants in New York City', *International Migration Review* 33, 55–78.

Karpathakis, A. (2001) 'The Greek Orthodox Church and identity politics', in *New York Glory: Religions in the City*. Carnes, T. and Karpathakis, A. (eds), New York: New York University Press, pp. 374–87.

Karskens, M. (1999) 'The foreign homeland', unpublished paper, History of the Present Seminar Series, London.

Kastoryano, R. (1998) 'Transnational participation and citizenship', in *Transnational Communities Working Papers Series, WPTC 98–12*. Available online at: http//www.transcomm.ox.ac.uk/wwwroot/frames1.htm.

Katsas, G. (1992) 'Differential self-employment among the foreign-born and native-born: the case of Greeks in New York', unpublished Ph.D. dissertation, Fordham University.

Kearney, M. (1995) 'The local and the global: the anthropology of globalization and transnationalism', *Annual Review of Anthropology* 24, 547–65.

Keith, M. and Pile, S. (1993) 'Introduction Part 1 and Part 2', in *Place and the Politics of Identity*. Keith, M. and Pile, S. (eds), London: Routledge.

Kenney, M. and Florida, R. (1994) 'Japanese maquiladoras: production organization and global commodity chains', *World Development* 22, 27–44.

Kenney, M. and Lowe, N. (1999) 'Too far from Asia, too close to the United States: the decline of Mexico's consumer electronics industries 1965–1985'. University of California, Davis, unpublished manuscript.

Kenney, M., Goe, W.R., Contreras, O., Romero, J. and Bustos, M. (1998) 'Learning factories or reproduction factories? Labor–management relations in the Japanese consumer electronics maquiladoras in Mexico', *Work and Occupations* 25, 269–304.

Kipp, S., Clyne, M. and Pauwels, A. (1995) *Immigration and Australia's Language Resources*. Monash University and National Languages and Literacy Institute of Australia. Canberra: Australian Government Publishing Service.

Kiriazis, J.W. (1989) *Children of the Colossus: The Rhodian Greek Immigrants in the United States*. New York: AMS Press.

Kirshenblatt-Gimblett, B. (1994) 'Spaces of dispersal', *Cultural Anthropology* 9, 339–44.

Kloos, P. (2000) 'The dialectics of globalization and localization', in *The Ends of Globalization. Bringing Society Back In*. Kalb, D., Van Der Land, M., Staring, R., van Steenbergen, B. and Wilterdin, N. (eds), Lanham: Rowman & Littlefield, pp. 281–97.

Kogut, B. and Zander, U. (1993) 'Knowledge of the firm and the evolutionary theory of the multinational corporation', *Journal of International Business Studies* 24, 25–45.

Kolar-Panov, D. (1997) *Video, War and the Diasporic Imagination*. London: Routledge.

Kopan, A.T. (1990) *Education and Greek Immigrants in Chicago 1892–1973: A Study in Ethnic Survival*. New York: Garland.

Kopinak, K. (1996) *Desert Capitalism*. Tuscon: University of Arizona Press.

Kopp, R. (1994) 'International human resource policies and practices in Japanese, European, and United States multinationals', *Human Resource Management* 33, 581–99.

Kubik, J, (1994) 'The role of decentralization and cultural revival in post-communist transformations. The case of Cieszyn Silesia, Poland', *Communist and Post-Communist Studies* 27, 331–55.

Kubica-Heller, G. (1996) *Luteranie na Śląsku Cieszyńskim*. Bielsko-Biała: Głos Życia.

Kunkelman, G.A. (1990) *The Religion of Ethnicity: Belief and Belonging in a Greek American Community*. New York: Garland.

Kuo, C.-T. (1995) *Global Competitiveness and Industrial Growth in Taiwan and the Philippines*. Pittsburgh, PA: University of Pittsburgh Press.

Kymlicka, W. and Norman, W. (1994) 'Return of the citizen: a survey of recent work of citizenship theory', *Ethics* 104, January, 352–81.

Lacoste, Y. (1989) 'Editorial: Geopolitique des diasporas', *Herodote* 53.

Laghi, B. (1998) 'Ottawa to tighten citizenship rules', *Globe and Mail* 13 November, A1, A8.

Lahickey, B. (ed.) (1997) *All Ages: Reflections on Straight Edge*, Huntington Beach, CA: Revelation Books.

Lam, D.K.-K. (1992) *Explaining Economic Development: A Case Study of State Polices Towards the Computer and Electronics Industry in Taiwan (1960–1980)*. Ph.D. dissertation, Carleton University. Ann Arbor, MI: University Microfilms International.

Lash, S. (1994) 'Reflexivity and its doubles: structure, aesthetics, community' and 'Expert-systems or situated interpretation? Culture and institutions in disorganized capitalism', in *Reflexive Modernization: Politics, Tradition and Aesthetics in the Modern Social Order*. Beck, U., Giddens, A. and Lash, S. (eds), Cambridge: Polity Press, pp. 110–75 and 198–215.

Lash, S. and Urry, J. (1994) *Economies of Signs and Space*. London: Sage.

Lavie, S. and Swedenburg, T. (1996) 'Introduction', in *Displacement, Diaspora, and Geographies of Identity*. Lavie, S. and Swedenburg, T. (eds), Durham: Duke University Press, pp. 1–25.

Lefebvre, H. (1991) *The Production of Space*. Oxford: Blackwell Publishers.

Lim, S.G-L. and Dissanayake, W. (1999) 'Introduction', in *Transnational Asia Pacific: Gender, Culture, and the Public Sphere*. Lim, S.G-L., Smith, L. and Dissanayake, W. (eds) Chicago, IL: University of Illinois Press, pp.1–9.

Lindo, F. (1999) *Heilige wijsheid in Amsterdam: Aya Sofia, stadsdeel De Baarsjes en de strijd om het Riva-terrein*. Amsterdam: Het Spinhuis.

Lowe, L. (1996) *Immigrant Acts. On Asian American Cultural Politics*. Durham: Duke University Press.

Mach, Z. (1993) *Symbols, Conflict, and Identity. Essays in Political Anthropology*. Albany, NY: State University of New York Press.

McKendrick, D.G., Doner, R.F. and Haggard, S. (2000) *From Silicon Valley to Singapore: Location and Competitive Advantage in the Hard Disk Drive Industry*. Stanford, CA: Stanford University Press.

McNeill, W.H. (1985) *Polyethnicity and National Unity in World History*. Toronto: University of Toronto Press.

Madden, R. and Young, S. (1992) *Women and Men Immigrating to Australia: Their Characteristics and Immigration Decisions*. Bureau of Immigration Research. Canberra: Australian Government Publishing Service.

Mahler, S. (1998) 'Theoretical and empirical contributions toward a research agenda for transnationalism', in *Transnationalism from Below*. Smith, M. and Guarnizo, L. (eds), New Brunswick, NJ: Transaction Publishers.

Manas (2001) *The Indian Diaspora*. Available online at: http://www.sscnet.ucla.edu/southasia/diaspora/diaspora.html.

Marcus, G.E. and Fischer, M.J. (1986) *Anthropology as Cultural Critique: An Experimental Moment in the Human Sciences*. Chicago, IL: University of Chicago.

Marienstras, R. (1975) *Etre un peuple en diaspora*. Paris, Maspero.

Martínez, R. (1992) 'Corazon del Rocanrol', in *The Other Side: Fault Lines, Guerrilla Saints, and the True Heart of Rock 'n' Roll*. Martínez, R. (ed.), London: Routledge.

Marx, K. (1967) *Capital*, vol. 1. London: L & W.

Massey, D. (1995) 'Making spaces, or, geography is political too', *Soundings* 1, 192–203.

Matthews, K.C. (2000) 'Deconstructing place and space: towards a deeper understanding of the "social"', *The Colloquium* 1, 203–12.

Matykowski, R. (1997) '*Śląsku Cieszyński* a Podbeskidzie. Świadomość regionalna mieszkańców województwa bielskiego (spojrzenie geograficzne)' in *śląsk Cieszyński i inne pogranicza w badaniach nad tożasamością etniczną, narodową i regionalną*, Bukowska-Floreńska, I. (ed.), Katowice: Silesia University Press, pp. 99–114.

Mauss, M. (1969) *The Gifts*. London: RKP.

Mayall, J. (1990) *Nationalism and International Society*. Cambridge: Cambridge University Press.

Meehan, E. (1993) *Citizenship and the European Community*. London: Sage Publications.

Menchini, C. (1974) *Giovanni Caboto, scopritore del Canada*. Montreal: Riviera.

Mercer, C. (1983) 'A poverty of desire: pleasure and popular politics', in *Formations of Pleasure*. London: RKP, pp. 84–100.

Mercer, C. (1986) 'Complicit pleasures', in *Popular Culture and Social Relations*. Bennett, T., Mercer, C. and Woollacott, J. (eds), Milton Keynes: Open University Press, pp. 50–68.

Mercer, C. (1986) 'Baudelaire and the city: 1848 and the inscription of hegemony' in *Literature, Politics and Theory*. Barker, F., Hulme, P., Iversen, M. and Loxley, D. (eds), London: Methuen.

Meznaric, S. (1991) *Osvajanje prostora, prekrivanje vremena: migracije umjesto razvoja (The Conquering of Space, the Covering of Time: Migration instead of Development)*. Zagreb: Sociolosko drustvo Hrvatske.

Meznaric, S. and Grdešic, I. (1990) 'Odljev mozgova iz Jugoslavije (Brain-drain from Yugoslavia)', *Politicka misao (Political Thought)* 27, 4, 136–63.

Mintz, S.W. (1998) 'The localization of anthropological practice: from area studies to transnationalism', *Critique of Anthropology* 18, 117–33.

Mirak, R. (1983) *Torn Between Two Lands: Armenians in America, 1890 to World War I*. Cambridge, MA: Harvard University Press.

Mitchell, K. (1997) 'Transnational discourse: bringing geography back in', *Antipode* 29, 2, 101–14.

Monos, D. (1986) *The Achievement of the Greeks in the United States*. Philadelphia, PA: Centrum.

Morawska, E. and Spohn, W. (1997) 'Moving Europeans in the globalizing world: contemporary migrations in a historical–comparative perspective (1955–1994 vs. 1870–1914)', in *Global History and Migrations*. Gungwu, W. (ed.), Boulder, CO: Westview, pp. 23–62.

Moskos, C. (1982) 'Greek American studies', in *The Greek American Community in Transition*. Psomiades, H.J. and Scourby, A. (eds), New York: Pella, pp. 17–64.

Moskos. C. (1989a) 'The Greek Orthodox Church in America', *Journal of Modern Hellenism* 6' 25–37.

Moskos, C. (1989b) *Greek Americans: Struggle and Success*. New Brunswick, NJ: Transaction Books.

Moskos, C. (1993) 'Faith, language, and culture', in *Project for Orthodox Renewal, Seven Studies of Key Issues Facing Orthodox Christians in America*. Sfekas, S.J. and Matsoukas, G.E. (eds), Chicago: Orthodox Christian Laity, pp. 17–32.

Muus, P.J. (1992) *Migration, Minorities and Policy in the Netherlands. Report for the O.E.C.D. SOPEMI-Netherlands*. Amsterdam: Institute for Social Geography, University of Amsterdam.

Muus, P.J. and Penninx, R. (1991) *Immigratie van Turken en Marokkanen in Nederland*. Den Haag: Ministerie van Binnenlandse Zaken.

Nejašmic, I. (1995) *Hrvatski gradjani na radu u inozemstvu i clanovi obitelji koji s njiam borave: Usporedna analiza statistickih podataka 1971., 1981. i 1991. godine (Croatian Citizens Who Work Abroad and the Members of their Families Staying with them: Comparative Analysis of the Census Data 1971, 1981, 1991)*. Zagreb: Institut za migracije i narodnosti.

O'Connor, A. (1999) 'Who's Emma and the limits of cultural studies', *Cultural Studies* 13, 691–702.

Odyssey Magazine (1993–6) *Odyssey Magazine*, various issues.

O'Hara, C. (1995) *The Philosophy of Punk: More Than Noise!!*. Edinburgh: AK Press.

Olwig, K.F. (1997) 'Cultural sites: sustaining a home in a deterritorialized world', in *Sitting Culture: The Shifting of the Anthropological Object*. Fog Olwig, K. and Hastrup, K. (eds), London: Routledge.

Ong, A. and Peletz, M.G. (eds) (1995) *Bewitching Women, Pious Men. Gender and Body Politics in Southeast Asia*. Berkeley, CA: University of California Press.

Oommen, T.K. (1997a) 'Social movements in the Third World', in *Social Movements in Development: The Challenges to Globalization and Democratization*. Lindberg, S. and Sverrisson, A. (eds), Basingstoke: Macmillan, pp. 44–66.

Oommen, T.K. (1997b) *Citizenship, Nationality and Ethnicity*. Cambridge: Polity Press.

Panic, I. (1994) 'Przyczynek do problemu świadomości narodowej mieszkań ców Księstwa Cieszyńskiego od średniowiecza do pocz ątków reformacji', in *Poczucie tożsamo ści narodowej m łodzieży*. Lewowicki, T. (ed.), Studium z pogranicza polsko-czeskiego, Cieszyn: Uniwersytet Śląski – Filia w Cieszynie.

Pantoja, J. (ed.) (1996) *Cuando el Chopo Despertó, El Dinosauro Ya No Estaba Ahí*. Mexico City: Ediciones Imposible.

Papaioannou, G. (1985) *The Odyssey of Hellenism in America*. Thessaloniki: Patriarchal Institute for Patristic Studies.

Patrinacos, N.D. (1982) 'The role of the church in the evolving Greek American community', in *The Greek American Community in Transition*. Psomiades, H.J. and Scourby, A. (eds), New York: Pella, pp. 123–36.

Patterson, G.J. (1989) *The Unassimilated Greeks of Denver*. New York: AMS Press.

Perin, R. (1982) 'Conflits d'identité et d'allégeance. La propagande du consulat italien à Montréal dans les années 1930', *Questions de culture 2: Migrations et communautés culturelles*. Montreal: IQRC/Leméac.

Perth Social Atlas (1997) *Perth Social Atlas*. Perth: Australian Bureau of Statistics.

Phizacklea, A. (ed.) (1983) *One Way Ticket: Migration and Female Labour*. London: Routledge & Kegan Paul.

Pile, S. and Thrift, N. (1995) 'Introduction', in *Mapping the Subject: Geographies of Cultural Transformation*. Pile, S. and Thrift, N. (eds), London: Routledge.

Pinches, M. (2000) 'Class and national identity: the case of Filipino migrant workers', in *Organising Labour Globalising Asia*. Hutchison, J. and Brown, A. (eds), London: Routledge.

Portes, A. (1997) *Globalization from Below: The Rise of Transnational Communities*. Princeton, NJ: WPTC.

Portes, A. (2000) 'Globalization from below: the rise of transnational communities', in *The Ends of Globalization: Bringing Society Back In*. Kalb, D., van der Land, M., Staring, R., van Steenbergen, B. and Wilterdink, N. (eds), Boulder, CO: Rowman and Littlefield, pp. 253–70.

Portes, A., Rapport, N. and A. Dawson (eds) (1998) *Migrants of Identity: Perceptions of Home in a World of Movement*. New York: Berg.

Portes, A., Guarzino, L.E. and Landolt, P. (1999) 'The study of transnationalism. Pitfalls and promises of an emergent research field', *Ethnic and Racial Studies* 22, 217–37.

Profane Existence (ed.) (1997) *Making Punk A Threat Again!: The Best Cuts 1989–1993*. Minneapolis, MN: Profane Existence.

Radhakrishnan, R. (1996) *Diasporic Mediations. Between Home and Location*. Minneapolis, MN: University of Minnesota Press.

Rapport, N. and Dawson, A. (1998) 'The topic and the book', in *Migrants of Identity Perceptions of Home in a World of Movement*. Rapport, N. and Dawson, A. (eds), New York: Berg.

Rasch, I. (2001) *Conversation with Grierson, E.M*. Auckland: Auckland University of Technology, *Te Wananga Aronui O Tamaki Makau Rau*, 4 May.

Rasiah, R. (1995) *Foreign Capital and Industrialization in Malaysia*. New York: St Martin's Press.

Rath, J., Penninx, R., Groenendijk, K. and Meijer, A. (1996) *Nederland en zijn Islam. Een ontzuilde samenleving reageert op het ontstaan van een geloofsgemeenschap*. Amsterdam: Het Spinhuis.

Reygadas, L. (1992) 'Obreros de Fin de Siglo: Los trabajadores de las Maquiladoras de Chihuahua', in *Crisis y Sujetos Sociales en México*. de la Garza, E. (ed.), Mexico: Miguel Angel Porrúa.

Ricoeur, P. (1991) *A Ricoeur Reader: Reflection and Imagination*, edited by M.J. Valdes. New York: Harvester and London: Wheatsheaf.

Robertson, R. (1992) *Globalization: Social Theory and Global Change*. Sage, London.

Roche, M. (1995) 'Citizenship and modernity', *British Journal of Sociology* 46, 715–33.

Rodman, K.A. (1998) '"Think globally, punish locally": nonstate actors, multinational corporations, and human rights sanctions', *Ethics and International Affairs* 12, 19–41.

Rosen, B.C. (1968) 'Race, ethnicity, and the achievement syndrome', in *Race, Class, and Power*. Mack, R.W. (ed.), New York: D. Van Nostrand Company, pp. 291–304.

Roseneil, S. (1997) 'The global commons: the global, local and personal dynamics of the women's peace movement in the 1980s', in *The Limits of Globalization*. Scott, A. (ed.), London: Routledge, pp. 55–71.

Rosenfeldt, M. (1989) *Assessment of Selected Operations Management Technologies in Maquiladoras: Complexities and Adaptations*. Texas: College of Business Administration North Texas State University.

Rosenfeldt, M. and Ponthieu, L.D. (1987) *Entrepreneurial Challenges in the Texas–Mexico Borderlands: The Need to Establish Supplier Industries*. Texas: Department of Management, North Texas State University.

Roudometof, V. (1996) 'Nationalism and identity politics in the Balkans: Greece and the Macedonian question', *Journal of Modern Greek Studies* 14, 253–301.

Roudometof, V. (1999) 'Nationalism, globalization, eastern orthodoxy: "unthinking" the "clash of civilizations" in Southeastern Europe', *European Journal of Social Theory* 2, 233–47.

Roudometof, V. (2001) 'Transnationalism and globalization: the Greek-Orthodox diaspora between orthodox universalism and transnational nationalism', *Diaspora*.

Safran, W. (1991) 'Diasporas in modern societies: myths of homeland and return', *Diaspora* 1, 83–99.

Said, E. (1994) *Culture and Imperialism*. London: Vintage.

Saloutos, T. (1964) *The Greeks in the United States*. Cambridge: Harvard University Press.

Salvatore, F. (1978) 'Three poems for Giovanni Caboto', in *Roman Candles. An Anthology of Poems by Seventeen Italo-Canadian Poets*. Di Cicco, P.G. (ed.), Toronto: Honslow Press, pp. 13–16.

Sanadjian, M. (1995) 'Temporality of "home" and spatiality of market in exile: Iranians in Germany', *New German Critique* 64, Winter, 3–36.

Sanadjian, M. (1998) 'Ethnography of spectacle, the reality of sport and its popular representation', paper presented at the Faculty of Leisure and Tourism, Buckinghamshire Chiltern University College.

Sanadjian, M. (2000) 'Food, articulation of identity and proletarianisation of Iranian middle classes in diaspora', paper presented at the Conference on cultural Change in Urban Context in Manchester.

Sandis, E.E. (1982) 'The Greek population of New York City', in *The Greek American Community in Transition*. Psomiades, H.J. and Scourby, A. (eds), New York: Pella, pp. 65–92.

Sassen, S. (1996) *Losing Control? Sovereignty in an Age of Globalization*. New York: Columbia University Press.

Sassen, S. (1998) *Globalization and Its Discontents*. New York: New York Press.

Scarce, R. (1990) *Eco-Warriors: Understanding the Radical Environmental Movement*. Chicago, IL: Noble Press.

Schein, L. (1998) 'Forged transnationality and oppositional cosmopolitanism', in *Transnationalism From Below*. Vol. 6. *Comparative Urban and Community Research*. Smith, M.P. and Guarnizo, L.E. (eds), New Brunswick, NJ: Transaction Publishers, pp. 291–313.

Schermerhorn, R.A. (1970) *Comparative Ethnic Relations*. New York: Random House.

Schiller, N.G., Basch, L. and Blanc-Szanton, C. (eds) (1992) *Towards a Transnational Perspective on Migration; Race, Class, Ethnicity, and Nationalism Reconsidered*. New York: The New York Academy of Sciences.

Schiller, N., Basch, L. and Blanc-Szanton, C. (1995) 'From immigrant to transmigrant: theorizing transnational migration', *Anthropological Quarterly* 68, 48–63.

Scourby, A. (1982) 'Three generations of Greek Americans: a study in ethnicity', in *The Greek American Community in Transition*. Psomiades, H.J. and Scourby, A. (eds), New York: Pella, pp. 111–22.

Scourby, A. (1984) *The Greek Americans*. Boston, MA: Twayne.

Sease, D. (1987) 'Taiwan's export boom to U.S. owes much to American firms', *Wall Street Journal* 27 May, 1, 21.

Settler Arrivals (1994–95) *Settler Arrivals 1994–95, Statistical report No. 18*. Bureau of Immigration, Multicultural and Population Research. Canberra: Australian Government Publishing Service.

Sfekas, S.J. and Matsoukas, G.E. (eds) (1993) *Project for Orthodox Renewal, Seven Studies of Key Issues Facing Orthodox Christians in America*. Chicago, IL: Orthodox Christian Laity.

Shaiken, H. and Browne, H. (1991) 'Japanese work organization in Mexico', in *Manufacturing Across Border and Oceans*. Szekely, G. (ed.), San Diego, CA: Center for US–Mexican Studies.

Sheffer, G. (1995) 'The emergence of new ethno-national diasporas', *Migration* 28, 5–28 (special issue 'Nationalism and Diaspora').

Sheffer, G. (1996) 'Wither the study of ethnic diasporas? Some theoretical, definitional, analytical and comparative considerations', in *The Networks of Diasporas, 37–46*. Prévélakis, G. (ed.), Nicosia: Cyprus Research Centre.

Simic, A. (1973) *The Peasant Urbanites: A Study of Rural–Urban Mobility in Serbia*. New York: Seminar Press.

Simon, A. (1977) 'The sacred sect and the secular church: symbols of ethnicity in Astoria's Greek community', unpublished Ph.D. dissertation, CUNY.

Simos, A. (1991) 'Greek American reaction to the Colonels', *The Greek American* 21 September, New York: Petallides-Holliday Publisher.

Skeldon, R. (1995) 'Emigration from Hong Kong, 1945–1994: the demographic lead-up to 1997', in *Emigration From Hong Kong: Tendencies and Impacts*. Skeldon, R. (ed.), Hong Kong: The Chinese University Press.

Sklair, L. (1993) *Assembling for Development: The Maquila Industry in Mexico and the U.S.* San Diego, CA: Center for US–Mexican Studies.

Sklair, L. (1995) *Sociology of the Global System*. London: Prentice Hall and Baltimore, MD: Johns Hopkins University.

Sklair, L. (2000) *The Transnational Capitalist Class*. London: Blackwell.

Sklair, L. (2001) *The Transnational Capitalist Class*. Oxford: Blackwell.

Skrbiš, Z. (1994) 'Ethno-nationalism, immigration and globalism, with particular reference to second generation Croatians and Slovenians in Australia', unpublished Ph.D. thesis, Flinders University of South Australia.

Slany, K. (1990), 'Immigrants from the European socialist countries in the USA and Canada: socio-demographic aspects', *Migracijske teme* 6, 223–47.

Smith, A.D. (1991) *National Identity*. London: Penguin Books.

Smith, A.D. (1995) *Nations and Nationalism in a Global Era*. Cambridge: Polity Press.

Smith, A.D. (1999) 'Secret territories and national conflict', *Israel Affairs* 5, 4, 13–31.

Smith, M.P. (1994) 'Can you imagine? Transnational migration and the globalization of grass-roots politics', *Social Text* 39, 15–33.

Smith, R.C. (1998) 'Transnational localities: community, technology and the politics of membership within the context of Mexico and US migration', in *Transnationalism From Below*. Vol. 6. *Comparative Urban and Community Research*. Smith, M.P. and Guarnizo, L.E. (eds), New Brunswick, NJ: Transaction Publishers, pp. 196–238.

Smith, M.P. and Guarnizo, L.E. (eds) (1998) *Transnationalism From Below*. Vol. 6. *Comparative Urban and Community Research*. New Brunswick, NJ: Transaction Publishers, pp. 3–34.

Soysal, Y.N. (1994) *The Limits of Citizenship: Migrants and Post-national Membership in Europe*. Chicago, IL: University of Chicago Press.

Statistics Canada (2000) *Statistical Profile of Canadian Communities*. Available online at: http://ceps.statcan.ca/english/profil/placesearchform1.cfm.

Stavrou, T.G. (1988) 'The Orthodox Church of Greece', in *Eastern Christianity and Politics in the Twentieth Century*. Ramet, P. (ed.), Durham: Duke University Press, pp. 183–207.

Strathern, M. (1984) 'The social meanings of localism', in *Locality and Rurality: Economy and Society in Rural Regions*. Bradleym, T. and Lowem, P. (eds), Norwich: Geo-Books.

Strout, C. (1963) *The American Image of the Old World*. New York: Harper and Row.

Stubbs, P. (1996) 'Nationalism, globalisation and civil society in Croatia and Slovenia', *Research in Social Movements, Conflicts and Change* 19, 1–26.

Sunier, T. (1996) *Islam in beweging. Turkse jongeren en islamitische organisaties*. Amsterdam: Het Spinhuis.

Swidler, A. (1986) 'Culture in action: symbols and strategies', *American Sociological Review* 51, 273–86.

Tardif, F., Beaudet, G. and Labelle, M. (eds) (1993) *Question nationale et ethnicité. Le discours de leaders d'origine italienne de la région de Montréal*. Université du Québec à Montréal, Département de sociologie, Les Cahiers du Centre de recherche sur les relations interethniques et le racisme, no 11.

Tautai Contemporary Pacific Arts Trust (1998) *Tautai/AIT Sculpture Symposium: Navigating Pacific Art in the Present, Testing Traditions, 2–9 March 1998* (brochure). Auckland: Tautai Trust & Auckland Institute of Technology, Te Whare Takiura O Tamaki Makau Rau.

Tautai Contemporary Pacific Arts Trust (2001) *Tautai Contemporary Pacific Arts Trust*. Available online at: http://www.tautaipacific.com/intro2.htm.

Tavuchis, N. (1972) *Family and Mobility Among Greek Americans*. Athens: National Center of Social Research.

Thomas, W.I. and Znaniecki, F. (1958 and 1918) *The Polish Peasant in Europe and America*. New York: Dover Publications (first printed in 1918).

Thompson, A. (1998) 'Liberals split on birthright proposal', *Toronto Star* 14 May.

Thompson, G. (1983) 'Carnival and the calculable: consumption and play at Blackpool', in *Formations of Pleasure*. London: RKP.

Thrift, N. (1997) ' "Us" and "Them": re-imagining places, re-imagining identities', in *Consumption and Everyday Life*. Mackay, H. (ed.), Milton Keynes: Open University Press and London: Sage.

Tiryakian, E.A. (1991) 'Modernization: exhumetur in pace (Rethinking macrosociology in the 1990s)', *International Sociology*, 6, 2, 165–80.

Tiryakian, E.A. and Nevitte, N. (1985) 'Nationalism and modernity', in *New Nationalisms of the Developed West*. Tiryakian, E.A. and Rogowski, R. (eds), Boston: Allen and Unwin, pp. 57–86.

Tölölyan, K. (1996) 'Rethinking diaspora(s): stateless power in the transnational moment', *Diaspora* 5, 3–36.

Tonks, R. and Paranjpe, A. (1999) 'Two sides of acculturation: attitudes toward multiculturalism and national identity amongst immigrant and Canadian born youth', paper presented at the Third National Metropolis Conference, 15 January, Simon Fraser University Harbour Centre, Vancouver, BC.

Tönnies, F. (1957 and 1887) *Community and Society (Gemeinschaft und Gesellschaft)*. Translated and edited by C.P. Loomis. East Lansing: Michigan State University Press.

Turner, B. (1990) 'Outline of a theory of citizenship', *Sociology* 24, 189–217.

Turner, B. (1993) 'Contemporary problems in the theory of citizenship', in *Citizenship and Social Theory*. Turner, B. (ed.), London: Sage Publications.

Turner, V. (1969) *The Ritual Process: Structure and Anti-Structure*. Harmondsworth: Penguin Books.

Tyler, J. and Miller, C. (eds) (1994) *Mexico on the Loose 1994*. New York: Foders.

Urry. J. (2000) 'Mobile sociology', *British Journal of Sociology* 51, 1.

Valenzuela, J.M. (1988) *A la Brava Ése: Cholos, Punks, Chavos Banda*. Tijuana: El Colegio de la Frontera Norte.

Van Hear, N. (1998) *New Diasporas: The Mass Exodus, Dispersal, and Regrouping of Migrant Communities*. Seattle, WA: University of Washington Press.

Vargas, R. (1998) *Reestructuración Industrial, Educación Tecnológica y Formación de Ingenieros*. Mexico: ANUIES.

Vegleris, A. (1988) 'Differential social integration among first generation Greeks in New York', *International Migration Review* XXII, 4.

Vercoe, C. (1999) 'A Pacific presence', in *Art New Zealand* 90, Autumn, 40–1 and 87.

Vertovec, S. (1999) 'Conceiving and researching transnationalism', *Ethnic and Racial Studies* 22, 447–62.

Vertovec, S. (2000). 'Rethinking remittances', plenary lecture at the 5th International Metropolis Conference. Vancouver, BC, November.

Vertovec, S. and Cohen, R. (1999) 'Introduction' in *Migration, Diasporas and Transnationalism*. Vertovec, S. and Cohen, R. (eds), Cheltenham: Edward Elgar Publishing, pp. viii–xxvii.

Vigil, M. (1990) 'The ethnic organization as an instrument of political and social change: MALDEF, a case study', *The Journal of Ethnic Studies* 18, 15–31.

Waters, M.C. (1991) *Ethnic Options: Choosing Identities in America*. Berkeley, CA: University of California Press.

Weale, A. (1991) 'Citizenship beyond borders', in *The Frontiers of Citizenship*. Vogel, U. and Moran, M. (eds), New York: St Martin's Press.

Weinfeld, M. (1985) 'Myth and reality in the Canadian Mosaic: "Affective Ethnicity"', in *Ethnicity and Ethnic Relations in Canada*. Bienvenue, R.M. and Goldstein, J.E. (eds), Toronto: Butterworths, pp. 65–86.

Welsh, W. (1999) 'Transculturality: the puzzling from of cultures today', in *Spaces of Culture: City–Nation–World*. Featherstone, M. and Lash, S. (eds), London: Sage, pp. 194–213.

Werbner, P. (1997) 'Introduction: the dialectics of cultural hybridity', in *Debating Cultural Hybridity*. Werbner, P. and Madood, T. (eds), London: Zed Books.

When I Realised I am a Greek Child (1997) *When I Realised I am a Greek Child* (Ti stigmi pou katalava oti eimai Ellinopoulo). New York: Seabury Press.

Wilden, A. (1977) *System and Structure: Essays in Communication and Exchange*. London: Tavistock Publications.

Wilson, P. (1992) *Exports and Local Development: Mexico's New Maquiladoras*. Austin, TX: University of Texas, Austin Press.

Wilson, R. and Dissanayake, W. (1996) 'Introduction: tracking the global/local' in *Global/Local: Cultural Production and the Transnational Imaginary*. Wilson, R. and Dissanayake, W. (eds), Durham: Duke University Press, pp. 1–18.

Wong, L. and Ng, M. (1998) 'Chinese immigrant entrepreneurs in Vancouver: a case study of ethnic business development', *Canadian Ethnic Studies* XXX, 64–85.

Yaeger, P. (1996) 'Introduction', in *The Geography of Identity*. Yaeger, P. (ed.), Ann Arbor, MI: The University of Michigan Press.

Zivkovic, I., Sekulic, D. and Sporer, Z. (1995) *Asimilacija i identitet (Assimilation and Identity)*. Zagreb: Skolska knjiga.

Index